Microsoft® SQL Server® 2008 Implementation and Maintenance (70-432)

Lab Manual

WILEY

EXECUTIVE EDITOR	John Kane
EDITORIAL PROGRAM ASSISTANT	Jennifer Lartz
DIRECTOR OF SALES	Mitchell Beaton
EXECUTIVE MARKETING MANAGER	Chris Ruel
CONTENT MANAGER	Micheline Frederick
SENIOR PRODUCTION EDITOR	Kerry Weinstein

To order books or for customer service, please call 1-800-CALL WILEY (225-5945).

ISBN   978-0-470-18368-7

Printed in the United States of America

10 9 8 7 6 5 4 3

BRIEF CONTENTS

Textbook Exercises

CONTENTS

Textbook Exercises

Hands-On Exercises

LESSON 2
TEXTBOOK
EXERCISES

This lab section contains the following exercises and activities:

Exercise 2-1   Installing SQL Server 2005

> **TAKE NOTE**
>
> You will find instructions for loading SQL Server 2008 in Hands-On Exercise 2.1.

1. Create a user account named **SmithB** with a password of **Pa$$w0rd,** and make it a member of the Administrators local group. You can perform this task using one of these tools: on a Windows member server or on Windows Workgroup, use Computer Management (right-click **My Computer →Manage**); on a Windows domain controller, use **Active Directory Users** and **Computers** (click **Start → Administrative Tools**). You will use this user in multiple exercises as you go through this course.

2. Insert the **SQL Server 2005 DVD**, and wait for the automenu to open. If it doesn't, find **setup.exe** and double-click it. For SQL Server, continue with the following steps.

3. Under Install, click **Server Components**, **Tools**, **Books Online**, and **Samples**.

4. You will then be asked to read and agree with the end-user license agreement (EULA); check the box to agree, and click **Next**.

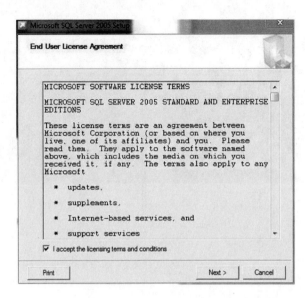

5. If your machine does not have all the prerequisites installed, the setup will install them for you at this time. Click **Install** if you are asked to do so. When complete, click **Next**.

6. Next you will see a screen telling you that the setup is inspecting your
    system's configuration again, after which the Welcome screen appears. Click
    Next to continue.

7. Another, more in-depth, system configuration screen appears letting you
    know whether any configuration settings will prevent SQL Server from being
    installed. Errors (marked with a red icon) need to be repaired before you can
    continue. Warnings (yellow icon) can optionally be repaired and will not
    prevent SQL Server from installing. Once you have made any needed
    changes, click **Next**.

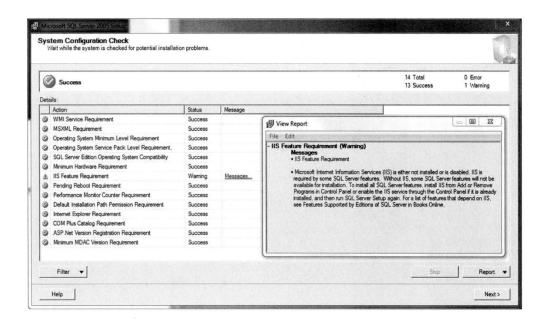

8.   After a few configuration setting screens appear, you will be asked for your product key. Enter it, and click **Next**.

9.   On the next screen, you need to select the components you want to install. Click the **Advanced** button to view the advanced options for the setup. For training, be sure to select the **AdventureWorks** database and all training tools.

10. Click the **Back** button to return to the basic options screen, and check the boxes next to **SQL Server Database Services**, **Integration Services**, and **Workstation components, Books Online, and development tools**. Then click **Next**.

11. On the Instance Name screen, choose **Default Instance**, and click **Next** (you'll install a named instance in the next exercise).

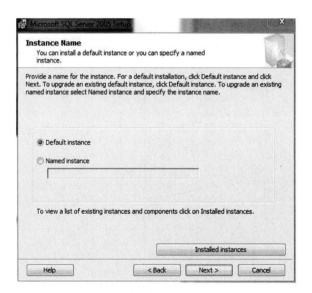

12. On the next screen, enter the account information for the service account you created in Step 1. You will be using the same account for each service in this exercise. When finished, click **Next**.

13. On the Authentication Mode screen, select **Mixed Mode**, enter a password of Pa$$w0rd for the sa account, and click **Next**.

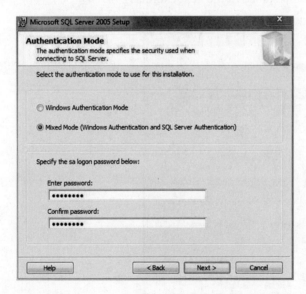

14. Select the **Latin1_General** collation designator on the next screen, and click **Next**.

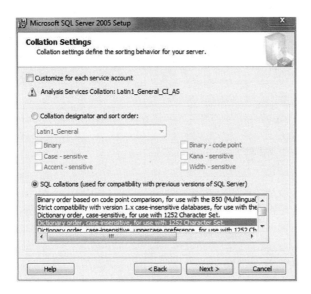

15. On the following screen, you can select to send error and feature usage information directly to Microsoft. This setting is entirely up to you, but you will not be checking it here. So, leave the defaults, and click **Next**.

16. On the **Ready to Install** screen, you can review your settings, and then click **Install**.

17. The setup progress appears during the install process. When setup is finished (which may take several minutes), click **Next**.

18. The final screen gives you an installation report, letting you know whether any errors occurred and reminding you of any postinstallation steps to take. Click **Finish** to complete your install.

19. Reboot your system if requested to do so.

Exercise 2-2   Installing a Named Instance of SQL Server 2005

TAKE NOTE

You will find instructions for loading a second instance of SQL Server 2008 in Hands-On Exercise 2.2.

1. Create a user account named Marketer with a password of Pa$$w0rd, and make it a member of the Users local group. You can perform this task using one of these tools: on a Windows member server or on Windows Workgroup, use Computer Management (right-click **My Computer → Manage**); on a Windows domain controller, use **Active Directory Users** and **Computers** (click **Start → Administrative Tools**). You will use this user in multiple exercises as you go through this course.

2. Insert the SQL Server **DVD** and wait for the automenu to open. SQL Server users, follow the next steps; SQL Server 2008 users skip to Step 16.

3.   Under Install, click **Server Components**, **Tools**, **Books Online**, and **Samples**.

4.   You will then be asked to read and agree with the EULA; check the box to agree, and click **Next**.

5.   Next you should see a screen telling you that the setup is inspecting your system's configuration again, and then the Welcome screen appears. Click **Next** to continue.

6.   Another, more in-depth, system configuration screen appears letting you know whether any configuration settings will prevent SQL Server from being installed. Errors (marked with a red icon) need to be repaired before you can continue. Warnings (yellow icon) can optionally be repaired and will not prevent SQL Server from installing. Once you have made any needed changes, click **Next**.

7.   Check the box next to SQL Server Database Services, and click **Next**.

8.   On the **Instance Name** screen, choose **Named Instance**, enter **Instance1** in the text box, and click **Next**.

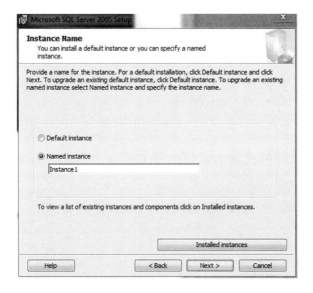

9.   On the next screen, enter the account information for the service account you created in Step 1 of Exercise 2-1. You will use the same account for each service in this exercise. When finished, click **Next**.

10.   On the **Authentication Mode** screen, select **Mixed Mode**, enter a password for the sa account, and click **Next**.

11.   Select the **Dictionary Order, Case-Insensitive, for Use with 1252 Character Set** option in the SQL Collations list, and click **Next**.

12.   On the following screen, you can select to send error and feature usage information directly to Microsoft. This setting is entirely up to you, but you will not be checking it here. So, leave the defaults, and click **Next**.

13.   On the **Ready to Install** screen, you can review your settings and then click **Install**.

14.   The setup progress appears during the install process. When setup is finished (which may take several minutes), click **Next**.

15.   The final screen gives you an installation report, letting you know whether any errors occurred and reminding you of any postinstallation steps to take. Click **Finish** to complete your install.

16.   Reboot your system if requested to do so.

LESSON 3 TEXTBOOK EXERCISES

This lab section contains the following exercises and activities:

Exercise 3-1   Investigating a Database Diagram

1. Click the **plus (+)** sign next to Databases.

2. Click the **plus (+)** sign next to AdventureWorks.

3. Right-click **Database Diagrams** and select **New Database Diagram**.

4. Select **ALL** by highlighting the first table and then scrolling to the last table. Holding down the **Shift** key, click on the **last entry**. Make sure that all tables have been highlighted in blue.

5. When the wizard finishes, click **Finish** or **Close**. You will probably have to change the scale to 10% to see all of the objects. The scale defaults to 100% as shown in the toolbar line directly above the diagram.

6. Grab a table by pressing the **left mouse key** and dragging it. Eventually, you will have tables organized well enough that you can increase the scale to 25%.

7. Right-click a table and from the menu choose **Table View** to see the various display options. Start with **Standard**. Then select **Column Names**.

8. Continue down the menu. You see all of the management aspects pertaining to a table presented. You can totally manage a database in this diagrammatic view.

9. Right-click any empty space. Note that the menu changes. Now you can create a new table.

Exercise 3-2 Executing a Query

1. In the query window, type the following code:

```
USE AdventureWorks
SELECT * FROM
```

2. At this point, open **Databases** → **AdventureWorks** → **Tables**, and with your left mouse button drag **Person.Contact** from the list onto the query pane immediately behind the FROM keyword separated with a space. It should look like this:

```
USE AdventureWorks
SELECT * FROM Person.Contact
```

3. Click the **Execute** box, press the **F5** key or press the combination of **CTRL** and **e** (**CTRL-e** because uppercase E doesn't work). Congratulations! You've executed your first query.

4. Let your mouse pointer hover over the icons across the toolbar in turn. Discover whether **Results to Grid** or **Results to Text** is selected. Whichever has a solid border, change to the other one and execute again. The display is quite different. The desired option depends on the data you retrieve.

5. Try:

```
SELECT @@VERSION
```

6. Again switch the Results to Grid and Results to Text back and forth executing the query after each switch. Decide which proves easier to read.

7. Add a new Query window by pressing **CTRL-n** (CTRL-SHIFT-N starts a new project). Note that you now have multiple query windows open. SQL Server now supports multiple active result sets. Click the black **X** to the immediate right of the query tabs. Decide whether you want to save your query and finish closing it.

Exercise 3-3   Storing a Script

1. Either press the **CTRL-SHIFT-N** keys or click on the **File** drop-down menu and select **New** and **Project**. Highlight **SQL Server Scripts**, change the name to **Practice** and specify a more convenient location than My Documents—how about C:\Practice? Make sure that the check box for **Create directory for solution** is selected. Click **OK**.

2. The Solution Explorer opens, displaying your **Practice** project. Although you can perform all administrative tasks by executing Transact-SQL statements, it is often easier to use SSMS. However, you should generate the corresponding Transact-SQL scripts and save them in the project for future reference or reuse.

3. Right-click on **Queries** in the Practice submenu and make a **New Query.**

4. Right-click the new query and **Rename** it as **Config1**.

5. Double left-click Config1 and connect to your server instance to open a new query window.

6. In the Object Browser, right-click **<your server>** and select **Properties**.

7. Select the **Security** page.

8. In the Login auditing section of the right-hand pane, click the **Both failed and successful logins** radio button.

9. Click the **down arrow** adjacent to the Script box in the upper left-hand corner of the Properties box and copy the internally generated script to the clipboard.

10. Right-click in the **Config1 Query window** and paste in the results.

11. Click **OK** in the server property box to effect the change.

12. Click the query window closed; save the change.

13. Finally, double-click your **Config1** to verify the change was stored.

Exercise 3-4 Searching Books Online

1. Once open, click the **Magnifying Glass** icon.

2. Enter this string in the **Search** text box: "Features Supported by Editions of SQL Server."

3. Double left-click the article of interest from the search results list.

4. Scroll through the article to verify the features you need to learn are included.

5. Click the **Sync with Table of Contents** button. Look in the contents window for other articles to browse.

6. Look up the details about @@VERSION that you executed in the Query window.

7. Notice that usage examples appear near the end of most syntax pages.

Exercise 3-5 Using Configuration Manager

1. Double-click the **SQL Server Configuration Manager** icon shortcut you placed on your desktop.

2. This opens the Microsoft Management Console for SQL Server Configuration Manager.

3. Click on **SQL Server Services** in the tree view.

4. Right-click **SQL Server Agent**. Select **Restart** from the context menu. This stops and starts the service. An operating system administrator would normally have to do this for you.

5. Click on **SQL Server Network Configuration** and then double left-click the **Protocols** for your listed service.

6. Right-click **TCP/IP** and choose **Properties** from the menu. Explore the options on the two tabs to understand the controls you can set.

7. Similarly, explore **SQL Native Client Configuration**.

8. Close the tool when you are done.

Exercise 3-6   Using sp_configure

1. In **SQL Server Management Studio**, start a **New Query**.

2. Execute the following code:

```
USE master;
GO
EXEC sp_configure 'show advanced option', '1';
GO
RECONFIGURE
GO
EXEC sp_configure
```

3. Examine the output.

4. Change the century pivot year using the following code:

```
USE master;
GO
EXEC sp_configure 'two digit year cutoff', '2030';
GO
RECONFIGURE
GO
EXEC sp_configure
```

5. Close Query Editor.

Exercise 3-7   Using the Surface Area Configuration Tool for SQL Server 2005

1. Start the tool.

2. Begin your tour by clicking on the **Surface Area Configuration for Services and Connections** link. Now ask yourself, "Do I need the Reporting Services service running?" If not, turn it off. If you don't need to allow remote connections, deny access.

3. Also click the **Surface Area Configuration for Features** link. Browse this list. If you don't need SQL Mail, leave the Enable SQL Mail stored procedures unchecked.

4. Close the tool after you have explored all options.

Exercise 3-8 Exploring the Facets View for SQL Server 2008

1. Open **SQL Server Management Studio**. Right-click <**your server**> and select **Facets**.

2. In the **View Facets** dialog box, click the down arrow in the **Facet** text box. Note the options. Select **Server Audit**. Note that **C2AuditTracingEnabled** is set to **False**.

3. In the **View Facets** dialog box, click the down arrow in the **Facet** text box. Select **Surface Area Configuration**. Note the settings. Click in the box containing **False** for **DatabaseMailEnabled**. Set it to **True**.

4. Examine the other Facets. What can you control with this tool? What can you learn?

Exercise 3-9 Examining a Catalog View

1. Open **Management Studio**. Navigate to **Databases** → **AdventureWorks** → **Views** → **System Views**, and scroll through the list.

2. Start a **New Query**. Use the following code:

```
USE AdventureWorks
SELECT * FROM sys.databases
```

3. Execute the query.

4. Examine the output. This is an example of the detail available about your database.

5. Try a few others.

Exercise 3-10 Using Metadata Functions

1. Open **Management Studio**. Navigate to **Databases** → **AdventureWorks** → **Programmability** → **Functions** → **System Functions** → **Metadata Functions**, and scroll through the list.

2. Start a **New Query**. Use the following code:

```
USE AdventureWorks
SELECT DB_ID()
-- This reports the internal database identifier
```

3. Execute the query.

4. Examine the output. This is an example of the detail available about your database.

5. Try a few others.

Exercise 3-11   Understanding Stored Procedures

1. Open **Management Studio**. Navigate to **Databases** → **AdventureWorks** → **Programmability** → **Stored Procedures** → **System Stored Procedures**, and scroll through the list.

2. Start a **New Query**. Use the following code:

```
USE AdventureWorks
EXEC sp_databases
```

3. Execute the query.

4. Examine the output. This is an example of the detail available about your database.

5. Try a few others. Try sp_HelpDB.

Exercise 3-12   Checking the Current Database

1. Open Management Studio.

2. Start a **New Query**. Use the following code:

```
USE AdventureWorks
DBCC CheckDB
```

3. Execute the query. This will take a few minutes.

4. Examine the output. This is an example of the detail available about your database.

5. Find DBCC CheckDB in Books Online (BOL). Sync with Table of Contents (sync is to the left of Ask a Question). Scroll through the list.

6. Try a few others.

LESSON 4 TEXTBOOK EXERCISES

This lab section contains the following exercises and activities:

Exercise 4-1   Summing Different Data Types

Exercise 4-2   Using the Convert Function

Exercise 4-3   Creating a Transact-SQL User-Defined Type

Exercise 4-1   Summing Different Data Types

1. Open **Management Studio**. Start a **New Query**. Enter the following code:

    ```
    SELECT 2 Result
    ```

2. Execute. You should see a result set of 2. Add a character 2 like this:

    ```
    SELECT 2 + '2' Result
    ```

3. Execute. You should see a result set of 4. This might be an unexpected result, and certainly something of which to be keenly aware.

Take Note

In Visual Studio, you have the ability to set OPTION EXPLICIT, which guards against these consequences. There is no OPTION EXPLICIT equivalent in Transact-SQL.

4. Continue this by adding a floating-point value, like this:

```
SELECT 2 + '2' + 2.0 Result
```

5. Execute. You should see a result set of 6.0. SQL Server converted all of the previous data types to floating point. Is that what you expected?

Exercise 4-2 Using the Convert Function

1. Open **SQL Server Management Studio**. Start a **New Query**. Enter this code:

```
SELECT CONVERT(nvarchar(30), GETDATE( ), 102) Date
```

2. Execute this code. You should get back a date in a format that looks like 2010.02.18.

3. Change the 102 to **111** and execute again. You should get back a date in a format that looks like 2010/02/18.

4. Change the nvarchar(30) to nvarchar(3) and execute again. You should get back a date in a format that looks like 200. SQL Server truncated the output to fit the specified field length.

5. Change the nvarchar(3) to just nvarchar (no parentheses) and execute again. You should get back a date in a format that looks like 2010/02/18. You just learned that the default length for an undefined nvarchar is 30.

Take Note

Other RDBMSs use different default values. This could lead to unexpected results if your code is run on different platforms.

6. Close the **Query Editor**.

Exercise 4-3 Creating a Transact-SQL User-Defined Type

1. Open a new database query window on the **AdventureWorks** database.

2. Create a user-defined type by using the following syntax:

```
CREATE TYPE ssn FROM varchar(11) NOT NULL
GO
```

3. Use the defined type in a CREATE TABLE statement:

```
USE AdventureWorks
CREATE TABLE HumanResources.Employees
(EmployeeID int identity (1,1)
, Employeename nvarchar(200)
, DepartmentID int
, EmployeeSSN ssn)
```

4. Add some data to your new table:

```
USE AdventureWorks
INSERT dbo.Employees
VALUES ('John Smith', 123, '123-45-6789')
INSERT dbo.Employees
VALUES ('Sally Jones', 456, '123456789')
SELECT * FROM Employees
GO
```

Take Note

You don't have the ability to alter the type once it is used in a table definition. What do you think of the two different formats used for the SSNs?

5. Delete the **HumanResources.Employees** table you just created. In Management Studio, highlight the table in the Object Browser and press the **Delete** key on your keyboard.

LESSON 5 TEXTBOOK EXERCISES

This lab section contains the following exercises and activities:

Exercise 5-1	Creating a Database Using Query Editor
Exercise 5-2	Creating a Database Using Management Studio
Exercise 5-3	Creating a Report

Exercise 5-1   Creating a Database Using Query Editor

1. In Query Editor, type:

    ```
    CREATE DATABASE MyFirstDB
    ```

2. Execute.

Exercise 5-2   Creating a Database Using Management Studio

1. Start Management Studio by selecting **Start → Programs → Microsoft SQL Server → Management Studio**.

2. Connect to your SQL Server.

3. Click the **plus (+)** sign next to Databases to expand your Databases folder.

4. Right-click either the **Databases** folder in the console tree or the white space in the right pane, and choose **New Database** from the context menu.

5. You should now see the General page of the Database properties sheet. Enter the database name, **MSSQL_Training**, and leave the owner as <default>.

6. In the data files grid, in the Logical Name column, change the name of the primary data file to **MSSQL_Training_data**. Use the default location for the file, and make sure the initial size is **3**.

7. Click the **ellipsis** button (the one with three periods) in the Autogrowth column for the MSSQL_Training_data file; then, in the dialog box that pops up, select the **Restricted File Growth (MB)** radio button, and restrict the file growth to **20** MB; then click **OK**.

8. To add the secondary data file, click the **Add** button, and change the logical name of the new file to **MSSQL_Training_Data2**. Here, too, use the default location for the file, and make sure the initial size is **3**.

9. Restrict the file growth to a maximum of 20 MB for MSSQL_Training_Data2 by clicking the **ellipsis** button in the Autogrowth column.

10. Leave all of the defaults for the MSSQL_Training_log file.

11. Click **OK** when you are finished. You should now have a new MSSQL_Training database.

Exercise 5-3   Creating a Report

1. From the last exercise, you should still be in Management Studio. Click the **plus (+)** sign next to Databases. Right-click **AdventureWorks,** and from the menu choose **Reports → Choose Standard Reports.** Finally, choose **Disk Usage**.

2. Examine the other report options.

LESSON 6 TEXTBOOK EXERCISES

This lab section contains the following exercises and activities:

Exercise 6-1   Creating the Products Table in Query Editor

1. Open a new query.

2. Enter the following Transact-SQL code:

```
USE MSSQL_Training
CREATE TABLE Products
(
ProdID          Int   NOT NULL          IDENTITY(1,1),
[Description]    nvarchar(100)           NOT NULL,
InStock         Int                     NOT NULL
)
```

3. Execute the query.

4.   Open and refresh **Object Explorer**.

5.   Verify the new table's creation.

Exercise 6-2   Creating the Customers Table

1.   Right-click the **Tables** icon, and select **New Table** to open the Table Designer.

2.   In the first row, under Column Name, enter **CustID**.

3.   Under Data Type, select **Int**.

4.   Make certain Allow Nulls is not checked.

5.   Under Column Properties and in the Table Designer section, expand **Identity Specification**, and then change **(Is Identity)** to **Yes**.

6.   Just under CustID, in the second row under Column Name, enter **Fname**.

7.   Just to the right of that, under Data Type, enter **nvarchar(20)**.

8.   Make certain Allow Nulls is unchecked.

9.   Using the parameters displayed earlier, fill in the information for the remaining columns. Don't allow nulls in any of the fields.

10.   Right click on the top of the Query Window where the name of the query is shown. Select the **Save Table…** entry.

11.   In the Choose Name box that pops up, enter **Customers** and click **OK**.

12.   Close the **Table Designer** query window.

Exercise 6-3   Creating the Orders Table

1.   Right-click the **Tables** icon, and select **New Table** to open the Table Designer.

2.   In the first row, under Column Name, enter **CustID**.

3.   Under Data Type, select **Int**.

4.   Make certain Allow Nulls is not checked.

5.   This won't be an identity column as it was in the Customers table, so don't make any changes to the Identity Specification settings.

6. Just under CustID and in the second row under Column Name, enter **ProdID** with a data type of **int**. Don't change the Identity Specification settings. Don't allow null values.

7. Just below ProdID, create a field named **Qty** with a data type of **int** that doesn't allow nulls.

8. Create a column named **OrdDate** with a data type of **smalldatetime**. Don't allow null values.

9. Right-click on the top of the Query Window where the name of the query is shown. Select the **Save Table...** entry.

10. In the Choose Name box that pops up, enter **Orders** and click **OK**.

11. Close the **Table Designer** query window.

Exercise 6-4   Creating a Partition Function and Scheme

1. In SQL Server Management Studio, right-click the **MSSQL_Training** database, and click **Properties**.

2. On the **Filegroups** page, click the **Add** button.

3. In the Name box, enter **TestPF1**.

4. Click **Add** again, and in the Name box, enter **TestPF2**.

5. Click **Add** again, and in the Name Box, enter **TestPF3**.

6. Click **OK**.

7. Select **MSSQL_Training** from the Object Explorer window. You may have to expand Databases to see the database names.

8. Open a new query window, and execute the following code to create the partition function:

```
CREATE PARTITION FUNCTION pfOrders (smalldatetime)
AS RANGE LEFT FOR VALUES (Getdate( ) - 30)
```

9. To create a partition scheme based on this function, execute this code:

```
CREATE PARTITION SCHEME pfOrders AS PARTITION pfOrders
TO (TestPF1, TestPF2, TestPF3);
```

LESSON 7 TEXTBOOK EXERCISES

This lab section contains the following exercises and activities:

Exercise 7-1   Creating the Contacts_in_398 View

1. Open **SQL Server Management Studio** by selecting it from the SQL Server group under Programs on your Start menu; connect with **Windows Authentication** if requested.

2. In Object Explorer, expand your **Server → Databases → AdventureWorks**; then right-click **Views**, and select **New View**.

3. In the Add Table dialog box, select **Contact (Person)**, and click **Add**.

4. Click **Close**, which opens the View Designer.

5. In the Transact-SQL syntax editor text box, under the column grid, enter the following:

```
SELECT LastName, FirstName, Phone FROM Person.Contact
WHERE (Phone LIKE '398%')
```

. the **Execute** button (the red exclamation point) on the toolbar to test
query.

Choose File → Save View → dbo.View_1.

8. In the Choose Name dialog box, enter **Contacts_in_398**, and click **OK**.

9. To test the view, click the **New Query** button, and execute the following
code:

```
USE AdventureWorks
SELECT * FROM Person.Contacts_in_398
```

10. To verify that the results are accurate, open a new query and execute the code
used to create the view:

```
USE AdventureWorks
SELECT lastname, firstname, phone
FROM Person.Contact WHERE (phone LIKE '398%')
```

Exercise 7-2   Creating an Updateable View

1. Open SQL Server Management Studio. Connect with Windows
Authentication if requested.

2. In Object Explorer, expand your **Server** → **Databases** → **AdventureWorks**;
right-click **Views**, and select **New View**.

3. In the Add Table dialog box, select **Location (Production)**, and click **Add**.

4. Click **Close** to open the View Designer.

5. In the Transact-SQL syntax editor text box, enter the following:

```
SELECT Name, CostRate, Availability
FROM Production.Location
```

6. Choose **File** → **Save View** → **dbo.View_1**.

7. In the Choose Name box, enter **Update_Product_Location**.

8. To test your view, open a new query and execute the following code:

```
USE AdventureWorks
SELECT * FROM dbo.Update_Product_Location
```

9. Now that you're sure the view is working the way you want, you'll create a new record. Open a new SQL Server query, then enter and execute the following code:

```
USE AdventureWorks
INSERT dbo.Update_Product_Location
VALUES ('Update Test Tool', 55.00, 10)
```

10. To verify that the record was inserted, and that you can see it in the view, execute the following code in the query window:

```
USE AdventureWorks
SELECT * FROM dbo.Update_Product_Location
WHERE Name = 'Update Test Tool'
```

11. To view the data as it was inserted into the base table, enter and execute the following code in the query window:

```
USE AdventureWorks
SELECT * FROM Production.Location WHERE Name = 'Update
Test Tool'
```

Exercise 7-3   Creating an Indexed View

1. Open SQL Server Management Studio; connect using Windows Authentication if requested.

2. Click the **New Query** button, and select **New SQL Server Query**. Connect using **Windows Authentication** if requested.

3. Create a view similar to dbo.Contacts_in_398 but without the XML column and ORDER BY and TOP clauses. Add the **ContactID** field and **SCHEMABINDING** so that the view can be indexed on the ContactID field, which is unique. To do all this, enter and execute the following code:

```
SET QUOTED_IDENTIFIER ON
GO
CREATE VIEW Person.Indexed_Contacts_in_398
WITH SCHEMABINDING
AS
SELECT c.ContactID, title as Title, lastname AS
Last Name, firstname as First Name, phone AS
Phone Number, c3.cardtype as Card Type
FROM Person.Contact c JOIN Sales.ContactCreditCard
c2 ON c.ContactID = c2.ContactID
JOIN Sales.CreditCard c3 ON c2.CreditCardID =
c3.CreditCardID
WHERE phone LIKE '398%'
```

4. To test the Person.Indexed_Contacts_in_398 view, enter and execute the following query:

```
USE AdventureWorks
SELECT * FROM Person.Indexed_Contacts_in_398
```

5. Now you'll create an index on the ContactID column, because it's unique. To do that, open a new query window and execute this code:

```
USE AdventureWorks
CREATE UNIQUE CLUSTERED INDEX CI_Indexed_View
ON Person.Indexed_Contacts_in_398(ContactID)
```

6. To make sure your index has been created, right-click **Views** under **AdventureWorks** in Object Explorer, and click **Refresh**.

7. Next, expand **Views → Person.Indexed_Contacts_in_398 → Indexes**. You should see the new CI_Indexed_View index listed.

8. To test the indexed view, execute this code:

```
USE AdventureWorks
SELECT * FROM Person.Indexed_Contacts_in_398
```

LESSON 8 TEXTBOOK EXERCISES

This lab section contains the following exercises and activities:

Exercise 8-1   Creating the Valid Zip Code Constraint

1. In Object Explorer, expand the **MSSQL_Training** database → **Tables** → **dbo.Customers**.

2. Right-click **Constraints**, and click **New Constraint**.

3. In the Check Constraint dialog box, enter **CK_Zip** in the (Name) text box.

4. In the Description text box, enter **Check** for valid zip codes.

5. To create a constraint that will accept only five characters that can be 0 through 9, enter the following code in the Expression text box:

    ```
    (zip like '[0-9][0-9][0-9][0-9][0-9]')
    ```

6. Click **Close**.

7. Click the **Save** button at the top left of the toolbar.

8. Close the **Table Designer** (which was opened when you started to create the constraint).

Exercise 8-2 Testing Your Constraint

1. In SQL Server Management Studio, click the **New Query** button.

2. Enter the following code into the query window:

```
USE MSSQL_Training
INSERT customers VALUES ('Gary', 'McKee', '111 Main',
'Palm Springs', 'CA', '94312', '7605551212')
```

3. Click the **Execute** button just above the query window to execute the query, and notice the successful results.

4. To see the new record, click the **New Query** button and execute the following code:

```
SELECT * FROM Customers
```

5. Notice that the record now exists with a CustID of 1 (because of the identity property discussed earlier, which automatically added the number for you).

6. To test the check constraint by adding characters in the Zip field, click the **New Query** button and execute the following code (note the letters in the Zip field):

```
USE MSSQL_Training
INSERT customers VALUES ('Amanda', 'Smith', '817 3rd',
'Chicago', 'IL', 'AAB1C', '8015551212')
```

7. Notice in the results pane that the query violated a constraint, which made it fail.

Exercise 8-3 Creating a Default Constraint

1. Open SQL Server Management Studio. In Object Explorer, expand **Server → Databases → MSSQL_Training → Tables → dbo.Customers → Columns**.

2. Right-click the **State** column, and click **Modify**.

3. In the bottom half of the screen, in the Default Value or Binding text box, type **'CA'** (with single quote marks).

4.   Click the **Save** button, and exit the Table Designer.

5.   To test the default, click the **New Query** button in SQL Server Management Studio. Select **New SQL Server Query**; connect with **Windows Authentication** if requested.

6.   Enter and execute the following code:

```
USE MSSQL_Training
INSERT customers (fname, lname, address, city,
zip, phone)
VALUES ('Tom', 'Smith', '609 Georgia', 'Fresno',
'33405', '5105551212')
```

Another Way

You may leave off the column names if you supply values in the correct column order and number. In this case, insert the keyword DEFAULT between Fresno and 33405.

7.   To verify that CA was entered in the State field, start a query.

8.   Enter and execute the following code:

```
SELECT * FROM customers
```

9.   Notice that the Tom Smith record has CA in the State field.

Exercise 8-4   Creating a Unique Constraint

1.   In SQL Server Management Studio, click the **New Query** button.

2.   Select **MSSQL_Training** in the database drop-down list on the toolbar.

3.   Enter and execute the following code:

```
ALTER TABLE customers
ADD CONSTRAINT CK_Phone UNIQUE (Phone)
```

4.   To test your new constraint, click the **New Query** button, and execute the following code to add a new record to the Customers table:

```
USE MSSQL_Training
INSERT customers VALUES ('Shane', 'Travis', '806 Star',
'Phoenix', 'AZ', '85202', '6021112222')
```

5. Click the **New Query** button, and try entering another customer with the same phone number by entering and executing the following:

```
USE MSSQL_Training
INSERT customers VALUES ('Janet', 'McBroom', '5403
Western', 'Tempe', 'AZ', '85103', '6021112222')
```

6. Notice that this fails, with a message that the UNIQUE_KEY constraint was violated by the duplicate phone number.

LESSON 9 TEXTBOOK EXERCISES

This lab section contains the following exercises and activities:

Exercise 9-1   Determining the Number of SQL Server Included Stored Procedures

1. Start SQL Server Management Studio.

2. Click the **plus (+)** sign next to Databases.

3. Click the **plus (+)** sign next to Master.

4. Click the **plus (+)** sign next to Stored Procedures.

5. Click the **plus (+)** sign next to System Stored Procedures.

6. Scroll down the list to appreciate how many stored procedures Microsoft makes available to you.

7. Do the same thing for the MSDB database.

8.   Execute this query just for fun:

```
USE Master
SELECT [Name] FROM Sys.SysObjects
WHERE [Name] LIKE 'sp_%' ORDER BY [Name]
```

Exercise 9-2   Examining Books Online for SP Explanations

1.   Launch Books Online.

2.   Click the **search icon** (it looks like a magnifying glass on the toolbar).

3.   Enter **sp_help** in the search field and press **Enter**.

4.   Double left-click the **sp_help (Transact-SQL)** article summary in Local Help.

5.   Press the **Sync with Table of Contents** button (to the left of **Ask a Question** where the icon looks like a book with arrows).

6.   Scroll through the list in the Contents pane. Stop every once in a while, double-click an article, and discover its functionality.

Exercise 9-3   Understanding sp_helptext

1.   Go to the Query Editor by clicking the **New Query** button on the upper left of Management Studio.

2.   Click **Connect**.

3.   In your query window, type the following code:

```
sp_helptext sp_helptext
```

More Information

You will use a system stored procedure to look at the code that created this system stored procedure. Make sure that the **Master Database** is selected in the context window to the left of the Execute button and that you have selected **Results to Text.** Then execute this command.

4.   Left-click in the results pane to set the focus on this area.

5.   Press **CTRL-a** to select all of the text.

6.   Press **CTRL-c** to copy the text to the clipboard.

7.   Press **CTRL-n** to open a new query window.

8.   Press **CTRL-v** to paste the text in the blank query window.

9.   Scroll to the top of the window to see the beginning of the code.

10. Examine this code. It shows the use of the CREATE PROC or CREATE PROCEDURE keywords, together with a name of your choice. In this example, the programmer chose the sys schema and sp_helptext object name.

    Lines 4 and 5 declare two parameter values with their data type. The @ symbol designates a local scope variable. The @objname now contains the text string sp_HelpText that you passed into the stored procedure.

    Lines 10 through 29 declare some local variables used mostly for manipulating the output. Text in green represents comments the author provided to help us understand code flow and intent.

    Line 34 creates a temporary table with two attributes: a line identifier and a line of text storage. Continue scrolling through the code. Examine the Transact-SQL code and the logic applied. Line 82 retrieves the object's text stored in a metadata table (sys.syscomments).

Exercise 9-4   Creating Your Own Stored Procedure Using Transact-SQL

1. Click the **plus (+)** sign next to AdventureWorks.

2. Click the **plus (+)** sign next to Programmability.

3. Right-click **Stored Procedures** and highlight to select the **New Stored Procedure** menu choice. This opens a new query window populated with a stored procedure template.

4. Use the template. Substitute the following Transact-SQL code to create a new procedure in the AdventureWorks database:

```
CREATE PROCEDURE up_ProductionLargeListPrices
AS BEGIN
SELECT Name, ListPrice
FROM Production.Product
WHERE ListPrice > (SELECT avg(ListPrice)
FROM Production.Product)
END
GO
```

Exercise 9-5   Executing a Stored Procedure

1. Open your **Query Editor**.

2. Enter the following code:

```
Exec Production.LargeListPrices
```

3. Execute.

Exercise 9-6 Creating and Deploying a CLR Procedure

1. If it does not exist already, create a new directory at the root of your C: drive named **Practice**. Copy the files **Lesson9.dll** and **Lesson9.sql** to C:\practice from the Wiley Companion Web site.

2. Open a database query window in the Mssql_Training database.

3. Configure the server to allow the use of CLR code to access objects stored outside of SQL Server and access the file system or network:

```
USE Master
GO
ALTER DATABASE Mssql_Training SET TRUSTWORTHY ON
```

4. Catalog the assembly:

```
USE Mssql_Training
CREATE ASSEMBLY Lesson9 FROM 'C:\Practice\Lesson9.dll'
WITH PERMISSION_SET = EXTERNAL_ACCESS
```

5. After you have cataloged the assembly, create a stored procedure that references the assembly and the method:

```
CREATE PROCEDURE [dbo].[up_CreateFolder] @foldername
nvarchar(200) OUTPUT WITH EXECUTE AS CALLER
AS EXTERNAL NAME
[Lesson9].[Chapter5.StoredProcedures].Createfolder
```

Take Note

The external name references are case sensitive.

6. Enable clr:

```
sp_configure 'clr_enabled', 1
RECONFIGURE
```

7. The stored procedure will create a folder in a specified location. Ensure that the folder "Lesson9" does not exist in C:\Practice and then test the stored procedure by executing this code:

```
EXEC up_CreateFolder 'C:\Practice\Lesson9'
```

8. Verify, through Windows Explorer, that the new folder was created.

LESSON 10 TEXTBOOK EXERCISES

This lab section contains the following exercises and activities:

Exercise 10-1   Examining Built-In Functions

1. Start SQL Server Management Studio. Click Connect.

2. Click the **plus (+)** sign next to **Databases**.

3. Click the **plus (+)** sign next to **AdventureWorks**.

4. Click the **plus (+)** sign next to **Programmability**.

5. Click the **plus (+)** sign next to **Functions**.

6. Click the **plus (+)** sign next to **System Functions**.

7. Click the **plus (+)** sign next to **Aggregate Functions**.

8. Explore and examine the available functions. Do a search for a few in Books Online. What do they do?

Exercise 10-2   Using the max( ) Function

1. You are already in Management Studio. Start a **New Query**.

2. Enter this code example in your query editor:

```
USE AdventureWorks
SELECT MAX(ListPrice) from Production.Product
```

3. Execute the query.

Exercise 10-3   Using the avg( ) Function

1. Enter this code example in your query editor:

```
USE AdventureWorks
SELECT Name, ListPrice FROM Production.Product
WHERE ListPrice > (SELECT avg(ListPrice)
FROM Production.Product)
ORDER BY ListPrice
```

2. Execute the query.

Exercise 10-4   Using the Version System Function

1. Now click the **plus (+)** sign next to Configuration Functions. Again, hover your mouse pointer over each in turn. You learn that @@Max_Precision returns the precision level used by decimal and numeric data types currently set in the server.

2. Return to your Query Editor.

3. Type **USE AdventureWorks**; press **ENTER**, then type **SELECT**, and a space.

4. Using your left mouse button, capture and drag @@Version from the Object Explorer to the Query window, so that it looks like this:

```
USE AdventureWorks
SELECT @@Version
```

5. Execute the query.

6. This is difficult to read in the Results to Grid mode, so if this is your setting, change it by clicking on the **Results to Text** button on the same row as the AdventureWorks database context display.

7. Execute your query again.

Exercise 10-5   Using the Cursor_Rows System Function

1. Now click the **plus (+)** sign next to Cursor Functions in the Object Browser.

2. Return to your Query Editor pane.

3. Type **SELECT** plus a space, and drag **@@Cursor_Rows** from the browser.

4. The code should look like this:

```
SELECT @@Cursor_Rows
```

5. Click **Execute** or press **F5**.

Exercise 10-6   Using the DateDiff( ) and GetDate( ) Functions

1. Click the **plus (+)** sign next to Date and Time Functions. And yet again, hover your mouse pointer over each function in turn.

2. Enter the following code in Query Manager:

```
USE AdventureWorks
GO
SELECT DATEDIFF(Day, OrderDate, GETDATE( )) AS
'Number of Days' FROM Sales.SalesOrderHeader
```

3. Execute your query

Exercise 10-7   Using the Rank( ) Function

1. Examine and enter this code:

```
USE AdventureWorks
GO
SELECT i.ProductID, p.Name, i.LocationID,
i.Quantity, RANK( ) OVER (PARTITION BY
i.LocationID ORDERBY i.Quantity DESC) as 'Rank'
FROM Production.ProductInventory i
INNER JOIN Production.Product p ON i.ProductID =
p.ProductID ORDER BY p.Name;
GO
```

2. Execute.

Exercise 10-8   Using the Rtrim( ) Function

1. Click the **plus (+)** sign adjoining String Functions. Hover your mouse pointer over each function to learn its purpose.

2. Enter the following code in your Query Editor.

```
USE AdventureWorks
SELECT RTRIM(LastName) FROM Person.Contact
```

3. Execute.

Exercise 10-9   Using the Substring( ) Function

1. Type the code shown next into your query window:

```
USE AdventureWorks
SELECT SUBSTRING(FirstName, 1, 1) Initial
FROM Person.Contact
```

```
WHERE LastName LIKE 'Barl%'
ORDER BY Last Name
```

2. Execute by pressing **CTRL-e**.

Exercise 10-10   Using the Stuff( ) Function

1. Enter this code:

```
SELECT STUFF('abcdef', 2, 3, 'ijklmn')
```

2. Execute by pressing **F5**.

Exercise 10-11   Using the Multistatement Table-Valued Function

1. Examine and enter this code:

```
USE AdventureWorks
GO
CREATE FUNCTION dbo.fn_Contacts
(@Length nvarchar(5))
RETURNS @tbl_Employees TABLE -- Note the data type
(ContactID int PRIMARY KEY NOT NULL,
[Contact Name] nvarchar(50) NOT NULL)
AS
BEGIN
IF @Length = 'Short'
INSERT @tbl_Employees SELECT ContactID, LastName
FROM Person.Contact
ELSE IF @Length = 'Long'
INSERT @tbl_Employees SELECT ContactID,
(FirstName + ' ' + Lastname) FROM Person.Contact
RETURN
END
```

2. Execute. This creates the function.

3. Use this function in the FROM clause of your query instead of using a table or a view.

```
SELECT * FROM dbo.fn_Contacts('Short')
```
or
```
SELECT * FROM dbo.fn_Contacts('Long')
```

Exercise 10-12   Using the Inline Table-Valued Function

1.   Enter the following code in your Query Editor:

```
USE AdventureWorks
GO
CREATE FUNCTION fn_CustomerNamesInStates
(@RegionParameter nvarchar(30))
RETURNS Table
AS
RETURN (
SELECT ContactID, LastName
FROM Person.Contact
WHERE ModifiedDate > '01/01/2005')
```

2.   Execute the statement.

Exercise 10-13   Determining Determinism

1.   Enter this code:

```
USE AdventureWorks
IF ObjectProperty (Object_ID
('dbo.ufnGetProductDealerPrice'), 'IsDeterministic') = 0
PRINT 'This function is not deterministic'
```

2.   Execute.

Exercise 10-14   Creating a CLR User-Defined Function

1.   Copy **Lesson10.dll** and **Lesson10.sql** from the Wiley Companion Web site to the Practice directory already created on the root of your C: drive.

2.   Open a new database Query Editor instance on the MSSQL_Training database context.

3.   Create a user-defined function by using the following syntax:

```
USE MSSQL_Training
CREATE ASSEMBLY Lesson10
FROM 'C:\Practice\Lesson10.dll'
WITH PERMISSION_SET = EXTERNAL_ACCESS
```

If you processed the assembly in a previous exercise, you will get an error message that the assembly is already cataloged.

4. Create a function from the Visual Basic code supplied as a dynamic linked library:

```
CREATE FUNCTION dbo.GetIP (@servername
nvarchar(4000)) RETURNS TABLE (IPaddress
nvarchar(20)) AS EXTERNAL NAME
Lesson10.[Chapter5.UserDefinedFunctions].GetIP
```

5. Test the CLR user-defined function:

```
SELECT * FROM Mssql_Training.dbo.GetIP
('localhost')
```

Exercise 10-15   Creating a Transact-SQL User-Defined Function

1. Use this example code:

```
CREATE FUNCTION FN_NMN
(@Null_Input nvarchar(30))
RETURNS char(30) -- Note the RETURNS with an S
BEGIN
IF @Null_Input IS NULL
SET @Null_Input = ' NMN '--Abbreviation for No
-- Middle Name
RETURN @Null_Input -- Note the RETURN without an S
END
```

2. Execute.

3. You then use it as follows:

```
USE MyDataBase
SELECT FName, FN_NMI(MName), LName
FROM MyTable
```

4. The result set then appears as:

```
Mary Tyler Moore
Sam NMN Snead
```

LESSON 11 TEXTBOOK EXERCISES

This lab section contains the following exercise and activity:

Exercise 11-1   Implementing a Service Broker Architecture

Exercise 11-1   Implementing a Service Broker Architecture

1. Open a **new query** window, and type the following syntax to enable the broker architecture in the MSSQL_Training database:

```
USE MASTER
GO
-- Enable the broker architecture
ALTER database MSSQL_Training
SET ENABLE_BROKER
GO
USE MSSQL_Training
GO
```

2. Execute the following code to create the message types:

```
-- Define broker architecture
-- Create message type on initiator and target
CREATE MESSAGE TYPE TicketRequest AUTHORIZATION dbo
VALIDATION = WELL_FORMED_XML
CREATE MESSAGE TYPE TicketStatus AUTHORIZATION
dbo VALIDATION = WELL_FORMED_XML
```

3. Execute the following code to create the sender and receiver queue:

```
-- CREATE QUEUES
-- Execute this statement on the sender
CREATE QUEUE SenderQUEUE
-- Execute this statement on the receiver
CREATE QUEUE ReceiverQUEUE
```

4. Execute the following code to create the contract:

```
-- Create the contract
CREATE CONTRACT TicketServicesContract
(TicketRequest SENT BY INITIATOR,
TicketStatus SENT BY TARGET)
```

5. Execute the following code to initiate the services:

```
-- Create the service on the sender
CREATE SERVICE SendTicketingService ON
Queue SenderQUEUE
(TicketServicesContract)
-- Create the service on the recipient
CREATE SERVICE ReceiveTicketingService ON
Queue ReceiverQUEUE
(TicketServicesContract)
```

6. Execute the following code to submit a message to the queue:

```
-- Test and submit an order to a queue
DECLARE @message xml
DECLARE @conversationhandle UNIQUEIDENTIFIER
SET @message =
'<TICKETREQUEST>
<Requestor>student@training.com</Requestor>
<Requestednumber>5</Requestednumber>
<RequestedShow>SQL Server Training</RequestedShow>
</TICKETREQUEST>' '
BEGIN DIALOG CONVERSATION @conversationHandle
FROM SERVICE SendTicketingService
TO SERVICE 'ReceiveTicketingService'
ON CONTRACT TicketServicesContract
WITH ENCRYPTION = OFF;
```

```
-- Send the message on the dialog
SEND ON CONVERSATION @conversationHandle
MESSAGE TYPE TicketRequest
(@message);
END CONVERSATION @conversationHandle
-- End the conversation
```

7.   Execute the following SELECT statement to check whether this message is, and perhaps other messages are, in the queue:

```
-- Check the content of the queue
SELECT * from ReceiverQUEUE
GO
```

8.   Create a stored procedure to process the messages from the queue:

```
-- CREATE PROCEDURE TO RETRIEVE MESSAGES FROM THE QUEUE
CREATE PROCEDURE up_ProcessQueue
AS
BEGIN
DECLARE @conversation_handle UNIQUEIDENTIFIER,
@message_body XML,
@message_type_name NVARCHAR(128);
RECEIVE TOP(1)
@conversation_handle = conversation_handle,
@message_type_name = message_type_name,
@message_body = message_body
FROM dbo.ReceiverQUEUE
-- DO SOMETHING with the message
IF @message_type_name = 'TicketRequest'
BEGIN
-- To process from the queue you would write a stored
   procedure to handle the message
-- EXEC up_processticketrequest @message_body
-- for exercise purposes you just select the message
SELECT @message_body
END
END CONVERSATION @conversation_handle ;
END
GO
```

9. Alter the queue, and enable automatic activation:

```
-- Alter the queue for automatic activation
ALTER QUEUE ReceiverQUEUE
WITH ACTIVATION (STATUS = ON,
PROCEDURE_NAME = up_ProcessQUEUE,
EXECUTE AS OWNER)
GO
```

10. Execute the stored procedure manually to check the queue processing:

```
-- EXECUTE the stored procedure manually
EXEC up_ProcessQUEUE
```

LESSON 13 TEXTBOOK EXERCISES

This lab section contains the following exercises and activities:

Exercise 13-1   Setting the Authentication Mode

1. Click **Start** → **All Programs** → **Microsoft SQL Server** → **SQL Server Management Studio**. Click **Connect**.

2. Right-click **<your server>** in Object Explorer and select **Properties** from the context menu. The dialog box that appears should be labeled Server Properties, followed by your server name. Select the **Security** page in the **Select a page** tree view.

3. In the Server Authentication section, select **SQL Server and Windows Authentication Mode**. SQL Server service must be restarted.

4a. For SQL Server 2005, click **Start** → **All Programs** → **Microsoft SQL Server** → **Configuration Tools** and launch **SQL Server Surface Area Configuration**. Click the **Surface Area Configuration for Services and Connections** link near the bottom of the page. After a moment, the View by

Instance tab is populated. Open, if necessary, the **Database Engine**. Make sure the black arrow points to **Service**, and in the dialogue box press the **Stop** and then the **Start** buttons.

4b.   For SQL Server 2008, open **Configuration Manager**, be sure to select **SQL Server Services**, click on **SQL Server** and on the toolbar click the clockwise blue arrow (restart service).

5.   Close all dialog boxes.

Exercise 13-2   Applying Statement Permissions

1.   Click **Start** → **All Programs** → **Microsoft SQL Server** → **SQL Server Management Studio**. Click **Connect**.

2.   To prepare SQL Server for the following exercises, you need to remove permissions from the public role because the existing permissions will interfere with your work. Open a **New Query** editor window in SQL Server Management Studio, and execute the following query:

```
USE AdventureWorks
REVOKE ALL from public
```

Take Note

You may see a warning that says, "The ALL permission is deprecated and maintained only for compatibility. It DOES NOT imply ALL permissions defined on the entity." You can safely ignore this because at the Database scope "ALL" means Backup Database, Backup Log, Create Database, Create Default, Create Function, Create Procedure, Create Rule, Create Table, and Create View.

3.   Close the **Query window** without saving changes. In Object Explorer, click **<your server>**, click the **plus (+)** sign next to Databases, right-click **AdventureWorks,** and select **Properties** from the menu. Make sure that the dialogue window title is "Database Properties—AdventureWorks." Select the **Permissions** page.

4a.   For SQL Server, grant RosmanD the Create Table permission by selecting **RosmanD** in the Users or Roles list and checking the **Grant** box next to Create Table. In a similar fashion, grant **Accounting** the permissions called **Backup Database and Backup Log**. If the guest user has any permissions granted, remove them by unchecking the boxes. Click **OK** to apply your changes.

4b.   For SQL Server 2008, grant RosmanD the Create Table permission by right-clicking the account in **Security** → **Users** and selecting **Properties**. Select **Securables**, click the **Search** button and select **All objects of the types...** and click **OK**. Select **Databases** and click **OK**. Click the Grant box for Create Table. In a similar manner, for Accounting scroll through the **Permissions for AdventureWorks** until you find Backup database and Backup log. Click **Grant** on both. Click **OK**.

5.   Log out of **Windows**, and log back in as **JonesB**.

6.   Open a new **SQL Server query** in SQL Server Management Studio, connect using **Windows Authentication**, and type the following query:

```
USE AdventureWorks
CREATE TABLE Statement1
(column1 varchar(5) not null,
column2 varchar(10) not null)
```

7.   From the Query drop-down menu, select **Execute Query**. Notice that the query is unsuccessful because JonesB (a member of the Accounting group) doesn't have permission to create a table.

8.   Close **SQL Server Management Studio**, log out of **Windows**, and log back in as **RosmanD**.

9.   Open a new **SQL Server query** in SQL Server Management Studio, and enter and execute the code from Step 6 again. This time it's successful, because RosmanD has permission to create tables.

Exercise 13-3   Applying and Testing Object Permissions

1.   Click **Start** → **All Programs** → **Microsoft SQL Server** → **SQL Server Management Studio**. Click **Connect**.

2.   Expand **<your server>**. Click the **plus (+)** sign next to Databases. Click the **plus (+)** sign next to AdventureWorks. Click the **plus (+)** sign next to Tables. Right-click the table **Person.Address** and select **Properties**. Make sure that the title of this dialog box is "Table Properties—Address."

3.   On the Permissions page, add **<Your Domain or Server Name>\Sales** and **SmithB** under the Users or Roles list.

4.   Select **<Your Domain or Server Name>\Sales** in the Users or Roles list, and grant Sales the Select permission by checking the **Grant** box next to Select.

5.   Select **SmithB** in the Users or Roles list, and grant SmithB the Select permission by checking the **Grant** box next to Select.

6.   If the guest user has any permissions granted, remove them by clicking each one until all check boxes are clear.

7.   Click **OK**, and close **SQL Server Management Studio**.

8.   Log out of **Windows**, and log back in as **JonesB**.

9.   Open a new **SQL Server query** in SQL Server Management Studio, and connect using **Windows Authentication**.

10. Execute the following query (it fails because Accounting doesn't have the Select permission):

```
USE AdventureWorks
SELECT * FROM Person.Address
```

11. Close **SQL Server Management Studio**, and repeat steps 8 through 10, but for ChenJ. The query succeeds this time because Sales (of which ChenJ is a member) has the Select permission.

12. Log out of **Windows**, and log back in as yourself.

Exercise 13-4   Testing Permission States

1.   Click **Start → All Programs → Microsoft SQL Server → SQL Server Management Studio**. Click **Connect**.

2.   Click the **plus (+)** sign next to Databases. Click the **plus (+)** sign next to AdventureWorks. Click the **plus (+)** sign next to Security. Expand **Users**. Right-click **SmithB** and select **Properties**. Select the **Securables** page. The dialog box title should be "Database User—SmithB."

3.   Click **Add** under the Securables list box, select the **Specific Objects** radio button, and click **OK**.

4.   Click the **Objects Type** button, select **Tables**, and click **OK**.

5.   Click **Browse**, check the **HumanResources.Department** box, and click **OK**.

6.   In the Explicit Permissions for HumanResources.Department list, check the **Grant** box next to Select, and click **OK**.

7.   Open a new **SQL Server query**, and connect as **SmithB** using **SQL Server Authentication**.

8. Execute the following query. It's successful because SmithB has the Select permission on the HumanResources.Department table:

```
USE AdventureWorks
SELECT * FROM HumanResources.Department
```

9. Right-click **SmithB** under Users in the AdventureWorks database, and select **Properties**.

10. On the Securables page, click **Add** under the Securables list box, select the **Specific Objects** radio button, and click **OK**.

11. Click the **Objects Type** button, select **Tables**, and click **OK**.

12. Click **Browse**, check the **HumanResources.Department** box, and click **OK**.

13. In the Explicit Permissions for HumanResources.Department list, uncheck the **Grant** box next to Select, and click **OK**.

14. Return to the query window and execute the query shown in Step 8. It fails because SmithB doesn't have the explicit Select permission.

15. Right-click **SmithB** under Users in the AdventureWorks database, and select **Properties**.

16. Under Role Membership, check the box next to the **db_datareader role**.

17. Return to the query window, and rerun the query from Step 8. Now it's successful, because SmithB has inherited the Select permission from the db_datareader role and doesn't need to have it explicitly applied.

18. Right-click **SmithB** under Users in the AdventureWorks database, and select **Properties**.

19. On the Securables page, click **Add** under the Securables list box, select the **Specific Objects** radio button, and click **OK**.

20. Click the **Objects Type** button, select **Tables**, and click **OK**.

21. Click **Browse**, check the **HumanResources.Department** box, and click **OK**.

22. In the Explicit Permissions for HumanResources.Department list, check the **Deny** box next to Select, and click **OK**.

23. Return to the query window, and again run the query from Step 8. It fails this time because you've specifically denied SmithB access; therefore, SmithB can no longer inherit the Select permission from the db_datareader role.

24. Right-click **SmithB** under Users in the AdventureWorks database, and select **Properties**.

25. Under Role Membership, uncheck the box next to the db_datareader role.

26. On the Securables page, click **Add** under the Securables list box, select the **Specific Objects** radio button, and click **OK**.

27. Click the **Objects Type** button, select **Tables**, and click **OK**.

28. Click **Browse**, check the **HumanResources.Department** box, and click **OK**.

29. In the Explicit Permissions for HumanResources.Department list, uncheck the **Deny** box next to Select, and click **OK**.

LESSON 14 TEXTBOOK EXERCISES

This lab section contains the following exercises and activities:

Exercise 14-1	Creating Standard Logins
Exercise 14-2	Creating Windows Accounts
Exercise 14-3	Creating SQL Server Logins for Windows Accounts
Exercise 14-4	Testing SQL Server Logins for Windows Accounts
Exercise 14-5	Creating User Accounts in AdventureWorks
Exercise 14-6	Examining the Built-In Permissions
Exercise 14-7	Adding Logins to Fixed Server Roles
Exercise 14-8	Adding Users to Fixed Database Roles
Exercise 14-9	Creating and Adding Users to Custom Database Roles
Exercise 14-10	Creating and Testing an Application Role

Exercise 14-1 Creating Standard Logins

1. Click **Start → All Programs → Microsoft SQL Server → SQL Server Management Studio**. Click **Connect**.

2. Click the **plus (+)** sign next to your server in Object Explorer. Click the **plus (+)** sign next to Security. Click the **plus (+)** sign next to logins to view the current users. Right-click **Logins** and select **New Login** from the menu. Select the **SQL Server Authentication** radio button.

3. In the Login Name box, type **SmithB**.

4. In the Password text box, type **Pa$$w0rd** (remember, passwords are case sensitive).

5. In the Confirm Password text box, type **Pa$$w0rd** again.

6. For the Default Database option, select **AdventureWorks** as the default database.

7. Uncheck the **User Must Change Password at Next Login** box.

8. Switch to the **User** mapping page by clicking **"User Mapping"** in the Select a Page view. On the User Mapping page, check the **Map** box next to AdventureWorks to give your user access to the default database.

9. Click **OK** to create your new login.

10. Repeat the process once more to add a second user, named GibsonH.

11. Test your registration success by clicking the **New Query** button located near the upper left in Management Studio.

12. Click the **Change Connection** button located just below the New Query button.

13. In the Connect to Database Engine dialog box, select **SQL Server Authentication** from the Authentication drop-down list.

14. In the Login box, type **SmithB**.

15. In the Password box, type **Pa$$w0rd**.

16. Click **Connect** to connect to AdventureWorks.

Exercise 14-2   Creating Windows Accounts

1a. For a Domain Controller: Click **Start → Administrative Tools → Active Directory Users and Computers.** Right-click **Users** and choose **New** from the menu and **User** from the pop-out menu.

1b. For a Stand-alone or Member Server: Click **Start.** Right-click **My Computer.** Click **Manage** from the context menu. Click the **plus (+)** sign next to Local Users and Groups. Right-click **Users** and select **New User**.

2. Create six new users with the criteria from the list in Table 14-1.

Table 14-1
User requirements

Username	Description	Password	Must Change	Never Expires
MorrisL	IT	Pa$$w0rd	Deselect	Select
RosmanD	Administration	Pa$$w0rd	Deselect	Select
JohnsonK	Accounting	Pa$$w0rd	Deselect	Select
JonesB	Accounting	Pa$$w0rd	Deselect	Select
ChenJ	Sales	Pa$$w0rd	Deselect	Select
SamuelsR	Sales	Pa$$w0rd	Deselect	Select

3a.   For a Domain Controller: Click **Start → Administrative Tools → Active Directory Users and Computers**. Right-click **Users**. Choose **New** from the menu and **Group** from the pop-out menu.

3b.   For a Stand-alone or Member Server: Click **Start**. Right-click **My Computer**. Choose **Manage**. Click the **plus (+)** sign next to Local Users and Groups. Right-click **Groups** and select **New Group**.

4.   Create a group called **Accounting**

5.   Add the new users you just created whose Description value is Accounting.

6.   While still in Computer Management or Active Directory Users and Computers, create a group named **Sales**.

7.   Add all the users whose Description value is Sales.

8.   Click **Start → Run**. Enter **MMC** and click **OK**. Click **File → Add/Remove Snap-in → Add → Group Policy Object Editor → Add**.

   a.   For a Domain Controller: Click **Browse → Domain Controllers** for your domain name. Highlight the **Default Domain Controller Policy** and click **OK**.

   b.   For a Stand-alone or Member Server: Make sure that **Local Computer** is listed in the Group Policy Object text box and click **Finish**.

9.   Click **Finish**. Click **OK**. Click **Close**. Click **OK**. Click the **plus (+)** sign to expand your policy. Click the **plus (+)** sign next to Computer Configuration. Click the **plus (+)** sign next to Windows Settings. Click the **plus** sign next to Security. Click the **plus (+)** sign next to Local Policies. Click **User Rights Assignment**.

10.   Double-click the **Allow Log on Locally** right, and click **Add User or Group**. Select the **Everyone** group, click **OK**, and then click **OK** again.

> **Take Note**
>
> On a production machine, this is not a best practice; this is only for this exercise.

11.   Close the **MMC**. Answer **No** to save console settings.

Exercise 14-3   Creating SQL Server Logins for Windows Accounts

1.   Click **Start → All Programs → Microsoft SQL Server → SQL Server Management Studio**. Click **Connect**.

2.   Click the **plus (+)** sign next to your server in Object Explorer. Click the **plus (+)** sign next to Security. Click the **plus (+)** sign next to Logins to view the current users. Right-click **Logins** and select **New Login** from the menu.

3.   In the **Login Name** box, type **<Your Domain or Server Name>\Accounting**—which you created earlier. For the Default Database option, select **AdventureWorks**.

4.   On the User Mapping page, check the **Map** box next to AdventureWorks to give your user access to the default database.

5.   Click **OK** to create the login.

6.   Right-click **Logins**, and select **New Login**.

7.   In the Login name box, type **<Your Domain or Server Name>\Sales**— which you also created earlier.

8.   For the Default Database option, select **AdventureWorks** as the default database.

9.   On the User Mapping page, check the **Map** box next to AdventureWorks to give your user access to the default database.

10.   Click **OK** to create the login.

11.   Right-click **Logins**, and select **New Login**.

12.   Fill in the Login Name field with **<YourServerName>\RosmanD**.

13.   For the Default Database option, select **AdventureWorks** as the default database.

14.   On the **User Mapping** page, check the **Map** box next to AdventureWorks to give your user access to the default database.

15. Click **OK** to create the login.

16. Right-click **Logins**, and select **New Login**.

17. Fill in the Login Name field with **<YourServerName>\MorrisL**.

18. For the Default Database option, select **AdventureWorks** as the default database.

19. On the **User Mapping** page, check the **Map** box next to AdventureWorks to give your user access to the default database.

20. Click **OK** to create the login.

Exercise 14-4   Testing SQL Server Logins for Windows Accounts

1. Log out of **Windows**, and log back in as **JonesB**.

2. Open a new **SQL Server query** in SQL Server Management Studio, and select **Windows Authentication** from the Authentication drop-down list.

3. Close **SQL Server Management Studio**, log out of **Windows**, and log back in as **RosmanD**.

4. Open a new **SQL Server query** in SQL Server Management Studio, and select **Windows Authentication** from the Authentication drop-down list.

Exercise 14-5   Creating User Accounts in AdventureWorks

1. Click **Start → All Programs → Microsoft SQL Server → SQL Server Management Studio**. Click **Connect**.

2. Click the **plus (+)** sign next to Databases. Click the **plus (+)** sign next to AdventureWorks. Click the **plus (+)** sign next to Security. Click the **plus (+)** sign next to Users. Right-click **Users** and select **New User**. Make sure the dialog box title is "Database User—New."

3. Click the **ellipsis** button next to the Login Name box, and click **Browse**. View all the available names; note that only logins you've already created are available.

4. Check the **GibsonH** box, and click **OK** twice.

5. Enter **GibsonH** in the User Name box and **dbo** in the Default Schema box.

6. Click **OK** to create the GibsonH database user account.

Exercise 14-6   Examining the Built-In Permissions

1.   Open your **Query Editor**. Type the following code:

```
USE Master
SELECT * FROM fn_builtin_permissions(default);
```

2.   Execute.

3.   Scroll through the list. You discover 186 built-in permissions!

4.   Now try this code:

```
USE AdventureWorks
SELECT * FROM fn_my_permissions('person.address',
'object');
```

5.   You now discover 35 permissions available for this specific table object.

Exercise 14-7   Adding Logins to Fixed Server Roles

1.   Click **Start** → **All Programs** → **Microsoft SQL Server** → **SQL Server Management Studio**. Click **Connect**.

2.   Click the **plus (+)** sign next to Security. Click the **plus (+)** sign next to Server Roles. This displays the built-in server roles. Double-click **Sysadmin** to open its properties. Make sure that your dialog box title is "Server Role Properties—sysadmin."

3.   Click **Add**, click **Browse**, check the **<YourServerName>\MorrisL** box, click **OK**, and click **OK** again.

4.   MorrisL should now appear in the Role Members list.

5.   Click **OK** to exit the Server Role Properties dialog box.

6.   Double-click **Serveradmin Server Role Properties**.

7.   Click **Add**, enter **GibsonH**, and click **OK**.

8.   Click **OK** to exit the Server Role Properties dialog box.

Exercise 14-8   Adding Users to Fixed Database Roles

1. Click **Start** → **All Programs** → **Microsoft SQL Server** → **SQL Server Management Studio**. Click **Connect**.

2. Click the **plus (+)** sign next to Databases. Click the **plus (+)** sign next to AdventureWorks. Click the **plus (+)** sign next to Security. Click the **plus (+)** sign next to Roles. Click the **plus (+)** sign next to Database Roles. Right-click **db_denydatawriter** and select **Properties**. Use the automatically selected **General** page. The Window should be entitled "Database Role Properties—db_denydatawriter."

3. Click **Add**.

4. Type **SmithB** in the Enter Object Names to Select box, and click **OK**.

5. Click **OK** again to return to SQL Server Management Studio.

6. Right-click **db_denydatareader**, and select **Properties**.

7. Click **Add**.

8. Type **GibsonH** in the Enter Object Names to Select box, and click **OK**.

9. Open a new **SQL Server query** in SQL Server Management Studio, and connect using **SQL Server Authentication**.

10. In the User Name box, type **SmithB**; in the Password box, type **Pa$$w0rd**.

11. The following query tries to update information in the HumanResources.Department table, but it fails because SmithB is a member of the db_denydatawriter role:

```
INSERT INTO HumanResources.Department
(DepartmentID, Name, GroupName, ModifiedDate)
values (200, 'Test','TestGroup',GetDate())
```

12. Close the query window.

Exercise 14-9 Creating and Adding Users to Custom Database Roles

1. Click **Start** → **All Programs** → **Microsoft SQL Server** → **SQL Server Management Studio**. Click **Connect**.

2. Click the **plus (+)** sign next to Databases. Click the **plus (+)** sign next to AdventureWorks. Click the **plus (+)** sign next to Security. Click the **plus (+)** sign next to Roles. Right-click **Database Roles** and select **New Database Role**. Accept the selection of the General Page. The dialog box title should be "Database Role—New."

3. In the Role Name box, type **SelectOnly**, and enter **dbo** in the Owner box.

4. Add **<YourServerName>\RosmanD** to the Role Members list.

5. On the Securables page, click **Add** under the Securables list box, select the **Specific Objects** radio button, and click **OK**.

6. Click the **Objects Type** button, select **Tables**, and click **OK**.

7. Click **Browse**, check the **HumanResources.Department** box, and click **OK**, then click **OK** again.

8. In the Explicit Permissions for HumanResources.Department list, check the **Grant** box next to Select, and click **OK**.

9. Click **OK** to create the role and return to SQL Server Management Studio.

10. Close all programs, log off **Windows**, and log back in as **RosmanD**.

11. Open a new **SQL Server query** in SQL Server Management Studio, and connect using **Windows Authentication**.

12. Notice that the following query succeeds because RosmanD is a member of the new SelectOnly role:

```
USE AdventureWorks
SELECT * FROM HumanResources.Department
```

13. Now notice the failure of the next query because RosmanD is a member of a role that is allowed to select only:

```
INSERT INTO HumanResources.Department
(DepartmentID, Name, GroupName, ModifiedDate)
values (200, 'Test','TestGroup',GetDate())
```

14. Close all programs, log out of **Windows**, and log back in as yourself.

Exercise 14-10   Creating and Testing an Application Role

1. Click **Start** → **All Programs** → **Microsoft SQL Server** → **SQL Server Management Studio**. Click **Connect**.

2. Click the **plus (+)** sign next to Databases. Click the **plus (+)** sign next to AdventureWorks. Click the **plus (+)** sign next to Security. Clickthe **plus (+)** sign next to Roles. Right-click **Application Roles** and select **New Application Role**. Accept the selection of the General Page. The dialog box title should be "Application Role—New."

3. In the Role Name box, type **EntAppRole**.

4. Enter **dbo** in the Default Schema box.

5. In the Password and Confirm Password boxes, type **Pa$$w0rd**.

6. On the Securables page, click **Add** under the Securables list box, select the **Specific Objects** radio button, and click **OK**.

7. Click the **Objects Type** button, select **Tables**, and click **OK**.

8. Click **Browse**, check the **HumanResources.Department** box, and click **OK**, then click **OK** again.

9. In the Explicit Permissions for HumanResources.Department list, check the **Grant** box next to Select, and click **OK**.

10. Open a new **SQL Server query** in SQL Server Management Studio, and connect using **SQL Authentication** with **GibsonH** as the username and **Pa$$w0rd** as the password.

11. Notice that the following query fails because GibsonH has been denied Select permissions due to membership in the db_denydatareader database role:

    ```
    USE AdventureWorks
    SELECT * FROM HumanResources.Department
    ```

12. To activate the application role, execute the following query:

    ```
    sp_setapprole @rolename='EntAppRole',
    @password='Pa$$w0rd'
    ```

13. Clear the query window, and don't save the changes; repeat Step 9 without opening a new query, and notice that the query is successful this time. This is because SQL Server now sees the user as EntAppRole, which has Select permission.

14. Close the query window.

LESSON 15 TEXTBOOK EXERCISES

This lab section contains the following exercises and activities:

Exercise 15-1   Creating a Database Master Key

Exercise 15-2   Using SQL Server Utility

Exercise 15-1   Creating a Database Master Key

1. In **Query Editor**, connect to the database by executing the following Transact-SQL command:

   ```
   USE AdventureWorks
   GO
   ```

2. Choose a password for encrypting the copy of the master key that will be stored in the database.

3. Add this code snippet:

   ```
   CREATE MASTER KEY ENCRYPTION BY PASSWORD = 'Pa$$w0rd'
   ```

4. Execute.

Exercise 15-2   Using SQL Server Utility

1. To start the **Create Utility Control Point Wizard**, you must be connected to the Database Engine, click **View** and choose **Utility Explorer**. In the upper left-hand corner under the title **Utility Explorer**, click the third from the left icon. The wizard starts. Click **Next** to begin.

2. Click on the **Connect** button or press **Enter**. The SQL Server Instance Name will be displayed. Give this job a descriptive name of your choice. Click **Next**.

3. You must enter a Windows domain account and click **Next**.

4. SQL Server verifies certain conditions that your classroom configuration fails to meet. You are not a domain member. Press **Cancel**.

5. Remember what you can do with this tool and plenty of additional study when you return to your enterprise installation.

LESSON 16 TEXTBOOK EXERCISES

This lab section contains the following exercises and activities:

Exercise 16-1   Creating a Permanent Backup Device

1. Open **SQL Server Management Studio** by selecting it from the SQL Server group under Programs on the Start menu. Expand your server and then **Server Objects**.

2. Right-click **Backup Devices** in Object Explorer, and select **New Backup Device**.

3. In the Device Name box of the Backup Device dialog box, enter **AdvWorksFull**. Notice that the filename and path are filled in for you; make sure you have enough free space on the drive SQL Server has selected.

4. Click **OK** to create the device.

5. Make note of the file path. You will need this information in a later lab exercise.

Exercise 16-2   Performing a Full Backup

1. Open **SQL Server Management Studio**. Expand your **server** and then **Databases**.

2. Right-click **AdventureWorks**, and select **Properties**.

3. On the **Options** page, change Recovery Model to **Full** so you can perform a transaction log backup later.

4. Click **OK** to apply the changes.

5. Right-click **AdventureWorks** under Databases, point to **Tasks**, and click **Backup**.

6. In the Backup dialog box, make sure **AdventureWorks** is the selected database to back up and Backup Type is **Full**.

7. Leave the default name in the Name box. In the **Description** box, type **Full Backup of AdventureWorks**.

8. Under **Destination**, a disk device may already be listed. If so, select the **device**, and click **Remove**.

9. Under Destination, click **Add**.

10. In the Select Backup Destination box, click **Backup Device**, select **AdvWorksFull**, and click **OK**.

11. You should now have a backup device listed under Destination.

12. Switch to the **Options** page, and select **Overwrite All Existing Backup Sets**. This option initializes a new device or overwrites an existing one.

13. Select **Verify Backup When Finished** to check the actual database against the backup copy, and be sure they match after the backup is complete.

14. Click **OK** to start the backup.

15. When the backup is complete, you will get a notification; click **OK** to close it.

16. To verify the backup, you can look at the contents of the backup device, so expand **Backup Devices** under Server Objects in Object Explorer.

17. Right-click **AdvWorksFull**, and select **Properties**.

18. On the Media Contents page, you should see the full backup of AdventureWorks.

19. Click **OK** to return to SQL Server Management Studio.

Exercise 16-3   Performing a Differential Backup

1. Open **SQL Server Management Studio**. Expand your **server** and then **Databases**.

2. Right-click **AdventureWorks**, point to **Tasks**, and select **Back Up**.

3. In the Back Up dialog box, make sure **AdventureWorks** is the selected database to backup and Backup Type is **Differential**.

4. Leave the default name in the Name box. In the Description box, type **Differential Backup of AdventureWorks**.

5. Under Destination, make sure the **AdvWorksFull** device is listed.

6. On the Options page, make sure **Append to the Existing Backup Set** is selected so you don't overwrite your existing full backup.

7. On the Options tab, select **Verify Backup When Finished**.

8. Click **OK** to start the backup.

9. When the backup is complete, you will get a notification; click **OK** to close it.

10. To verify the backup, you can look at the contents of the backup device, so expand **Backup Devices** under Server Objects in Object Explorer.

11. Right-click **AdvWorksFull**, and select **Properties**.

12. On the Media Contents page, you should see the differential backup of AdventureWorks.

13. Click **OK** to return to SQL Server Management Studio.

Exercise 16-4   Performing a Transaction Log Backup

1.   Open **SQL Server Management Studio**. Expand your **server** and then **Databases**.

2.   Right-click **AdventureWorks**, point to **Tasks**, and select **Back Up**.

3.   In the Back Up dialog box, make sure **AdventureWorks** is the selected database to back up and Backup Type is **Transaction Log**.

4.   Leave the default name in the Name box. In the Description box, type **Transaction Log Backup of AdventureWorks**.

5.   Under Destination, make sure the **AdvWorksFull** device is listed.

6.   On the Options page, make sure **Append to the Existing Backup Set** is selected so you don't overwrite your existing full backup.

7.   On the Options page, select **Verify Backup When Finished**.

8.   Click **OK** to start the backup.

9.   When the backup is complete, you will get a notification; click **OK** to close it.

10. To verify the backup, you can look at the contents of the backup device, so expand **Backup Devices** under Server Objects in Object Explorer.

11. Right-click **AdvWorksFull**, and select **Properties**.

12. On the Media Contents page, you should see the transactional log backup of AdventureWorks.

13. Click **OK** to return to SQL Server Management Studio.

Exercise 16-5   Preparing the MSSQL_Training Database for a Filegroup Backup

1.   Open **SQL Server Management Studio**. Expand your **server** and then **Databases**.

2.   Right-click the **MSSQL_Training** database, and select **Properties**.

3.   On the Filegroups page, click the **Add** button. In the Name text box, enter **Secondary**.

4. On the Files page, click the **Add** button, and enter this information:

   Name: MSSQL_Training_Data_3
   File Type: Rows Data (Click the **down** button to see the options.)
   Filegroup: Secondary (Click the **down** button to see the options.)
   Initial Size: 3

5. Click **OK** to create the new file on the Secondary filegroup.

6. Now, to add a table to the new filegroup, expand **MSSQL_Training** in Object Explorer, right-click **Tables**, and select **New Table**.

7. Under Column Name in the first row, enter **Emp_Name**.

8. Next to Emp_Name, select **varchar** as the data type. Leave the default length of 50.

9. Just below Emp_Name in the second row, enter **Emp_Number** as the column name with a type of **varchar**. Leave the default length of 50.

10. Select **View** → **Properties Window**.

11. Expand the **Regular Data Space Specification** section, and change the Filegroup or Partition Scheme Name property to **Secondary**.

12. Click the **Save** button (it looks like a floppy disk on the toolbar) to create the new table, and enter **Employees** for the table name.

13. Close the **Table Designer** by clicking the **X** in the upper-right corner of the window.

14. Now, to add some data to the new table, open a **new query**, and execute the following code (note that the second value is arbitrary):

```
USE MSSQL_Training
INSERT Employees
VALUES('Tim Hsu', 'VA1765FR')
INSERT Employees
VALUES('Sue Hernandez', 'FQ9187GL')
```

15. Close the **query window**.

Exercise 16-6   Performing a Filegroup Backup

1. Right-click the **MSSQL_Training** database in Object Explorer, point to **Tasks**, and select **Back Up**.

2. In the Back Up dialog box, make sure **MSSQL_Training** is the selected database to back up and Backup Type is **Full**.

3. Under Backup Component, select **Files and Filegroups**.

4. In the Select Files and Filegroups dialog box, check the **Secondary** box, and click **OK** (notice that the box next to MSSQL_Training_Data_3 is automatically checked).

5. Leave the default name in the Name box. In the Description box, type **Filegroup Backup of MSSQL_Training**.

6. Under Destination, make sure the **AdvWorksFull** device is the only one listed.

7. On the Options tab, make sure **Append to the Existing Backup Set** is selected so you don't overwrite your existing backups.

8. On the Options tab, select **Verify Backup When Finished**.

9. Click **OK** to start the backup.

10. When the backup is complete, you will get a notification; click **OK** to close it.

11. To verify the backup, you can look at the contents of the backup device, so expand **Backup Devices** under Server Objects in Object Explorer.

12. Right-click **AdvWorksFull**, and select **Properties**.

13. On the Media Contents page, you should see the filegroup backup of MSSQL_Training.

14. Click **Close**, and then click **OK** to return to SQL Server Management Studio.

Exercise 16-7   Backing Up to Multiple Devices

1. Open **SQL Server Management Studio**. Expand your **server** and then **Server Objects**.

2. Right-click **Backup Devices** in Object Explorer, and select **New Backup Device**.

3. In the Name box of the Backup Device dialog box, enter **PSDev1**. Notice that the filename and path are filled in for you; make sure you have enough free space on the drive that SQL Server has selected.

4. Click **OK** to create the backup device.

5. Right-click **Backup Devices** in Object Explorer, and select **New Backup Device**.

6. In the Name box of the Backup Device dialog box, enter **PSDev2**. Again, notice that the filename and path are filled in for you.

7. Click **OK** to create the backup device.

8. To start the backup, right-click **Model** under System Databases, point to **Tasks**, and click **Backup**.

9. In the Backup dialog box, make sure **Model** is the selected database to back up and Backup Type is **Full**.

10. Leave the default name in the Name box. In the Description box, type **Full Backup of Model**.

11. Under Destination, a disk device may already be listed. If so, select the **device**, and click **Remove**.

12. Under Destination, click **Add**.

13. In the Select Backup Destination box, click **Backup Device**, select **PSDev1**, and click **OK**.

14. Under Destination, click **Add**.

15. In the Select Backup Destination box, click **Backup Device**, select **PSDev2**, and click **OK**.

16. On the Options page, select **Overwrite All Existing Backup Sets**. This option initializes a new device or overwrites an existing one.

17. Check **Verify Backup When Finished** to check the actual database against the backup copy and be sure they match after the backup is complete.

18. Click **OK** to start the backup.

19. When the backup is complete, you will get a notification; click **OK** to close it.

20. To verify the backup, you can look at the contents of the backup device, so expand **Backup Devices** under Server Objects in Object Explorer.

21. Right-click **PSDev1**, and select **Properties**.

22. On the Media Contents page, you should see the first half of the full backup of Model. You should also note that the Media Family Count property is 2, denoting this is part of a multiple-device backup.

23. Click **OK** to return to SQL Server Management Studio.

Exercise 16-8   Creating Mirrored Backup Sets

1. In Windows Explorer, on an Enterprise Edition of SQL Server, create a new directory named **MirrorTest** on the C:\ drive.

2. Open a new **Query Editor** window.

3. Enter the following code:

```
BACKUP DATABASE AdventureWorks TO
DISK = 'c:\MirrorTest\AdventureWorks1A.bak',
DISK = 'c:\MirrorTest\AdventureWorks1B.bak',
DISK = 'c:\MirrorTest\AdventureWorks1C.bak'
MIRROR TO
DISK = 'c:\MirrorTest\AdventureWorks2A.bak',
DISK = 'c:\MirrorTest\AdventureWorks2B.bak',
DISK = 'c:\MirrorTest\AdventureWorks2C.bak'
GO
```

4. Wait until the backup completes and then go back to Windows Explorer and verify that you have six backup files in two media sets.

Exercise 16-9   Restoring a Database

1. Open the **SQL Server Configuration Manager** from the Start menu.

2. In the left pane, select **SQL Server Services**.

3. Right-click **SQL Server (MSSQLSERVER)** in the right pane, and click **Stop**. You'll be asked whether you want to stop the SQL Server Agent service as well; click **Yes**.

4. Find the file **AdventureWorks_Data.mdf** (The location depends on the release of SQL Server you are using.).

5. Rename the file as **AdventureWorks_Data.old**.

6. Find the file **AdventureWorks_Log.ldf**, and rename it as **AdventureWorks_Log.old**.

7. From the Configuration Manager, restart the **SQL Server Agent** and **SQL Server services**.

8. Open **SQL Server Management Studio**, and expand **Databases** under your
    server name. AdventureWorks cannot be expanded and has no summary; it is
    now inaccessible.

9. To restore the database, right-click **Databases**, and select **Restore Database**.

10. In the Restore Database dialog box, select **AdventureWorks** from the To
    Database drop-down list box.

11. Under Source for Restore, select **From Device**. Click the **ellipsis (…)** button
    next to the text box to select a device.

12. In the Specify Backup dialog box, select **Backup Device** from the Backup
    Media drop-down list box, and click **Add**.

13. In the Select Backup Device dialog box, select **AdvWorksFull**, and click
    OK.

14. Click **OK** to close the Specify Backup dialog box.

15. Under Select the Backup Sets to Restore, check **all three backups** (full,
    differential, and transaction log). Doing so returns the database to the most
    recent state.

16. On the Options page, make sure the **RESTORE WITH RECOVERY**
    option is selected, because you have no more backups to restore.

17. Click **OK** to begin the restore process.

18. In SQL Server Management Studio, right-click **Database**, and click **Refresh**.

19. Expand **Databases**, and you should see AdventureWorks as usual.

Exercise 16-10   Preparing for a Point-in-Time Restore

1. You need to add a record that will survive the restore. Open a new query in
    SQL Server Management Studio by clicking the **New Query** button on the
    toolbar.

2. To create a new record, enter and execute the following code:

```
USE AdventureWorks
INSERT HumanResources.Shift (Name, StartTime, EndTime,
ModifiedDate) VALUES('Test Shift 1', getdate( ) + 1,
getdate( ) + 2, getdate( ))
```

3. Note the time right now.

4.   Wait two minutes, clear the query window, and then enter a new record using the following code:

```
USE AdventureWorks
INSERT HumanResources.Shift (Name, StartTime, EndTime,
ModifiedDate) VALUES('Test Shift 2', getdate( ) + 1,
getdate( ) + 2, getdate( ))
```

5.   To see both records, clear the query window, and enter and execute the following code:

```
USE AdventureWorks
SELECT * FROM HumanResources.Shift
```

6.   To perform a point-in-time restore, you must perform a transaction log backup. Open **SQL Server Management Studio**. Expand your **server** and then **Databases**.

7.   In Object Explorer, right-click **AdventureWorks**, point to **Tasks**, and select **Back Up**.

8.   In the Back Up dialog box, make sure **AdventureWorks** is the selected database to back up and Backup Type is **Transaction Log**.

9.   Leave the default name in the Name box. In the Description box, type **Point-in-time Backup of AdventureWorks**.

10.   Under Destination, make sure the **AdvWorksFull** device is listed.

11.   On the Options page, make sure **Append to the Existing Backup Set** is selected so you don't overwrite your existing full backup.

12.   On the Options page, select **Verify Backup When Finished**.

13.   Click **OK** to start the backup.

Exercise 16-11   Performing a Point-in-Time Restore

1.   Open **SQL Server Management Studio**. Expand **your server** and then **Databases**.

2.   Right-click **AdventureWorks**, point to **Tasks**, move to **Restore**, and select **Database**.

3.   Click the **ellipsis (...)** button next to the Point-in-Time restore text box.

4. In the Point-in-Time Restore dialog box, enter the time from Step 3 of Exercise 16-10, and click **OK**.

5. Make sure you're restoring from the **AdvWorksFull** device, select **all available backups** in the device, and click **OK** to perform the restore. Return to the **Options** page and check **Overwrite**.

6. To test the restore, open a **new query** in SQL Server Management Studio, and enter and execute the following code:

```
USE AdventureWorks
SELECT * FROM HumanResources.Shift
```

7. Notice that **Test Shift 2** is no longer there, but that **Test Shift 1** remains.

Exercise 16-12   Performing a Piecemeal Restore

1. Right-click the **MSSQL_Training** database in Object Explorer, point to **Tasks**, and select **Backup**.

2. In the Backup dialog box, make sure **MSSQL_Training** is the selected database to back up and Backup Type is **Full**.

3. Under Backup Component, select **Files and Filegroups**.

4. In the Select Files and Filegroups dialog box, check the **MSSQL_Training** box, and click **OK** (notice that all the other boxes in the list are automatically checked for you).

5. Leave the default name in the Name box. In the Description box, type **Piecemeal Backup of MSSQL_Training**.

6. Under Destination, make sure the **AdvWorksFull** device is the only one listed.

7. On the Options page, make sure **Append to the Existing Backup Set** is selected so you don't overwrite your existing backups.

8. On the Options tab, select **Verify Backup When Finished**.

9. Click **OK** to start the backup.

10. Look up the filename and path used in Exercise 16-1 Step 3. You need this data in the RESTORE script code in the next step.

11. To perform a partial restore of the MSSQL_Training database to a new database named MSSQL_Training_part, execute the following code in a new query window:

```
RESTORE DATABASE MSSQL_Training_Part
FILEGROUP = 'PRIMARY'
FROM DISK='<InsertYourFilePath>\AdvWorksFull.bak'
WITH FILE=6, RECOVERY, PARTIAL,
MOVE 'MSSQL_Training_data' TO
'C:\MSSQL_Training_part_data.mdf',
MOVE 'MSSQL_Training_data2' TO
'C:\MSSQL_Training_part_data2.ndf',
MOVE 'MSSQL_Training_log' TO
'C:\MSSQL_Training_part_log.log'
```

12. To test the restore, enter and execute the following code:

```
USE MSSQL_Training_Part
SELECT * FROM Employees
```

13. This code should fail because the filegroup containing the Employees table wasn't restored. Enter and execute this code:

```
USE MSSQL_Training_Part
SELECT * FROM Customers
```

14. Close the query window.

LESSON 18 TEXTBOOK EXERCISES

This lab section contains the following exercise and activity:

Exercise 18-1   Remotely Accessing AdventureWorks

Exercise 18-1   Remotely Accessing AdventureWorks

1. Open **SQL Server Management Studio → Server Objects,** and right-click **Linked Servers**.

2. Select **New Linked Server…** from the context menu.

TAKE NOTE

When asked to insert a product name, put in anything.

3. Enter the server name of someone else in the classroom. If your teacher has assigned partners, use your partner's server name.

4. For the Other Data Source, select **SQL Native Client**.

5. Select the **Security** option in the tree view of **Select a page**.

6. Choose **Be made using the login's current security context**.

7. Accept **all** of the Server Options.

8. Click **OK** to accept this new linked server assignment.

9. Start a new query by clicking on the **New Query** button.

10. Enter the following code (substituting values appropriate to you where needed):

```
SELECT * FROM <YourPartner'sServerName>
.AdventureWorks.Person.Contact
```

11. Scan the results and note they did not come from your database.

LESSON 19 TEXTBOOK EXERCISES

This lab section contains the following exercise and activity:

Exercise 19-1   Creating a DDL Trigger

Exercise 19-1   Creating a DDL Trigger

1. Open a new database query window in the **MSSQL_Training** database.

2. Create a trigger on the database that will roll back every DDL event:

```
CREATE TRIGGER trg_block_ddl ON DATABASE
FOR DDL_DATABASE_LEVEL_EVENTS AS
RAISERROR ('Database locked for DDL events', 16, 1)
ROLLBACK TRANSACTION
```

3. Test the trigger functionality by creating a table:

```
USE MSSQL_Training
CREATE TABLE Test (testid int)
```

4. Drop the existing trigger:

```
DROP TRIGGER trg_block_ddl ON DATABASE
```

LESSON 20 TEXTBOOK EXERCISES

This lab section contains the following exercises and activities:

Exercise 20-1   Installing a Distribution Server

1. Open **Management Studio**, and connect to your server.

2. Right-click **Replication**, and click **Configure Distribution**.

3. You are presented with a welcome page; click **Next** to continue.

4. The **Select Distributor** page appears. Select the server that will act as its own distributor option, and click **Next**.

5. You are now asked to specify the snapshot folder. The only reason to change this is if you are replicating over the Internet and need to specify a folder that is accessible via FTP. Accept the **defaults**, and click **Next**.

6. The Distribution Database page appears next. You can supply a name for the distribution database, as well as location information for its database file and transaction log. Keep the defaults, and click **Next** to continue.

7. Now you are on the Publishers page, where you can choose which servers you want to configure as publishers. The **ellipsis (...)** button allows you to specify security credentials such as login ID and password, as well as the location of the snapshot folder. Be sure to place a check mark next to your local **SQL Server** system, and then click **Next** to continue.

8. On the **Wizard Actions** page, you can have the wizard configure distribution, write a script to configure distribution that you can run later, or both. Leave the Configure distribution box checked, and click **Next** to continue.

9. On the **Complete the Wizard** page, review your selections, and click **Finish**.

10. When the wizard is finished, click **Close**.

Exercise 20-2   Creating a Publication

1. Connect to your **SQL Server** system in Management Studio.

2. Expand **Replication**, right-click **Local Publications**, and click **New Publication**. This brings you to the New Publication Wizard welcome page.

3. Click **Next** to continue.

4. On the Publication Database page, highlight **AdventureWorks**, and click **Next** to continue.

5. On the Publication Type page, you can choose the type of publication to create. For this exercise, choose **Transactional Publication**, and click **Next** to continue.

6. On the **Articles** page, you can select the data and objects you want to replicate. Expand **Tables**, and check the **ProductCategory** box.

7. You can also set the properties for an article from this page. Make sure **ProductCategory** is highlighted, click **Article Properties**, and then click **Set Properties of Highlighted Table Article**.

8. In the Destination Object section, change the Destination Object name to **ReplicatedCategory**, change the Destination Object Owner to **dbo**, and click **OK**.

9. Back at the Articles page, click **Next** to continue.

10. On the next page, you can filter the data that is replicated. You do not want to filter the data in this case, so click **Next** to continue.

11. On the **Snapshot Agent** page, check the box to create a snapshot immediately, and click **Next**.

12. On the **Agent Security** page, you are asked how the agents should log on and access data. To set this for the snapshot agent, click the **Security Settings** button next to **Snapshot Agent**.

13. Ordinarily, you would create an account for the agent to run under, but to make the exercise simpler, you will run the agent using the **SQL Server Agent** service account, so select the radio button for that option, and click **OK**.

14. Back at the Agent Security page, click **Next** to continue.

15. On the Wizard Actions page, you can have the wizard create the publication, write a script to create the publication that you can run later, or both. Leave the **Create the Publication** box checked, and click **Next** to continue.

16. On the **Complete the Wizard** page, you need to enter a name for the new publication, so enter **CategoryPub**, and click **Finish**.

17. When the wizard is finished, click **Close**.

Exercise 20-3   Creating a Subscription

1. Connect to your **SQL Server** system in **SQL Server Management Studio**.

2. Expand **Replication**, right-click **Local Subscriptions**, and click **New Subscription**. This brings you to the New Subscription Wizard welcome page. Click **Next** to continue.

3. On the **Publication** page, select your **server** from the Publisher drop-down list, select **CategoryPub** from the **Databases and Publications** list, and click **Next** to continue.

4. On the **Distribution Agent Location** page, you are asked which machine should run the replication agents, at the distributor or at the subscriber. Because you want to create a pull subscription, select the **Run Each Agent at Its Subscriber** option, and click **Next**.

5. On the **Subscribers** page, you can choose a subscriber for the publication. Check the box next to <**your server**>.

6. The drop-down list is populated with all the available databases on the subscriber. Select the **MSSQL_Training** database, and click **Next**.

7. On the next page, you need to set the distribution agent security. To do so, click the **ellipsis (…)** button in the **Subscription Properties** list.

8. Ordinarily, you would create an account for the agent to run under, but to make the exercise simpler, you will run the agent using the **SQL Server Agent** service account, so select the radio button for that option, and click **OK**.

9. Back at the Distribution Agent Security page, click **Next** to continue.

10. The next step is to set the synchronization schedule. For snapshots, it might be wise to set up some type of regular schedule. For merge replication, you will most likely use a manual form of synchronization called *on demand*. Because you are using transactional replication, select **Run Continuously**, and click **Next** to continue.

11. On the next page, you can tell SQL Server when to initialize the subscription, if at all. If you have already created the schema on the subscriber, you do not need to initialize the subscription. In this case, you should select **Immediately** from the drop-down list, make sure the **Initialize** box is checked, and click **Next** to continue.

12. On the Wizard Actions page, you can have the wizard create the subscription, write a script to create the subscription that you can run later, or both. Leave the **Create the Subscription** box checked, and click **Next** to continue.

13. On the Complete the Wizard page, you can review your options and click **Finish** to create the subscription.

14. When the wizard is finished, click **Close**.

Exercise 20-4   Testing Replication

1. You should have four records in the **ReplicatedCategory** table. To verify that, open a **New Query**, and execute the following code:

```
USE MSSQL_Training
SELECT * FROM ReplicatedCategory
GO
```

2. Now add a new record to the **ProductCategory** table in the AdventureWorks database. Run the following code to add a new record:

```
USE AdventureWorks
INSERT INTO Production.ProductCategory (Name)
VALUES('Tools')
GO
```

3. You should get the message that one row was added. Give the server about a minute to replicate the transaction, then run the following query:

```
USE MSSQL_Training
SELECT * FROM ReplicatedCategory
GO
```

4. You should get five records back. The last record should be the new **Tools** record.

Exercise 20-5   Using Replication Monitor

1. Open **SQL Server Management Studio** on the distribution server.

2. Right-click **Replication**, and select **Launch Replication Monitor**.

3. Expand your **server** to view the publications available.

4. Switch to the **Subscription Watch List** tab. From here you can view reports about the performance of all publications and subscriptions that this distributor handles.

5. Switch to the **Common Jobs** tab. On this tab you can view the status of replication jobs that affect all publications and subscriptions handled by this distributor.

6. Select the **CategoryPub** publication in the left pane.

7. On the All Subscriptions tab, you can view reports about all of the subscriptions for this particular publication.

8. Switch to the **Tracer Token** tab. From here you can insert a special record called a *tracer token* that is used to measure performance for this subscription.

9. To test it, click the **Insert Tracer** button, and wait for the results.

10. Switch to the **Warnings and Agents** tab. From here you can change settings for agents and configure replication alerts.

11. Click the **Configure Alerts** button, select **Replication: Agent Failure**, and click **Configure**.

12. Notice that this opens a new alert dialog box. Check the **Enable** box, and click **OK** to enable this alert.

13. Click **Close** to return to Replication Monitor.

14. Close **Replication Monitor**.

LESSON 21 TEXTBOOK EXERCISES

This lab section contains the following exercises and activities:

Exercise 21-1   Generating a Table Scan

1. Open **SQL Server Management Studio**, and connect using **Windows Authentication**.

2. To force SQL Server to perform a table scan, you need to delete an index (which you'll re-create later in this lesson). In Object Explorer, expand **Server → Databases → AdventureWorks → Tables**.

3. Right-click **HumanResources.EmployeePayHistory**, and select **Modify**.

4. Right-click the **EmployeeID** column, and click **Remove Primary Key**.

5. Click the **Save** button on the toolbar.

6. Open a new query and enter, but do not execute, the following code:

    ```
    USE AdventureWorks
    SELECT * FROM HumanResources.EmployeePayHistory
    ```

7. On the Query menu, click **Display Estimated Execution Plan** (third to the right of the Execute button). This will show you how SQL Server goes about finding your data.

8. Scroll down to the bottom of the results pane, and hover your mouse pointer over the Table Scan icon to view the cost of the scan—this tells you how much CPU time the scan should take (in milliseconds).

Exercise 21-2   Creating an Index

1. Open **SQL Server Management Studio**, and connect using **Windows Authentication**.

2. Expand your server in Object Explorer, and then choose **Databases** → **AdventureWorks** → **Tables** → **HumanResources.EmployeePayHistory**.

3. Right-click **Indexes**, and select **New Index**.

4. Limber up your typing fingers, and in the Index Name box, enter **idx_ModifiedDate**.

5. Select **Nonclustered** for the Index Type option.

6. Click the **Add** button next to the Index Key Columns grid.

7. Select the boxes next to the **ModifiedDate** column.

8. Click **OK** to return to the New Index dialog box.

9. Click **OK** to create the index.

Exercise 21-3   Creating a Primary Key

1. Open **SQL Server Management Studio** and connect using **Windows Authentication**.

2. In Object Explorer, expand **Databases** → **AdventureWorks** → **Tables**.

3. Right-click the **HumanResources.EmployeePayHistory** table, and select **Modify**.

4. Hold down the **Shift** key, and click the **EmployeeID** and **RateChangeDate** columns.

5. Right-click **EmployeeID** under Column Name, and select **Set Primary Key**. Notice that just to the left of both fields a small key icon now denotes that this is the primary key.

6. When you click the **Save** icon on the toolbar, SQL Server will create a new unique index, which ensures that no duplicate values can be entered in the custid field.

7. Close the **Table Designer**.

Exercise 21-4   Creating a Full-Text Catalog and Index

1. Open **SQL Server Management Studio**, and in Object Explorer expand **Databases → AdventureWorks → Tables**.

2. Right-click **Production.Document**, move to **Full-Text Index**, and click **Define Full-Text Index**.

3. On the first screen of the Full-Text Indexing Wizard, click **Next**.

4. For full-text searching to work, each table on which you create a full-text index must already have a unique index associated with it. In this instance, select the default **PK_Document_DocumentID** index, and click **Next**.

5. On the next screen, you are asked which column you want to full-text index. DocumentSummary is the only nvarchar(max) column in the table, so it is the best candidate; select it here by checking the box next to it, then click **Next**.

6. On the next screen, you are asked when you want changes to the full-text index applied. These are your options:

    •   **Automatically:** Means that the full-text index is updated with every change made to the table. This is the easiest way to keep full-text indexes up to date, but it can tax the server because it means changes to the table and index and the associated overhead take place all at once.

    •   **Manually:** Means changes to the underlying data are maintained, but you will have to schedule index population yourself. This is a slightly slower way to update the index, but it is not as taxing on the server because changes to the data are maintained but the index is not updated immediately.

    •   **Do Not Track Changes:** Means changes to the underlying data are not tracked. This is the least taxing, and slowest, way to update the full-text index. Changes are not maintained, so when the index is updated, the FullText Search service must read the entire table for changes before updating the index.

> **Take Note**
>
> Indexing can be dramatically processor-intensive and can noticeably interfere with productivity. Scheduling at a minimum-use period might make sense in your environment.

7. Choose **Automatically**, and click **Next**.

8. The next screen asks you to select a catalog. You'll need to create a new one here, because there are none available. In the Name field, enter **AdventureWorks Catalog**. You can also select a filegroup to place the catalog on. Leave this as default, and click **Next**.

9. On the next screen, you are asked to create a schedule for automatically repopulating the full-text index. If your data is frequently updated, you will want to do this more often, maybe once a day. If it is read more often than it is changed, you should repopulate less frequently. You can schedule population for a single table or an entire catalog at a time. Here, you will set repopulation to happen just once for the entire catalog by clicking the **New Catalog Schedule** button.

10. On the New Schedule Properties screen, enter **Populate AdventureWorks**, and click **OK**.

11. When you are taken back to the **Full-Text Indexing Wizard**, click **Next**.

12. On the final screen of the wizard, you are given a summary of the choices you have made. Click **Finish** to create the index.

13. To see your new catalog and index, in Object Explorer expand the **AdventureWorks → Storage → Full-Text Catalogs**.

14. Double-click the **AdventureWorks** catalog to open its properties.

15. Click **Cancel** to close the Properties window.

Exercise 21-5   Examining Full-Text Search Output

1. Install the Northwind database using the instnwnd.sql file you downloaded from the Wiley Companion site and placed in your C:\Practice folder. Open your **Query Editor**, load the script, and execute. Keeping your Query Editor open, run each of these code blocks in turn—one at a time (this script should also be in your Practice folder). Examine the results of each. Remember that a return value of 0 means false while a return value of 1 indicates true:

   a. ```
   USE Northwind
   SELECT FullTextServiceProperty('IsFullTextInstalled')
   GO
   ```
   ```

b.
```
USE Northwind
SELECT DatabaseProperty('Northwind,
'IsFullTextEnabled')
GO
```

c.
```
USE Northwind
SELECT ColumnProperty
(Object_ID('Employees'),'Notes', 'IsFullTextIndexed')
GO
```

d.
```
USE Northwind
CREATE UNIQUE INDEX ui_EmpID ON
dbo.employees(employeeid)
GO
CREATE FULLTEXT CATALOG ft AS DEFAULT
GO
CREATE FULLTEXT INDEX ON dbo.Employees(Notes)
KEY INDEX ui_EmpID
WITH STOPLIST = SYSTEM;
GO
CREATE FULLTEXT STOPLIST Nwind
```

e.
```
USE Northwind
Exec sp_Help_FullText_Tables
GO
```

f.
```
USE Northwind
Exec sp_Help_FullText_Columns
GO
```

g.
```
USE Northwind
SELECT LastName, Title, HireDate, Notes
FROM Employees
WHERE Contains (Notes, '"University" AND "French"')
GO
```

h.
```
USE Northwind
SELECT LastName, Title, HireDate, Notes
FROM Employees
WHERE Contains (Notes, '"University" OR "French"')
GO
```

i.
```
USE Northwind
SELECT LastName, Title, HireDate, Notes
FROM Employees
WHERE Contains(Notes, '"St. Andrews" NEAR()
"Scotland"')
GO
```

j.
```
USE Northwind
SELECT LastName, Title, HireDate, Notes
FROM Employees
WHERE Contains(Notes, 'FormsOf(Inflectional,
"Graduate")')
GO
```

k.
```
USE Northwind
SELECT LastName, Title, HireDate, Notes
FROM Employees
WHERE Contains (Notes, 'IsAbout (University
Weight(0.8), French Weight(0.2))')
GO
```

l.
```
USE Northwind
SELECT LastName, Title, HireDate, Notes
FROM Employees
WHERE Freetext (Notes, 'John came in from the cold')
GO
```

m.
```
USE Northwind
SELECT e.LastName, e.Title, e.HireDate, KEY_TBL.RANK
FROM Employees e Inner JOIN
ContainsTable(Employees, Notes,
'IsAbout (University weight (.8),
French weight (.4))' ) KEY_TBL
On e.EmployeeId = KEY_TBL.[KEY]
Order By KEY_TBL.RANK Desc
GO
```

n.
```
USE Northwind
SELECT LastName, Title, HireDate, Notes
FROM Employees
WHERE Contains (Notes, 'between')
GO
```

o. Use **Management Studio → Databases → Northwind → Storage → FullText Stoplists**. Right-click **Nwind** and select **Properties**. Examine the user interface. Add a stopword.

p. To see the stopwords in your stoplist, execute the following:

```
USE Northwind
GO
SELECT display_term, column_id, document_count
FROM sys.dm_fts_index_keywords
(DB_ID('Northwind'), OBJECT_ID('dbo.Employees'))
```

2. Clean up after yourself:

```
DROP FULLTEXT STOPLIST Nwind
DROP FULLTEXT INDEX ON dbo.employees
DROP FULLTEXT CATALOG ft

DROP INDEX ui_EmpID ON dbo.employees
```

3. Close your Query Editor.

LESSON 22 TEXTBOOK EXERCISES

This lab section contains the following exercises and activities:

Exercise 22-1   Examining User Options

Exercise 22-2   Viewing the Current Activity Window

Exercise 22-3   Querying a Dynamic Management View

Exercise 22-4   Working with a TRY...CATCH Block

Exercise 22-1   Examining User Options

1. Migrate to a new **Query Editor** session.

2. In the Query Editor, enter the following code:

    ```
    SET TRANSACTION ISOLATION LEVEL READ UNCOMMITTED
    DBCC USEROPTIONS
    ```

3. Examine the output. Near the bottom of the 13 rows returned you should see confirmation of isolation level setting.

Exercise 22-2   Viewing the Current Activity Window

1.   Open **SQL Server Management Studio**.

2.   Click the **plus (+)** sign next to Management in your Object Browser, and double left-click **Activity Monitor**.

3.   Note that in the **Select a page view** you have three choices. Click on **Locks by Object**.

4.   You are presented with a result set identifying the Process ID in the first column and the Request Mode in the eighth column. Note the entries. Go back to Table 22-3, if necessary, and identify each lock type.

5.   Change to **Locks by Process**. Examine the information. Note the Request Mode column is repeated, but the other entries give you slightly different information.

6.   Click on **Process Info**. Perhaps you detected a problem with Process ID 54. Right-click that row, and note that you can kill the process to remove the errant blockage from holding up the rest of your users. Note also that this display indicates the user owning the process. You might talk to him or her prior to bumping him or her off.

Exercise 22-3   Querying a Dynamic Management View

1.   Return to **SQL Server Management Studio**.

2.   Start a **New Query**.

3.   Set up some activity by entering and executing the following T-SQL code:

```
USE TempDB
GO
-- Create a test table and index
CREATE TABLE t_lock (c1 int, c2 int);
GO
CREATE INDEX t_lock_ci on t_lock(c1);
GO
-- Insert values into the test table
INSERT INTO t_lock VALUES (1, 1);
INSERT INTO t_lock VALUES (2, 2);
INSERT INTO t_lock VALUES (3, 3);
INSERT INTO t_lock VALUES (4, 4);
INSERT INTO t_lock VALUES (5, 5);
INSERT INTO t_lock VALUES (6, 6);
```

```
-- Session 1
SET TRANSACTION ISOLATION LEVEL READ COMMITTED;
BEGIN TRAN
-- The next line shows the use of query hints
SELECT c1 FROM t_lock WITH (holdlock, rowlock);
-- Session 2
BEGIN TRAN
UPDATE t_lock SET c1 = 10;
-- Note that both transactions are held open
```

4. Get the identification of TempDB:

```
-- Get TempDB id
SELECT Name, Database_id FROM sys.databases
WHERE Name = 'tempdb'
```

5. Query the dynamic management view:

```
-- Query for lock information.
-- In the query substitute the actual database id
-- you just received for <dbid> in the WHERE
-- clause
SELECT resource_type, resource_associated_entity_id,
request_status, request_mode, request_session_id,
resource_description FROM sys.dm_tran_locks WHERE
resource_database_id = <dbid>
```

6. Examine the output. Both transactions are held open; both must maintain their locks until complete.

7. Return to **SQL Server Management Studio** and the **Current Activity** window. Kill the process listed in the request_session_id column.

Exercise 22-4   Working with a TRY...CATCH Block

1. Type the following code in a new query window:

```
DECLARE @col1 int
DECLARE @col2 int
DECLARE @result decimal (9, 2)
SET @col1 = 5
SET @col2 = 2
SET @result = convert(decimal(9,2),@col1) / @col2
PRINT @result
```

2. When you execute the previous code, you get a result set of 2.5.

3.   Modify the code as follows:

```
DECLARE @col1 int
DECLARE @col2 int
DECLARE @result decimal (9,2)
SET @col1 = 5
SET @col2 = 0
SET @result = convert(decimal(9,2),@col1) / @col2
PRINT @result
```

4.   When you execute the previous code, you will get an error message stating you cannot divide by zero. Your next step is to prevent this error message from occurring by adding a TRY...CATCH block. Modify the code to display this:

```
BEGIN TRY
DECLARE @col1 int
DECLARE @col2 int
DECLARE @result decimal (9,2)
SET @col1 = 5
SET @col2 = 0
SET @result = convert(decimal(9,2),@col1) / @col2
PRINT @result
END TRY
BEGIN CATCH
SELECT error_message( ), error_number( )
END CATCH
```

LESSON 23 TEXTBOOK EXERCISES

This lab section contains the following exercises and activities:

Exercise 23-1   Importing Data from a Text File Using bcp

1. Open a new database query window in **SQL Server Management Studio**.

2. Type the following syntax to create the Countries table:

```
USE MSSQL_Training
CREATE TABLE Countries
(CountryCode char(2), CountryName varchar(50))
```

3. After you execute the **CREATE TABLE** statement (by clicking the **Execute** button or pressing the **F5** function key), you may close SQL Management Studio.

4.   Open a command prompt window, and change the directory location to your C:\Practice directory and locate the countries.txt file.

5.   You will now use the bcp utility to import data from a text file by typing the following command:

```
bcp MSSQL_Training.dbo.countries in
C:\Practice\countries.txt -f
C:\Practice\countries.fmt -T
```

6.   When you execute this command, you will get the following result set:

```
Starting copy...
4 rows copied.
Network packet size (bytes): 4096
Clock Time (ms.): total 1
```

7.   Now use the sqlcmd command to verify that the records have successfully been inserted using the bcp utility:

```
sqlcmd -E -Q "SELECT * FROM SSQL_Training.dbo.countries"
```

8.   This results in the following:

```
countrycode countryname
----------- ------------------------------

BE Belgium
CA Canada
US USA
FR France
(4 rows affected)
```

9.   Close the command prompt window.

Exercise 23-2   Importing Data

1.   Open an existing package and review its content.

2.   In your C:\Practice directory, double-click **DemoSolution.ssln**.

3.   View the **Data Flow** panel:

   a.   View the data coming from the Excel spreadsheet (BabyNames.xls).
   b.   View the two data sources going to SQL Server.

4. Execute the SSIS package by deploying it and then executing it using **dtsexec**. You will only debug the package and check its execution, rather than compile it and run it using dtsexec or schedule it to run as a job.

5. To debug the package, hit the **F5** function key to execute it. You will see that the package executes successfully.

6. On the Data Flow panel, review the inserted number of records.

Exercise 23-3   Exporting Data

1. Click **Start**, point to **All Programs**, point to **Microsoft SQL Server**, and then click **SQL Server Management Studio**.

2. In the Connect to Server dialog box, specify the values in the following table and click **Connect**.

Property	Value
Server type	Database engine
Server name	<YourComputerName>
Authentication	Windows Authentication

3. If Object Explorer is not visible, click **Object Explorer** on the View menu.

4. In Object Explorer, expand **Databases**.

5. Right-click **AdventureWorks**, point to **Tasks**, and then click **Export Data**.

6. Click **Next** on the Welcome to SQL Server Import and Export Wizard page.

7. In the Choose a Data Source page, specify the values in the following table, and then click **Next**.

Property	Value
Data source	SQL Native Client
Server name	<YourComputerName>
Authentication	Windows Authentication
Database	AdventureWorks

8. In the Choose a Destination page, specify the values in the following table, and then click **Next**.

Property	Value
Destination	Flat-file destination
Filename	C:\Contacts.txt
Locale	English (United States)
Code page	1252 (ANSI Latin 1)
Format	Delimited
Text qualifier	<None>
Column names in the first data row	Select the check box

9. In the Specify Table Copy or Query page, select **Write a query** to specify the data to transfer, and then click **Next**.

10. In the Provide a Source Query page, type:

```
SELECT Firstname, Lastname FROM Person.Contact
WHERE ContactID < 10
```

and then click **Next**.

11. In the Configure Flat File Destination page, accept the default file settings, and then click **Next**.

12. In the Save and Execute Package page, make sure **Execute immediately** is selected, and then click **Finish**.

13. In the Complete the Wizard page, click **Finish**. When execution has completed successfully, click **Close**.

14. Open **C:\Contacts.txt** in Notepad, and then make sure that you have exported the correct data.

15. Close **Notepad** and **SQL Server Management Studio**.

Exercise 23-4   Running the Copy Database Wizard

1. Open **SQL Server Management Studio**, expand your server, and expand **Databases**.

2. Right-click the **MSSQL_Training database**, go to **Tasks**, and select **Copy Database**. You will see the welcome page.

3.   Click **Next**.

4.   On the second page, you are asked to select a source server. Select the default instance of your server and the proper authentication type (usually Windows Authentication), and click **Next**.

5.   On the next page, you need to select a destination. Here you will choose the **(local) instance** of the server as the destination. Choose the appropriate security, and click **Next**.

6.   Next you are asked which mode you would like to use. Attach/detach is useful for copying databases between servers that are in remote locations from each other and requires the database to be taken offline. The SQL Management Object transfer method allows you to keep the database online and gives you the flexibility to make a copy on the same server, so select the **SQL Management Object Method** option, and click **Next**.

7.   Next you are asked which database you would like to move or copy. Check the **Copy** box next to MSSQL_Training, and click **Next**.

8.   On the **Database Destination** page, you need to make a few changes:

     a.   Change the destination database name to **MSSQL_Training_Copy**.
     b.   Change MSSQL_Training.mdf to **MSSQL_Training_copy.mdf**.
     c.   Change MSSQL_Training_log.ldf to **MSSQL_Training_log_copy.ldf**.

9.   Click **Next**. You now have the option to change the name of the package that will be created. This only matters if you plan to save the package and execute it later. Accept the defaults, and click **Next**.

10. On the next page, you are asked when you would like to run the SSIS job created by the wizard. Select **Run Immediately**, and click **Next**.

11. The final page summarizes the choices you have made. Click **Finish** to copy the MSSQL_Training database.

12. You will see the **Log Detail** page, which shows you each section of the job as it executes. Clicking the **Report** button will show each step of the job and its outcome.

13. Click **Close** on the Performing Operation page to complete the wizard. The Copy Database Wizard is a simple tool that makes a complex task much easier.

Exercise 23-5   Moving User Databases

Take Note

The following example moves a database named AdventureWorks. This database contains one data file, AdventureWorks_Data.mdf, and one log file, AdventureWorks_Log.ldf. If the database that you move in your production environment has more data files or log files, specify the files in a comma-delimited list in the sp_attach_db stored procedure. The sp_detach_db procedure does not change regardless of how many files the database contains because the sp_detach_db procedure does not list the files.

1. Detach the database as follows:

    ```
    USE master
    GO
    sp_detach_db 'AdventureWorks'
    GO
    ```

2. Next, create a new folder at the root of your C: drive (C:\Sqldata). Copy the data files and the log files from the current location to the new location (C:\Sqldata).

3. Reattach the database. Point to the files in the new location as follows:

    ```
    USE master
    GO
    sp_attach_db 'AdventureWorks',
    'C:\Sqldata\AdventureWorks_Data.mdf',
    'C:\Sqldata\AdventureWorks_Log.ldf'
    GO
    ```

4. Verify the change in file locations by using the sp_helpfile stored procedure:

    ```
    USE AdventureWorks
    go
    sp_helpfile
    GO
    ```

    The filename column values should reflect the new locations.

LESSON 24 TEXTBOOK EXERCISES

This lab section contains the following exercises and activities:

Exercise 24-1   Creating a Table Containing an XML Column

Exercise 24-2   Decomposing XML into Relational Data

Exercise 24-1   Creating a Table Containing an XML Column

1. Create a table with an XML column:

    ```
    CREATE Table Publishers (PublisherID int, PublisherName
    varchar(50), Publishercontactdetails XML)
    ```

2. Insert valid XML in the table:

    ```
    INSERT INTO publishers
    VALUES (1,'Wiley','<ROOT><Publisher>
    John Wiley &amp; Sons</Publisher></ROOT> ')
    ```

3. Insert valid XML in the table:

    ```
    INSERT INTO publishers VALUES (1,'Wiley',
    '<invalid>Wrong Format>')
    ```

4. The previous INSERT statement will result in an error message:

    ```
    Msg 102, Level 15, State 1, Line 2
    Incorrect syntax near '<invalid>Wrong Format>'.
    ```

Exercise 24-2   Decomposing XML into Relational Data

1. In SQL Server Management Studio, open a new query window, and connect to the **MSSQL_Training database**.

2. Type and execute the following syntax to create a new schema:

```
CREATE SCHEMA EventFunctions
GO
```

3. After you have created the schema, you will create a function that decomposes the Eventdata:

```
-- Create a function that decomposes the Transact-SQL
-- statement out of Eventdata
CREATE FUNCTION EventFunctions.fn_Eventtype (@eventdata
xml)
RETURNS nvarchar(max)
AS
BEGIN
RETURN @eventdata.value
('(/EVENT_INSTANCE/EventType)[1]','nvarchar(max)')
END
GO
```

4. Type the following syntax to decompose the Transact-SQL statement from the XML collection:

```
-- Create a function that decomposes the Transact-SQL
-- statement out of Eventdata
CREATE FUNCTION EventFunctions.fn_TSQLStatement
(@eventdata xml)
RETURNS nvarchar(max)
AS
BEGIN
RETURN
@eventdata.value
('(/EVENT_INSTANCE/TSQLCommand/
CommandText)[1]','nvarchar(max)')
END
GO
```

5. Create a DDL trigger in which you will call the two functions you created:

```
-- Create a ddl trigger to test the functionality
CREATE TRIGGER TRG_DDL_event ON DATABASE
FOR DDL_DATABASE_LEVEL_EVENTS
AS
declare @eventdata xml
SET @eventdata = EVENTDATA()
SELECT EventFunctions.fn_TSQLStatement (@eventdata),
EventFunctions.
fn_TSQLStatement (@eventdata)
```

6. Test the trigger's functionality by creating a table:

```
CREATE TABLE tbl_test (test int)
```

7. This will give you the following result set:

```
CREATE TABLE tbl_test (test int)
```

8. Drop the trigger you created:

```
DROP TRIGGER TRG_DDL_event ON DATABASE
```

LESSON 25
TEXTBOOK
EXERCISES

This lab section contains the following exercises and activities:

Exercise 25-1   Configuring Database Mirroring

Exercise 25-2   Implementing Database Snapshots

Exercise 25-1   Configuring Database Mirroring

Before starting, determine the connection string required for each of the three instances you will be using. It's likely to be <YourComputerName> \ <InstanceName>, for example, SERVER\INSTANCE1. The service name takes a different form, for example, MSSQL$INSTANCE1.

Instance Name	Service Name	Role
		Principle <Instance1>
		Mirror <Instance2>
		Witness <Instance3>

1. Log on to the operating system as **Administrator** with the password **Pa$$w0rd**. To complete this lab, you must start each instance of SQL Server running on your computer.

2. Open a **command prompt**.

3. Enter the following command:

    ```
    ECHO %COMPUTERNAME%
    ```

4. The name of your computer will be displayed on the screen. Note this name and use it whenever the placeholder text <Instance*x*> is used in this exercise.

5. Enter the following command to stop the default instance of SQL Server 2005 without any service packs:

    ```
    NET STOP <Instance1>
    ```

    Otherwise, skip this step and Step 6.

6. For SQL Server 2005 editions without any service packs, enter the following command to start the default instance of SQL Server on your computer with trace flag 1400 on. Trace flags are used to start the server with nonstandard behavior. This flag enables the creation of the database mirroring endpoint, which is required for setting up and using database mirroring:

    ```
    NET START <Instance1> /T1400
    ```

7. Enter the following command to start SQL Server <Instance1> on your computer:

    ```
    NET START <Instance1>
    ```

8. Enter the following command to start the SQL Server <Instance2> on your computer:

    ```
    NET START <Instance2>
    ```

9. Close the **Command Prompt** window.

10. Open **SQL Server Management Studio**.

11. In the Connect to SQL Server dialog box, enter or confirm the following details, and then click **Connect**.

User Interface Element	*Value*
Server type	Database Engine
Server name	<Instance1>
Authentication	Windows Authentication

12. Using Object Explorer, view the **properties** of the **AdventureWorks** database on the localhost server.

13. On the **Options** page of the Database Properties dialog box, set the recovery model of the database to **Full**. Click **OK** to implement the change.

14. Create a new **SQL Server query** (connecting to the localhost server using Windows Authentication), and add **Transact-SQL code** to back up the AdventureWorks database using the settings itemized in the following table:

Setting	Value
Database	AdventureWorks
Backup device	C:\Practice\AWBackup.bak
Options	CHECKSUM, NOFORMAT

15. It probably looks like this; if so, execute it:

```
USE master
GO
BACKUP DATABASE AdventureWorks TO DISK =
N'C:\Practice\AWBackup.bak' WITH CHECKSUM, NOFORMAT
GO
```

16. When the backup has completed, view the contents of the **C:\Practice** folder and verify that a file named **AWBackup.bak** has been created.

17. Create a new **SQL Server query** (connecting to the <Instance2> server using Windows Authentication), and add a **RESTORE DATABASE** statement using the settings described in the following table. Check that the pathnames for the databases are correct for your instance configuration:

Setting	Value
Database	AdventureWorks
Backup device	C:\Practice\AWBackup.bak
File	1
Move	C:\Program Files\Microsoft SQL Server\<Instance1>\ MSSQL\DATA\AdventureWorks_Data.NDF and C:\Program Files\Microsoft SQL Server\<Instance1> \MSSQL\DATA\AdventureWorks_Log.NDF
Options	CHECKSUM, NORECOVERY, REPLACE (Note: The replace is in case AdventureWorks is already loaded; in this lesson, it's probably not needed.

18. The code probably looks like this; if so, execute it to restore the database to the mirror server:

```
-- Restore database on mirror server
-- Run on Instance2
USE master
GO
```

TAKE NOTE

The following file paths may not even be correct for your installation of SQL Server 2005. Adjust the path to fit your installation.

```
RESTORE DATABASE AdventureWorks FROM  DISK =
N'C:\Practice\AWBackup.bak' WITH  FILE = 1,
MOVE N'AdventureWorks_Data' TO N'C:\Program
Files\Microsoft SQL Server
\<Instance2>\MSSQL\DATA\AdventureWorks_Data.MDF',
MOVE N'dat1' TO N'C:\Program Files\Microsoft SQL
Server\<Instance2>\MSSQL\DATA\dat1.ndf',
MOVE N'dat2' TO N'C:\Program Files\Microsoft SQL
Server\<Instance2>\MSSQL\DATA\dat2.ndf',
MOVE N'AdventureWorks_Log' TO N'C:\Program
Files\Microsoft SQL
Server\<Instance2>\MSSQL\DATA\AdventureWorks_Log.LDF',
CHECKSUM, NORECOVERY
GO
```

Take Note

When multiple instances of SQL Server are participating in mirroring sessions on the same computer, each instance requires an endpoint configured with a unique port. In this exercise, you will use port 5022 for the principal server <Instance1>, port 5023 for the mirror server <Instance2>, and port 5024 for the witness server <Instance3>. You should not use mirroring with multiple instances on the same computer in a production environment because this configuration does not provide adequate protection against hardware failure.

19. In the query window connected to <Instance1>, add **Transact-SQL code** to add a mirroring endpoint by using the settings listed in the following table.

Setting	Value
Endpoint Name	AdvWorksEndpoint_1
State	STARTED
TCP Listener Port Role	5022
Role	PARTNER

20.   Run the code that you just added, which probably looks like this:

```
USE master
GO
CREATE ENDPOINT AdvWorksEndpoint_1 STATE = STARTED AS
TCP ( LISTENER_PORT = 5022 ) FOR DATABASE_MIRRORING
(ROLE=PARTNER)
GO
```

21.   In the query window connected to <Instance2>, add **Transact-SQL code** to
add a mirroring endpoint by using the settings listed in the following table:

Setting	*Value*
Endpoint Name	AdvWorksEndpoint_2
State	STARTED
TCP Listener Port	5023
Role	PARTNER

22.   Run the code that you just added, which, again, probably looks like this:

```
USE master
GO
CREATE ENDPOINT AdvWorksEndpoint_2
STATE = STARTED
AS TCP ( LISTENER_PORT = 5023 )
FOR DATABASE_MIRRORING (ROLE=PARTNER)
GO
```

23.   Create a new **SQL Server query** (connecting to <Instance3> by using
Windows Authentication).

24.   In the query window connected to <Instance3>, add **Transact-SQL code** to
add a mirroring endpoint by using the settings shown in the following table:

Setting	*Value*
Endpoint Name	AdvWorksEndpoint_3
State	STARTED
TCP Listener Port	5024
Role	WITNESS

25. Run the code you just added, which probably looks like this:

```
USE master
GO
CREATE ENDPOINT AdvWorksEndpoint_3
STATE = STARTED
AS TCP ( LISTENER_PORT = 5024 )
FOR DATABASE_MIRRORING (ROLE=WITNESS)
GO
```

26. In the query window connected to <Instance2>, add **Transact-SQL code** to identify the principal server (TCP://<YourComputerName>:5022) as the mirror server's partner.

27. Run the script. It looks something like this, right?

```
USE master
GO
ALTER DATABASE AdventureWorks
SET PARTNER = 'TCP://<YourComputerName>:5022'
```

28. In the query window connected to <Instance1>, add **Transact-SQL code** to identify the mirror server (TCP://<YourComputerName>:5023) as the principal server's partner.

29. Run this script:

```
USE master
GO
ALTER DATABASE AdventureWorks
SET PARTNER = 'TCP://<YourComputerName>:5022'
```

30. In the query window connected to <Instance1>, add **Transact-SQL code** to retrieve the following columns from the sys.database_mirroring catalog view:

- mirroring_state_desc
- mirroring_partner_name
- mirroring_witness_name
- mirroring_witness_state_desc
- mirroring_role_desc
- mirroring_safety_level_desc

31. Run this script and review the results that describe the mirroring partnership:

```
-- Run on <Instance1> and
-- <Instance2>
```

```
SELECT mirroring_state_desc
, mirroring_partner_name
, mirroring_witness_name
, mirroring_witness_state_desc
, mirroring_role_desc
, mirroring_safety_level_desc
FROM sys.database_mirroring
```

32. In the query window connected to <Instance1>, add **Transact-SQL code** to specify TCP://<YourComputerName>:5024 as a witness server.

33. Execute this script:

```
USE master
GO
ALTER DATABASE AdventureWorks
SET WITNESS = 'TCP://<YourComputerName>:5024'
```

34. Create a new **SQL Server query** (connecting to the <Instance2> server using Windows Authentication), and add **Transact-SQL code** to retrieve the following columns from the sys.database_mirroring_witnesses catalog view:

   - database name
   - principal_server_name
   - mirror_server_name
   - safety_level_desc

35. Run the script and review the results:

```
-- View session properties
-- Run on the third instance
SELECT database_name
, principal_server_name
, mirror_server_name
, safety_level_desc
FROM sys.database_mirroring_witnesses
```

36. Open the **Performance** tool from the Administrative Tools group on the Start menu.

37. Delete any performance counters that are currently displayed.

38. Click the **Add** button on the toolbar.

39. In the Add Counters dialog box, in the Performance object list, click **SQL Server:Database Mirroring**.

40.   In the counters list, click **Send/Receive Ack Time**, and then click **Add**.

41.   Click **Close** to close the dialog box.

42.   In the query window connected to <Instance1>, add the following Transact-SQL code to update the AdventureWorks database:

```
USE AdventureWorks
UPDATE Person.Contact
SET LastName = 'Smith'
WHERE LastName = 'Abercrombie'
```

43.   Execute the script.

44.   Switch to the **Performance** tool.

45.   Note the spike in the Send/Receive Ack counter.

46.   Close the **Performance** tool.

47.   In the query window connected to <Instance2>, add the following **Transact-SQL code** to query the Adventure Works database:

```
USE AdventureWorks
SELECT * FROM Person.Contact
```

48.   Execute the script. Note the query cannot execute because the database is acting as a mirror database.

49.   In the query window connected to <Instance1>, add **Transact-SQL code** to initiate manual failover to the mirror server. It should look something like this:

```
-- Run on <Instance1>
USE master
GO
ALTER DATABASE AdventureWorks
SET PARTNER FAILOVER
GO
```

50.   Execute the script.

51.   In the query window connected to <Instance2>, add **Transact-SQL code** to retrieve the following columns from the sys.database_mirroring_witnesses catalog view:

- Database_name
- Principal_server_name

- Mirror_Server_name
- Safety_level_desc

52. Execute the script and review the results. Verify that the original mirror server (computer name:5023) is now the principal server, and vice versa.

```
-- View session properties
-- Run on <YourComputerName>\<Instance2>
SELECT database_name
, principal_server_name
, mirror_server_name
, safety_level_desc
FROM sys.database_mirroring_witnesses
```

53. In the query window connected to <Instance2>, add the following **Transact-SQL code** to query the AdventureWorks database:

```
USE AdventureWorks
SELECT * FROM Person.Contact
```

54. Execute the script and verify that the data is available.

55. In the query window connected to <Instance1>, add the following **Transact-SQL code** to query the AdventureWorks database:

```
USE AdventureWorks
SELECT * FROM Person.Contact
```

56. Execute the script. Note that the query cannot be executed because the database is now acting as a mirror database.

57. In the query window connected to <Instance1>, add **Transact-SQL code** to terminate the mirror session.

58. Execute the following script:

```
-- Run on <YourComputerName>\<Instance1>
USE master
GO
ALTER DATABASE AdventureWorks
SET PARTNER OFF
```

59. In the query window connected to <Instance3>, add Transact-SQL code to retrieve the following columns from the sys.databases_ mirroring_witnesses catalog view:

- Database_name
- Principal_server_name

- Mirror_server_name
- Safety_level_desc

60. Execute the script and review the results. Note that no rows exist because the database is no longer mirrored:

```
-- View session properties
-- Run on <YourComputerName>\<Instance2>
SELECT database_name
, principal_server_name
, mirror_server_name
, safety_level_desc
FROM sys.database_mirroring_witnesses
```

61. In Object Explorer, expand **Databases** and note that the AdventureWorks database is still in a restoring state.

62. In the query window connected to the <Instance1>, add **Transact-SQL code** to recover the database.

63. Execute this script:

```
-- Run on <Instance1>
RESTORE DATABASE AdventureWorks
WITH RECOVERY
```

64. Refresh the **Object Explorer** window to verify the new state of the database.

65. In the query window connected to <Instance1>, add **Transact-SQL code** to update the AdventureWorks database:

```
USE AdventureWorks
SELECT * FROM Person.Contact
```

66. Execute the script to confirm that the database is now accessible.

67. Close **SQL Server Management Studio** without saving changes.

68. Open a **command prompt**.

69. Enter the following command:

```
NET STOP <Instance1> /Y
```
This will stop SQL Server <Instance1> on your computer.

70. Enter the following command to stop SQL Server <Instance2> on your computer:

```
NET STOP <Instance2> /Y
```

71.   Enter the following command to stop the default instance of SQL Server on your computer:

```
NET STOP <Instance3> /Y
```

72.   Enter the following command to start the default instance of SQL Server without trace flag 1400:

```
NET START <Instance1>
```

73.   Close the **Command Prompt** window.

More Information

As the cost of bandwidth falls lower and lower, it could be interesting to combine a clustered environment with database mirroring on specific user databases.

In an ideal scenario, a company would then be able to keep its business running from a remote location when an entire region or area goes down. One of the key problems with clustering is that a company is limited to a geographical location that requires servers to be close to each other because of the cluster "heartbeat" and shared data store.

In previous editions of SQL Server, a lot of companies used a similar method via replication. They would replicate an entire user database to a remote server, which was hosted in an external data center that would allow them to switch over to the remote server in case of a server or database outage. This, however, caused a lot of implications once the "principal" server came up again, as they had to resynchronize and, essentially, break the replication.

Exercise 25-2   Implementing Database Snapshots

1.   Connect to **SQL Server Management Studio**, and open a **new query** window.

2.   In the new query window, type the following syntax to create a database snapshot. If you have multiple files, you need to list each logical name and filename separately. (See "How to Create a Database Snapshot" in Books Online.)

```
CREATE DATABASE MSSQL_Training_snapshot ON
( NAME = MSSQL_Training_data , FILENAME =
'C:\MSSQL_TrainingSnapshot.mdf' )
AS SNAPSHOT OF MSSQL_Training;
```

3.   After you have created the snapshot, insert a record into the actual database:

```
USE MSSQL_Training
INSERT INTO Countries values ('ES', 'Spain')
```

4.   Review the data stored in the snapshot:

```
USE MSSQL_Training_SNAPSHOT
SELECT * FROM Countries
```

5.   This will result in the following:

```
countrycode countryname
---------- --------------------
BE Belgium
CA Canada
US USA
FR France
(4 row(s) affected)
```

6.   Update a record in the MSSQL_Training database:

```
USE MSSQL_Training
UPDATE Countries
SET countryname = 'BelUSA'
WHERE countrycode = 'BE'
```

7.   Review the data stored in the snapshot:

```
USE MSSQL_Training_SNAPSHOT
SELECT * FROM Countries
```

8.   This will result in the following:

```
countrycode countryname
---------- ----------------------
BE Belgium
CA Canada
US USA
FR France
(4 row(s) affected)
```

9.   Drop the table in the MSSQL_Training database:

```
USE MSSQL_Training
DROP TABLE Countries
```

10.   Review the table existence in the Snapshot database.

```
USE MSSQL_Training_SNAPSHOT
SELECT * FROM Countries
```

11. This will result in the following:

```
countrycode countryname
----------- ----------------------
BE Belgium
CA Canada
US USA
FR France
(4 row(s) affected)
```

12. Perform a bulk insert to re-create the object in the MSSQL_Training database:

```
USE MSSQL_Training
SELECT * INTO Countries
FROM MSSQL_Training_snapshot.dbo.Countries
```

13. You have now successfully re-created a dropped object using database snapshots.

LESSON 26 TEXTBOOK EXERCISES

This lab section contains the following exercises and activities:

Exercise 26-17   Creating a WMI Alert

Exercise 26-18   Running the Maintenance Plan Wizard

Exercise 26-1   Reconstructing an Index

1. Open a **new query** in **SQL Server Management Studio**, and execute the following code to find the current amount of fragmentation on the Production.Product table:

```
USE AdventureWorks;
SELECT INDEX_ID, AVG_FRAGMENTATION_IN_PERCENT
FROM sys.dm_db_index_physical_stats (db_id(),
Object_ID(N'Production.Product'),
Default, Default, 'DETAILED');
```

2. Enter and execute the following code to reconstruct the index on the Products table:

```
USE AdventureWorks;
ALTER INDEX ALL
ON Production.Product
REBUILD WITH (FILLFACTOR = 80, ONLINE = ON,
-- ONLINE = ON only works with Enterprise Edition
STATISTICS_NORECOMPUTE = ON);
```

3. Query the sys.DM_DB_INDEX_PHYSICAL_STATS statement to see whether the fragmentation is gone:

```
USE AdventureWorks;
SELECT INDEX_ID, AVG_FRAGMENTATION_IN_PERCENT
FROM sys.dm_db_index_physical_stats
(db_id(),Object_ID(N'Production.Product') ,
Default, Default, 'DETAILED');
```

4. You should see 0 percent fragmentation.

Exercise 26-2   Updating Index Statistics

1. Open a **new query** in **SQL Server Management Studio**.

2. Enter and execute the following code to reconstruct the index on the Sales.SalesOrderDetail table:

```
USE AdventureWorks
UPDATE STATISTICS Sales.SalesOrderDetail
```

Exercise 26-3   Using DBCC CHECKDB on AdventureWorks

1. Open a **new query** in **SQL Server Management Studio**.

2. Enter and execute the following code to check the **AdventureWorks** database for errors:

```
USE AdventureWorks
DBCC CHECKDB
```

3. You should see the results in the Messages pane.

Exercise 26-4   Shrinking the AdventureWorks Database

1. Open **SQL Server Management Studio**, and expand **<your server>** and then **Databases**.

2. You need to add some space to the database, so right-click **AdventureWorks**, and select **Properties**.

3. On the **Files** page, add **10 MB** to the size of the AdventureWorks_Data file.

4. Click **OK**.

5. Right-click **AdventureWorks**, go to **Tasks**, select **Shrink**, and finally click **Database**. You should see about 10 MB of free space.

6. Check the **Reorganize Files...** box, and click **OK**.

7. Right-click **AdventureWorks**, go to **Tasks**, select **Shrink**, and finally click **Database**. You should see very little free space.

8. Click **Cancel** to close the dialog box.

Exercise 26-5   Configuring a Mailhost

1. Open **SQL Server Management Studio**, and connect to your server.

2. Expand **Management** in Object Explorer, right-click **Database Mail**, and select **Configure Database Mail**.

3. On the Select Configuration Task page, select **Set Up Database Mail by Performing the Following Tasks**, and click **Next**.

4. If a dialog box opens and asks you whether you would like to enable Database Mail, click **Yes**.

5. On the **New Profile** page, create a mail profile, and associate it with a mail server account:

   a. Enter **SQLAgentProfile** in the Profile Name box.
   b. Under SMTP Accounts, click **Add**.
   c. In the Account Name box, enter **Mail Provider Account 1**.
   d. In the Description box, enter **e-mail account information**.
   e. Fill in your outgoing mail server information using the information provided by your ISP or network administrator.
   f. If your email server requires you to log in, check the **SMTP Server Requires Authentication** box, and enter your login information.
   g. Click **OK** to return to the wizard. Your account should now be listed under SMTP Accounts.

6. Click **Next**.

7. On the **Manage Profile Security** page, check the **Public** box next to the mail profile you just created to make it accessible to all users. Set the Default Profile option to **Yes**, and click **Next**.

8. On the **Configure System Parameters** page, accept the defaults, and click **Next**.

9. On the **Complete the Wizard** page, review all your settings, and click **Finish**.

10. When the system is finished setting up Database Mail, click **Close**.

Exercise 26-6   Configuring the SQL Server Agent to Use the Mailhost

1. In **Object Explorer**, right-click **SQL Server Agent**, and select **Properties**.

2. On the **Alert System** page, check the **Enable Mail Profile** box.

3. Select **Database Mail** from the Mail System drop-down list.

4. Select **SQLAgentProfile** from the Mail Profile drop-down list.

5. Click **OK**.

6. From **SQL Server Configuration Manager**, stop and restart the **SQL Server Agent** service.

Exercise 26-7   Configuring an Operator

1. Open **SQL Server Management Studio**.

2. In Object Explorer, expand **<your server>** and then **SQL Server Agent**.

3. Right-click **Operators**, and select **New Operator**.

4. In the Name box, enter **Administrator**.

5. Enter your **e-mail address** as the email name.

6. If you carry a pager that is capable of receiving email, you can enter your pager's email address in the Pager E-mail Name box.

7. At the bottom of the page, you can select the days and times this operator is available for notification. If a day is checked, the operator will be notified on that day between the start and end times noted under Start Time and End Time. Check the box for each day, and leave the default workday times of 8:00 AM to 6:00 PM.

8. For now, click **OK** to create the operator.

Exercise 26-8   Configuring a Fail-Safe Operator

1. In **SQL Server Management Studio**, right-click the **SQL Server Agent** icon in Object Explorer, and select **Properties**.

2. On the **Alert System** page, check the **Enable Fail-Safe Operator** box.

3. Select **Administrator** in the Operator drop-down list.

4. Check the box next to **E-mail** so you'll receive email messages as a fail-safe operator.

5. Click **OK** to apply the changes.

Exercise 26-9   Creating a Job

1. Open **SQL Server Management Studio**.

2. Expand **your server** in Object Explorer, and then expand **SQL Server Agent**.

3. Right-click **Jobs**, and select **New Job**.

4. In the **Name** box, type **Create Test Database** (leave the rest of the boxes on this page with the default settings).

5. Go to the **Steps** page, and click the **New** button to create a new step.

6. In the **Step Name** box, type **Create Database**.

7. Leave **Type** as **Transact-SQL**, and enter the following code to create a database named **Test** on the C:\Practice drive:

```
CREATE DATABASE TEST ON
PRIMARY (NAME = test_dat,
FILENAME = 'C:\Practice\test.mdf',
SIZE = 10MB,
MAXSIZE = 15,
FILEGROWTH = 10%)
```

8. Click the **Parse** button to verify you entered the code correctly, and then move to the **Advanced** page.

9. On the **Advanced** page, verify that **On Success Action** is set to **Go to the Next Step** and that **On Failure Action** is set to **Quit the Job Reporting Failure**. Click **OK**.

10. To create the second step of the job, click the **New** button.

11. In the Name box, enter **Backup Test**.

12. Leave **Type** as **Transact-SQL Script**, and enter the following code to back up the database once it's created:

```
EXEC sp_addumpdevice 'disk', 'Test_Backup',
'C:\Practice\Test_Backup.dat'
BACKUP DATABASE TEST TO Test_Backup
```

13. Click **OK** to create the step; you should now have two steps listed on the **Steps** page.

14. Move to the **Schedules** page, and click the **New** button to create a schedule that will instruct SQL Server when to fire the job.

15. In the Name box, type **Create and Back Up Database**.

16. Select **One Time** from the Schedule Type drop-down list. Set the time to be five minutes from the time displayed in the system tray (usually, at the bottom-right corner of your screen).

17. Click **OK** to create the schedule and move to the **Notifications** tab.

18. On the **Notifications** tab, check the boxes next to **E-mail**, choosing **Administrator** as the operator to notify. Next to each, select **When the Job Completes** from the list box (this will notify you no matter what the outcome of the job is).

19. Click **OK** to create the job. Wait until the time set in Step 16 to verify completion. You should see a message pop up on your screen, notifying you of completion.

Exercise 26-10   Creating an Alert for a Standard Error

1. Open **SQL Server Management Studio**, expand <**your server**>, and then expand **SQL Server Agent**.

2. Right-click **Alerts**, and select **New Alert**.

3. In the Name box, enter **Number Alert**.

4. Select **SQL Server Event Alert** from the Type list.

5. Select <**all databases**> from the Database Name list.

6. Check the **Error Number** radio button, and enter **14599** in the text box.

7. On the Response page, check the **Notify Operators** box, and check the **E-mail** box next to Administrator.

8. On the **Options** page, check the **E-mail** box under Include Error Alert Text In, and click **OK**.

Exercise 26-11   Testing an Alert with RAISERROR( )

1. Open a new SQL Server query by clicking the **New Query** button in **SQL Server Management Studio**.

2. Enter and execute the following code to fire the error (the WITH LOG option forces SQL Server to write the event to the Windows Application Event log):

```
RAISERROR(14599,10,1) WITH LOG
```

3. When your email message arrives, note the detail it gives you, including the error number, description, and additional text.

Exercise 26-12 Modifying an Alert to Run a Job

1. First you need a job to run, so in SQL Server Management Studio, expand **SQL Server Agent**, right-click **Jobs**, and select **New Job**.

2. Enter **Backup Test** in the Job name box.

3. On the Steps page, click the **New** button, and enter this information:

    a. Enter **Backup AdventureWorks** in the Step Name box.
    b. Enter this code in the Command box:

    ```
    BACKUP DATABASE AdventureWorks
    TO DISK = 'C:\Practice\AdventureWorks.bak'
    ```

    c. Click **OK**, and then click **OK** again to create the backup job.

4. To create the alert, expand **Alerts** under SQL Server Agent.

5. Right-click **Number Alert**, and select **Properties**.

6. Select the **Response** page.

7. Check the **Execute Job** box, and enter Backup Test in the Job name box.

8. Click OK to apply the changes.

9. To test the alert, open a new query, and execute this code:

    ```
    RAISERROR(14599, 10, 1) WITH LOG
    ```

10. When your email message arrives, note the message at the bottom stating that the Backup Test job has run.

Exercise 26-13 Creating and Firing an Alert Based on a Custom Error

1. Open a new SQL Server query by clicking the **New Query** button in **SQL Server Management Studio**.

2. Enter and execute the following code to create the new error:

    ```
    USE master
    GO
    EXEC sp_addmessage @msgnum = 50001, @severity = 10,
    @msgtext = N' This is a custom error.',
    @with_log = 'TRUE'
    GO
    ```

3. In Object Explorer, expand **<your server>**, and then expand **SQL Server Agent**.

4. Right-click **Alerts**, and select **New Alert**.

5. In the Name box, enter **Custom Alert**.

6. Select the **Error Number** radio button, and enter **50001** in the Error Number text box.

7. On the Response page, check the **Notify Operators** box, and check the **E-mail** box next to Administrator.

8. On the Options page, check the **E-mail** box, and click **OK** to create the alert.

9. To test the new alert, open a new query, and execute the following code (WITH LOG is not required because you specified that this event is always logged when you created it):

```
RAISERROR(50001,10,1)
```

10. When your email message arrives, note the detail it gives you.

Exercise 26-14   Modifying an Error to Use Parameters

1. Open a new query by clicking the **New Query** button in **SQL Server Management Studio**.

2. Enter and execute the following code to create the new error:

```
USE master
GO
EXEC sp_addmessage @msgnum = 50001, @severity = 10,
@msgtext = N' This is a custom error by %ls',
@with_log = 'TRUE',
@replace = 'replace'
GO
```

3. To fire the error, enter and execute the following code:

```
RAISERROR(50001, 10, 1, 'SQL Guru')
```

4. When your email message arrives, note that the description now mentions "SQL Guru," which replaced the %ls in the message text.

Exercise 26-15   Creating a Performance Alert

1. Open **SQL Server Management Studio**, expand **<your server>**, and then expand **SQL Server Agent**.

2. Right-click **Alerts**, and select **New Alert**.

3. In the Name box, enter **Performance Alert**.

4. In the Type list, select **SQL Server Performance Condition Alert**.

5. In the Object box, select **SQLServer:Databases**.

6. In the Counter box, select **Percent Log Used**.

7. In the Instance box, select **AdventureWorks**.

8. Make sure the Alert If Counter is set to **Falls Below**.

9. In the Value box, type **100**.

10. Select the **Response** tab, check the **Notify Operators** box, and check the **E-mail** box next to your operator name.

11. Click **OK** to create the alert.

12. When your email message arrives, note the detail that is provided.

Exercise 26-16   Disabling an Alert

1. In SQL Server Management Studio, under Alerts in SQL Server Agent, double-click **Performance Alert** to expose its properties.

2. Uncheck the **Enable** box, and click **OK** to apply the changes.

Exercise 26-17   Creating a WMI Alert

1. Open **SQL Server Management Studio**, expand **<your server>**, and then expand **SQL Server Agent**.

2. Right-click **Alerts**, and select **New Alert**.

3. In the **Name** box, enter **WMI Alert**.

4. In the **Type** list, select **WMI Event Alert**.

5. Make sure Namespace is set to **\\.\root\Microsoft\SqlServer\ServerEvents\ MSSQLSERVER.**

6. Enter this query in the query box:

```
SELECT * FROM DDL_DATABASE_LEVEL_EVENTS
WHERE DatabaseName = 'AdventureWorks'
```

7. Select the **Response** tab, check the **Notify Operators** box, and check the **E-mail** box next to your operator name.

8. On the **Options** page, check the **E-mail** box under **Include Alert Error Text In**, and click **OK** to create the alert.

9. Open a new SQL Server query in SQL Server Management Studio by clicking the **New Query** button.

10. Enter and execute the following code to fire the new alert:

```
USE AdventureWorks
ALTER TABLE Person.Address
ADD WMI_Test_Column VARCHAR(20) NULL
```

11. When your email message arrives, note the detail that is provided.

12. To return the AdventureWorks database to normal, execute the following command (note that the WMI alert will fire again):

```
USE AdventureWorks
ALTER TABLE Person.Address DROP COLUMN WMI_Test_Column
```

13. To disable the alert, open it, uncheck the **Enable** box, and click **OK**.

Exercise 26-18   Running the Maintenance Plan Wizard

1. In **SQL Server Management Studio**, expand **Management**, right-click **Maintenance Plans**, and select **Maintenance Plan Wizard**.

2. On the first screen entitled **Maintenance Plan Wizard**, click the **Next** button.

3. On the **Select Plan Properties** page, enter **Maintenance Plan 1** in the Name box, enter a description if you'd like, select your local server, and click **Next**.

4. On the **Select Maintenance Tasks** page, check the boxes for all the available tasks, and click **Next**.

5. On the next page, you can set the order in which these tasks are performed. Leave the default, and click **Next**.

6. The next page allows you to select the databases you want to include in your maintenance plan. When you click the drop-down list, you're presented with several choices:

   - **All Databases:** This encompasses all databases on the server in the same plan.
   - **All System Databases:** This choice affects only the master, model, and MSDB databases.
   - **All User Databases:** This affects all databases (including AdventureWorks) except the system databases.
   - **These Databases:** This choice allows you to be selective about which databases to include in your plan.

7. For this exercise, select **All Databases**, and click **Next**.

8. On the **Define Shrink Database Task** page, select **All Databases**, and then click **Next**.

9. On the **Define Reorganize Index Task** page, select **All Databases** from the Databases drop-down list, and click **Next**.

10. The **Define Rebuild Index Task** page gives you a number of options for rebuilding your indexes, two of which are:

    - **Reorganize Pages with the Original Amount of Free Space:** This regenerates pages with their original fill factor.
    - **Change Free Space per Page Percentage To:** This creates a new fill factor. If you set this to 10, for example, your pages will contain 10 percent free space.

11. Again, select **All Databases**, accept the defaults, and click **Next**.

12. Next comes the **Define Update Statistics Task** page. Here, too, select **All Databases**, and click **Next**.

13. Next is the **Define Cleanup History Task** page. All the tasks performed by the maintenance plan are logged in the MSDB database. This list is referred to as the *history*, and it can become quite large if you don't "prune" it occasionally. On this page, you can set when and how the history is cleared from the database so you can keep it in check. Again, accept the defaults, and click **Next**.

14. On the **Define Execute SQL Server Agent Job Task** page, you can tell SQL Agent to run a job every time the maintenance plan runs. Because you have to select a job, check the **Backup Test** job, and click **Next**.

15. The next page allows you to control how *full* backups are performed. Select **All Databases** from the drop-down list, accept the defaults, and click **Next**.

16. The next page allows you to control how *differential* backups are performed. Select **All Databases** from the drop-down list, accept the defaults, and click **Next**.

17.   The next page allows you to control how *transaction log* backups are performed. Select **All Databases** from the drop-down list, accept the **defaults**, and click **Next**.

18.   On the **Select Plan Properties** page, click the **Change** button to create a schedule for the job.

19.   Enter **Maintenance Plan 1 Schedule** for the schedule name, accept the rest of the **defaults**, and click **OK** to create the schedule.

20.   Click **Next** to continue.

21.   On the **Select Report Options** page, you can write a report to a text file every time the job runs, and you can e-mail the report to an operator. In this case, write a report to **C:\Practice**, and click **Next**.

22.   On the next page, you can view a summary of the tasks to perform. Click **Finish** to create the maintenance plan.

23.   Once SQL Server is finished creating the maintenance plan, you can click **Close**.

LESSON 27 TEXTBOOK EXERCISES

This lab section contains the following exercises and activities:

Exercise 27-1   Working with Performance Monitor

1. Log on to **Windows** as **Administrator**.

2. From the Start menu, select **Programs → Administrative Tools → Performance**. Notice that the graph is already populated with counters.

3. On the toolbar, click the **Add** button (it looks like a plus (**+**) sign) to open the Add Counters dialog box.

4. In the **Performance Object** box, select **Memory**.

5. In the **Select Counters from List** box, select **Available Bytes**, and click **Add**.

6. Click **Close**, and notice the graph being created on the screen.

7. Press **Ctrl+H**, and notice the current counter turns white. This makes the chart easier to read.

8. On the toolbar, click the **View Report** button (it looks like a sheet of paper), and notice how the same data appears in report view.

9. In the left pane, expand **Performance Logs and Alerts**, right-click **Alerts**, and select **New Alert Settings**.

10. Enter **Test Alert** in the Name box, and click **OK**.

11. In the Alert Settings dialog box, enter **Test Alert** in the **Comment** field.

12. Click **Add**.

13. Select the **Processor** object and the **% Processor Time** counter, and click **Add**; then click **Close**.

14. Select **Under** from the **Alert When Value Is** drop-down list, enter **70** for the Limit, and click **OK**. This will generate an alert if the processor is not busy 70 percent of the time. In the real world, you would set this to more than 70 percent, thus warning you just before it becomes a serious problem.

15. Click **OK** to create the alert.

16. To view the alerts, open **Event Viewer**, and look for them in the Application log, then double-click the **event** to view its properties.

17. Watch the alerts generated for a short time, then select the **alert**, and finally press the **Delete** key. If asked whether you want to continue deleting a running alert; click **OK**.

18. Exit **System Monitor** and **Event Viewer**.

Exercise 27-2   Creating a Trace with Profiler

1. From the Start menu, go to **Programs → Microsoft SQL Server → Performance Tools → SQL Server Profiler**.

2. From the File menu, select **New Trace**.

3. Connect to your **default server instance** using the proper authentication; this opens the Trace Properties dialog box.

4. In the **Trace Name** box, type **Monitor**.

5. Use the **TSQL_Replay** template (you'll replay this later).

6. Check the **Save to File** box, and click **Save** to accept the default name and location. Leave the **Enable File Rollover** box checked and the **Server Processes Trace Data** box unchecked.

7. Check the **Save to Table** box, log on to your **default server instance**, and fill in the following:

    Database: **AdventureWorks**
    Owner: **dbo**
    Table: **Monitor**

8. Click the **Events Selection** tab, and check the **Show All Events** box toward the bottom of the tab.

9. In the **Events** grid, expand **Security Audit** (if it is not already expanded), and check the box to the left of **Audit Schema Object Access Event**. This will monitor the opening and closing of objects, such as tables.

10. Click **Run** to start the trace.

11. Leave **Profiler** running, and open a new **SQL Server query** in **SQL Server Management Studio**.

12. Execute the following query:

    ```
    USE AdventureWorks
    SELECT * FROM Person.Contact
    ```

13. Switch to **Profiler**, and click the **Pause** button (double blue lines). In the Profiler, notice the amount of data that was collected.

14. Close **Profiler** and **Management Studio**.

Exercise 27-3   Replaying a Trace

1. Open **Profiler.** From the File menu, select **Open** and **Trace File**.

2. In the **Open File** dialog box, select **Monitor.trc**, and click **OK**.

3. On the toolbar in the trace window, click the **Execute One Step** button (a blue arrow pointing to a gray line). This will execute a single step at a time.

4. Log on to your default instance of SQL Server.

5. In the **Replay** dialog box that opens, you can choose to create an output filename, which will store all error messages and output for later review. Leave this blank.

6. Under **Replay Options**, you can opt to enable debugging by replaying events in the order they were recorded, or disable debugging by replaying multiple events at the same time. Select the option to **Replay events in the order they were traced**. This option enables debugging. Click **OK**.

7. Scroll down, and select the first line you find that contains SQL:BatchCompleted.

8. On the toolbar, click the **Run to Cursor** button (an arrow pointing to double braces). This will execute all steps between the current position and the event you have selected.

9. Click the **Start Execution** button (a yellow arrow) to finish replaying the trace.

10. Close **Profiler**.

Exercise 27-4   Creating a Workload File

1. First you need to remove the indexes from the test table, so open **Management Studio** and expand **Databases** → **AdventureWorks** → **Tables**.

2. Right-click **Monitor**, and select **Modify**.

3. Right-click the **key icon** by the RowNumber column, and select **Remove Primary Key**.

4. Click the **Save** button on the toolbar to remove the indexes from the table.

5. To stop any excess traffic on the server, right-click **SQL Server Agent** in Object Explorer, and select **Stop**.

6. From the Start menu, go to **Programs** → **Microsoft SQL Server** → **Performance Tools** → **Profiler**.

7. From the **File** menu, select **New Trace** to open the Trace Properties dialog box.

8. Connect to your **default server instance** using the proper authentication.

9. In the **Trace Name** box, type **Tuning**.

10. Use the **Tuning** template.

11. Check the **Save to File** box, and click **Save** to accept the default name and location. Leave the **Enable File Rollover** box checked and the **Server Processes Trace Data** box unchecked.

12. Click **Run** to start the trace.

13. Leave **Profiler** running, and open a new **SQL Server query** in Management Studio.

14. Execute the following query:

```
USE AdventureWorks
SELECT textdata FROM monitor
WHERE DatabaseName = 'AdventureWorks'
```

15. Switch to **Profiler**, click the **Stop** button (red box), and then close **Profiler**.

Exercise 27-5   Using the Database Engine Tuning Advisor

1. From the Start menu, go to **Programs → Microsoft SQL Server → Performance Tools → Database Engine Tuning Advisor**.

2. Connect to **<your server>** using the appropriate authentication method. This will create a new session in the advisor.

3. In the Session Name box, enter **Tuning Session**.

4. In the Workload section, click the **browse** button (it looks like a pair of binoculars), and locate the **Tuning.trc** trace file created earlier.

5. In the databases and tables grid, check the box next to **AdventureWorks**.

6. Switch to the **Tuning Options** tab. From here you can instruct the advisor which physical changes to make to the database; specifically, you can have the advisor create new indexes (clustered and nonclustered) and partition the database.

7. Leave the **Limit Tuning Time** option checked and set for the default time; this prevents the advisor from taking too many system resources.

8. Leave the default options for Physical Design Structures (PDS) Options to Use in Database, Partitioning Strategy to Employ, and Physical Design Structures (PDS) to Keep in Database.

9. Click the **Advanced Options** button. From here you can set these options:

   • **Define Max. Space for Recommendations (MB)** will set the maximum amount of space used by recommended physical performance structures.

   • **All Recommendations Are Offline** will generate recommendations that may require you to take the database offline to implement the change.

   • **Generate Online Recommendations Where Possible** will return online recommendations even if a faster offline method is possible. If there is no online method, then an offline method is recommended.

   • **Generate Only Online Recommendations** will return only online recommendations.

10. Click **Cancel** to return to the advisor.

11. Click the **Start Analysis** button on the toolbar.

12. You should see a progress status screen during the analysis phase.

13. After analysis is complete, you will be taken to the Recommendations screen; you should see a recommendation for creating an index on the monitor table.

14. You can also check the **Reports** screen for more detailed information on the analysis process.

15. To apply these recommendations, select **Apply Recommendations** from the **Actions** menu.

16. On the dialog box that pops up, click **Apply Now**, and click **OK**.

17. When the index has been created, click **Close**.

18. Close the **Database Engine Tuning Advisor**.

LESSON 28 TEXTBOOK EXERCISES

This lab section contains the following exercise and activity:

Exercise 28-1   Running Database Consistency Checks (DBCCs)

Exercise 28-1   Running Database Consistency Checks (DBCCs)

1. Open **SQL Server Management Studio**, and connect to your SQL Server instance using Windows authentication.

2. Click the **New Query** toolbar button to open a new query window.

3. First check the allocation structures of the AdventureWorks database. Type the following Transact-SQL code, execute it, and observe the results:

```
USE master ;
GO
DBCC CHECKALLOC ('AdventureWorks')
```

4. Next, you'll check the system tables (or the metadata) of the AdventureWorks database. Type the following Transact-SQL code, execute it, and observe the results:

```
USE master ;
GO
DBCC CHECKCATALOG ('AdventureWorks')
```

5. In certain cases, you might need to check the integrity of only a specific table, so here you'll check the [Person].[Contact] table of the AdventureWorks database. Type the following Transact-SQL code, execute it, and observe the results:

```
USE AdventureWorks ;
GO
DBCC CHECKTABLE ('[Person].[Contact]')
```

6. In most cases you would check the integrity of your entire database, so now you'll check the AdventureWorks database. Execute the following Transact-SQL script in the query pane, and observe the results:

```
USE master ;
GO
DBCC CHECKDB ('AdventureWorks') ;
```

7. Another important performance troubleshooting technique is to examine the level of both internal and external fragmentation of a table, because this could be the cause of poor query performance and indicate a need to rebuild the appropriate indexes. To check the fragmentation level of the [Person].[Contact] table of the AdventureWorks database, type the following Transact-SQL code, execute it, and observe the results:

```
USE AdventureWorks ;
GO
DBCC SHOWCONTIG ('[Person].[Contact]')
```

8. As discussed earlier, however, you should be querying sys.dm_db_index_physical_stats in lieu of using the DBCC SHOWCONTIG command. Type the following Transact-SQL code, execute it, and observe the results:

```
USE AdventureWorks ;
GO
sys.dm_db_index_physical_stats(DB_ID('AdventureWorks'),
OBJECT_ID('Person.Contact'),
NULL, NULL, 'DETAILED' ) ;
```

LESSON 29 TEXTBOOK EXERCISES

This lab section contains the following exercises and activities:

Exercise 29-1   Reading SQL Server Error Logs

1. Open **SQL Server Management Studio**.

2. In **Object Explorer**, expand **<your server>** and then expand **Management**.

3. Under **Management**, expand **SQL Server Logs**.

4. Under **SQL Server Logs**, you should see a current log and up to six archives. Double-click the **current log** to open it.

5. In the **Log File Viewer**, you should see a number of messages. Many of these are informational, but some will be error messages. To find the errors, just read the description to the right of each error.

6. Click one of the errors to read more detail in the lower half of the right pane.

7. To view archive logs from here, check the box next to one of the logs.

8. To view Windows event logs, check the box next to an event log.

9. To filter the logs, click the **Filter** button on the toolbar, enter your filter criteria, and then click **OK**.

Exercise 29-2   Reading Windows Event Logs

1. Select **Event Viewer** from the **Administrative Tools** group on the **Start** menu.

2. In **Event Viewer**, click the **Application Log** icon.

3. In the contents pane (on the right), you will see a number of messages. Some of these are for other applications, and a great deal of them are informational. You are primarily interested in yellow or red icons that mention SQL Server in the description.

4. Double-click **one of the messages** to get more details about it.

5. Close **Event Viewer**.

Exercise 29-3   Using sys.dm_exec_requests and KILL

1. To start a locking session, open a **new query** in **SQL Server Management Studio**, and execute this command:

```
BEGIN TRAN
SELECT * FROM monitor WITH (TABLOCKX, HOLDLOCK)
-- Note the use of query hints
```

2. Now, to create a blocked session, open a **new query**, and execute this code:

```
UPDATE monitor SET textdata = 'test'
WHERE rownumber = 1
```

3. Notice that the second query does not complete because the first query is holding an exclusive lock on the table. To find the session that is doing the blocking, open a **third query** window.

4. In the third query window, query the **sys.dm_exec_requests** system view for any session that is being blocked with this code:

    ```
    SELECT session_id, status, blocking_session_id
    FROM sys.dm_exec_requests
    WHERE blocking_session_id > 0
    ```

5. The blocking_session_id is the session causing the problem. To end it, execute the **KILL** command with the **blocking_session_id** value. For example, if the blocking_session_id is 53, you would execute:

    ```
    KILL 53
    ```

6. Switch to the **second query** (from Step 2); it should now be complete, with one row affected.

Exercise 29-4   Finding Out When a Job Last Fired

1. Open **SQL Server Management Studio**.

2. Make sure your **SQL Server Agent** is started by right-clicking it in Object Explorer and selecting **Start**. Click **Yes** in the dialog box that opens.

3. To create a job to run, expand **SQL Server Agent**, right-click **Jobs**, and select **New Job**.

4. Enter **Test History** in the Name box.

5. Go to the **Steps** page, and click the **New** button.

6. Enter **History Step** in the Step Name box.

7. Select **AdventureWorks** from the database drop-down list.

8. Enter this code in the command box:

    ```
    SELECT * FROM Person.Contact
    ```

9. Click **OK**, and then click **OK** again to create the job.

10. When you return to **SQL Server Management Studio**, right-click the **Test History** job, and click **Start Job**.

11. When the job has finished, click **Close**.

12. To find out when the job last ran, right-click the **Test History** job, and click **View History**.

13. In the Log File Viewer, expand the log file entry by clicking the **plus (+)** sign. This will show you when the job last ran and which step last completed.

14. Close the **Log File Viewer**.

Exercise 29-5   Querying AdventureWorks Using PowerShell

1. From your operating system, start a Command Prompt (cmd.exe). At the prompt type **powershell** and press enter. Note the **PS** in front of the current prompt. You have entered the PowerShell environment.

2. At the current prompt, type **get-help.** PowerShell returns instructions on how to use this tool. Note that by drilling down you may find additional information. For example, type **get-help about*.** Now you see a list of topics to further refine your search and learn more. PowerShell contains full documentation in the same way that **man** pages work in the Unix shell. And like Unix, if the scrolling output bothers you, type **get-help about* | more.** A screen's worth of information is displayed followed by this line: **-- More --.** And you can press the space bar to see more.

3. Close the **Command Prompt**.

4. From **SQL Server Management Studio** and from the **Object Explorer**, open Databases. Right-click on **AdventureWorks** and select **Start Power Shell** from the context menu. **PS SQLSERVER** is displayed, and its in the context of **AdventureWorks**. Rather than a Windows context you now have cmdlets and snap-ins appropriate for working with SQL Server.

5. At the prompt, type **SQLCMD –?**. All of the options (switches) are now displayed. This time type **SQLCMD –E** (note that the switches are case sensitive). You have now entered the SQLCMD environment as indicated by the **1>** prompt. Type this SQL code:

```
1> USE adventureworks <enter>
2> SELECT * FROM humanresources.employee <enter>
3> GO <enter>
```

The humanresources.employee table data is displayed. This data can be output to an operating system text file as a really quick way to pass table data to an analyst (use the –o output file switch).

6. Type **exit** to return to the PowerShell environment. Note that you remain in the AdventureWorks context.

7. At the PS SQLSERVER prompt, type:

```
invoke-sqlcmd "select * from humanresources.employee" |
more
```

The same data is displayed but instead of rapidly scrolling through the data, the more command causes the display to pause at each screen's worth.

8.   Type **exit** to quit PowerShell.

Exercise 29-6   Connecting to the DAC

1.   Open a **PowerShell prompt** on your server.

2.   The following command connects to the server specified with the –S parameter using a trusted connection as specified by the –E parameter. The –A parameter specifies the DAC, or an administrative connection. Run the following command now:

```
Sqlcmd -S (local) -A -E
```

Another Way

Open a new connection to your Database Engine and connect as admin:<YourServerName> in the Server name text box.

3.   You should see a 1> prompt. From here you can enter a query. Type the following, and hit **Enter**:

```
SELECT session_id, status, blocking_session_id
FROM sys.dm_exec_requests
```

4.   You should now see a 2> prompt. Type **GO**, and hit **Enter** to execute the query.

5.   You should now be back at the 1> prompt. Type **Exit**, and hit **Enter** to exit the DAC.

Exercise 29-7   Entering Single-User Mode

1.   Stop all services (use **Configuration Manager**).

2.   Start a **Command Prompt**. Navigate to C:\Program Files\Microsoft SQL Server\<Your Path>\MSSQL\Binn (or something similar depending on your particular environment). Type **sqlservr –?** to see the switch options for this command.

3.   Select the single-user mode switch (sqlservr –m) and press **enter.** The Command Prompt appears to freeze after scrolling through some informational messages; this is the expected behavior. Leave it open (and do not shrink it—sitting on the taskbar consumes too many resources).

4.   Start **SQL Server Management Studio** and try to connect. If you see an error dialog box reporting that your attempt to connect failed because "*Server is in single-user mode. Only one administrator can connect at this time,*" check that all services are indeed stopped. SQL Server Agent is most likely the culprit.

5.   To verify single-user mode, click **Connect** (upper left-hand corner of Object Explorer). In the **Connect to Server** dialog box, click **Connect**. Now you should correctly see the message shown in Step 4.

TAKE NOTE

Object Explorer sometimes makes multiple connections. Since these efforts will fail, not all features will work. Clicking on a New Query will also fail. If you need to perform SQL code, connect initially with a New Query request although that will render the Object Browser inoperable. To go from one to the other, click Disconnect (next to the connect icon) and reopen with the other option.

6.   When you have completed your work, close **SQL Server Management Studio**, click on the **Command Prompt**, type **Ctrl-c**, press **y** and restart all those services you stopped earlier.

Exercise 29-8   Using the SQLdiag Utility

1.   Start a **PowerShell** instance. Type **SQLdiag /?** to see the help menu and thus the options available.

2.   At the prompt, type **sqldiag /B +00:01:00 /E +00:03:00**. This will start the collection in one minute to last for two minutes. If you don't specify otherwise with the /O option, the results will be placed in C:\Program Files\Microsoft SQL Server\<Your Version>\Tools\Binn\SQLDIAG. This, typically, creates trace files that will be displayed to you in SQL Profiler.

LAB 1
INTRODUCING THE COURSE

This lab contains the following exercise and activity:

Exercise 1.1   Checking for Background (Prerequisite) Knowledge

Exercise 1.1	Checking for Background (Prerequisite) Knowledge
Scenario	You need to develop or upgrade your administrative skills to include SQL Server. This course presumes you have fundamental knowledge in three areas: database concepts, structured query language constructs, and Windows Server administration.
Duration	This task should take less than one hour.
Procedure	In this task, you will answer background questions about concepts that apply to the prerequisites.
Equipment	This is a paper and pencil exercise.
Objective	To make certain you have the knowledge needed to successfully complete this course.
Criteria for Completion	You have completed this task when you've answered all of the questions.

■ PART A: Determining Prerequisites

1. What is an RDBMS?

_____

2. What are normalization rules?

_____

3. What is entity integrity?

_____

4. What is referential integrity?

_____

5. What is OLTP?

_____

6. What is OLAP?

_____

7. What is a field?

_____

8. What is a transaction?

_____

9. What is a domain?

_____

10. What is a user database?

_____

11. What is unicode?

_____

12. What is a select query?

_____

13. What is a join condition?

_____

14.   What is a calculated column?

_____

15.   What is does the SELECT statement return?

_____

16.   What is a self-join?

_____

17.   What is DDL?

_____

18.   What is UPDATE?

_____

19.   What is parameterization?

_____

20.   What is a search argument?

_____

21.   What is an SPN?

_____

22.   What is Windows Management Instrumentation?

_____

23.   What is a domain?

_____

24.   In Group Policy, passwords must meet complexity requirements. What are these requirements?

_____

25.   When you delete a user and then re-create the same user, what happens?

_____

26.   Identify six logs in Event Viewer for a domain controller.

_____

27. In System Monitor, what Performance Object/Counter will report the available free space on a specific hard drive?

_____

28. What utility permits you to change computer passwords?

_____

29. What is a stand-alone server?

_____

30. You check the Log On property of MSSQLSERVER from the Administrative Tools/Services menu and discover it is set to Log on as: Local System Account. Can *remote* users access this instance of SQL Server? Can *local* users access this instance of SQL Server?

_____

LAB 2
INSTALLING SQL SERVER 2008

This lab contains the following exercises and activities:

Exercise 2.1   Installing SQL Server 2008 Manually

Exercise 2.2   Installing a Second Instance

Exercise 2.1	Installing SQL Server 2008 Manually
Scenario	You are the database administrator (DBA) for a mid-sized company with offices in various cities throughout the United States and Canada. The company has decided to use SQL Server for data storage and retrieval, and you have been asked to install the software and get it running.
	As an experienced DBA, you understand the importance of installing the software right the first time, because if you install SQL Server incorrectly or on the wrong hardware, it will work slowly or not at all. Therefore, you have decided to verify the prerequisites and then install the software.
Duration	This task should take less than one hour.
Setup	This task requires little setup. You will need access to a copy of SQL Server Enterprise or Developer Edition and a computer that meets the requirements to run it.
Caveats	It seems redundant, but SQL Server runs better on faster hardware. So, remember that the minimum requirements listed later in this task are just that, minimum. If you have access to a faster machine with more random access memory (RAM), use it.
Procedure	In this task, you will verify that your computer meets the requirements for running SQL Server and then install the default instance.

Equipment	Although several editions of SQL Server exist, you will be working with the Enterprise Edition in this book because it has the widest range of available features. You can download a 180-day trial copy of Enterprise Edition from the Microsoft Web site (http://www.microsoft. com/sql) for your use in your home training environment. You will also need access to a machine that meets the prerequisites for Enterprise Edition.
Objective	To make certain your server meets the requirements for installing SQL Server. Refer to your text or Books Online for the information.
Criteria for Completion	You have completed this task when you have a running instance of SQL Server installed on your system.

■ PART A: Determining Prerequisites

1. Do you have a 32-bit, a 64-bit, or multiple CPUs?

2. How much memory do you have?

3. Do you have a DVD drive?

4. How much hard drive space is available?

5. What operating system do you have?

6. Do these answers meet the minimum requirements for SQL Server?

■ PART B: Installing SQL Server 2008

1. Create a user account named **SmithB** with a password of **Pa$$w0rd**, and make it a member of the Administrators local group. You can perform this task using one of these tools: on a Windows member server or on Windows Workgroup, use Computer Management (right-click **My Computer → Manage**); on a Windows domain controller, use **Active Directory Users** and **Computers** (click **Start → Administrative Tools**). You will use this user in multiple exercises as you go through this course.

> **NOTE**
>
> *In a production environment you should make the service account owner a user with the necessary permissions and name it just like any other user so hackers can't determine the account owner by inspection.*

2. Setup starts with a menu of options on the left. Explore these for a moment and then click on **Planning**. Run the **System Configuration Checker**. See if your system passes muster.

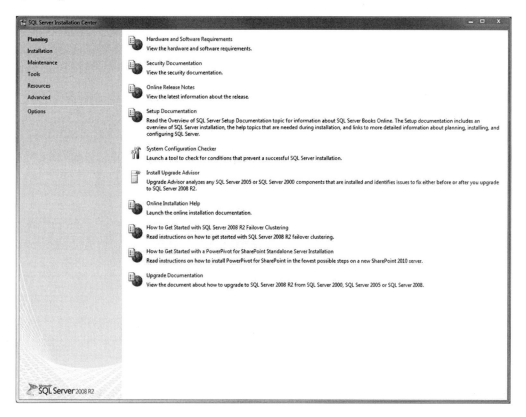

3. If yes, click on **Installation** and choose **New Installation or add features to an existing installation**.

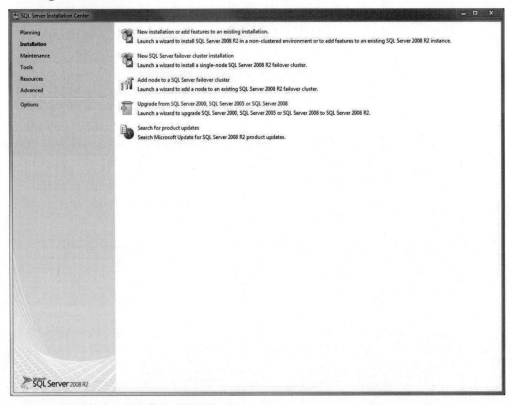

4. Setup does some initial system checks.

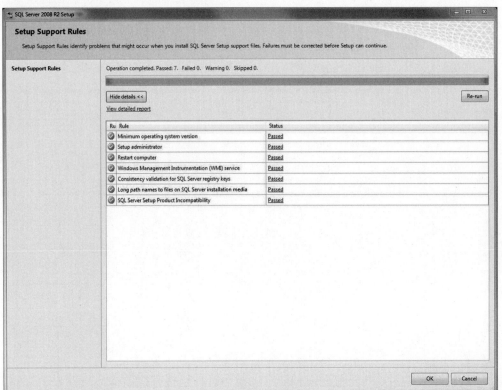

5. On the **Product Key** screen, select **Evaluation** or enter your Product Key, as appropriate. Click **Next**.

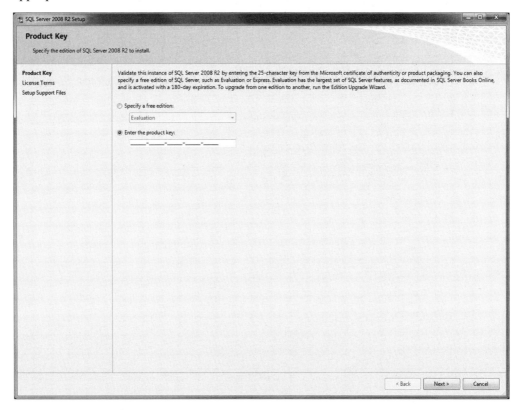

6. On the **License Terms** screen, select **I accept the license terms**. Click **Next**.

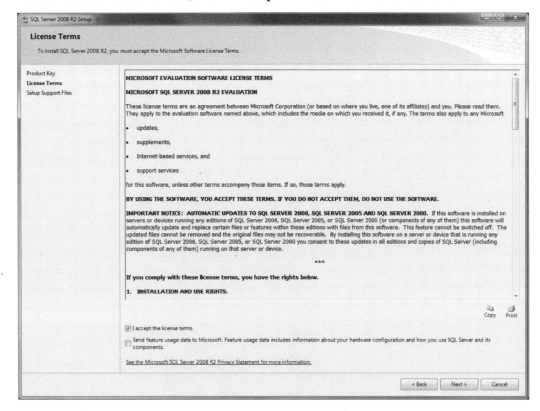

7. Next, setup wants to load some **Setup Support Files**. Click **Install**.

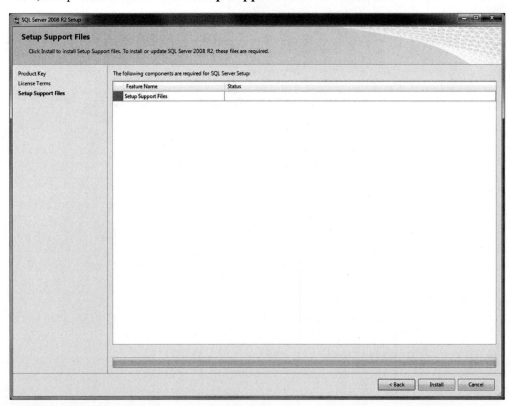

8. The **Setup Support Rules** screen checks conditions. If you didn't turn off your firewall, do so and **Rerun** the check. Click **Next**.

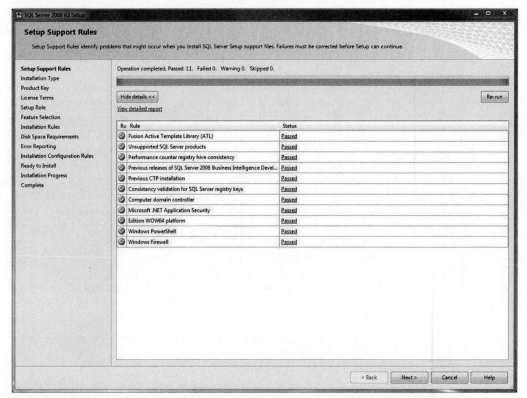

9. The **Setup Role** screen asks how you want to configure SQL Server. Select **All Features with Defaults**. Click **Next**.

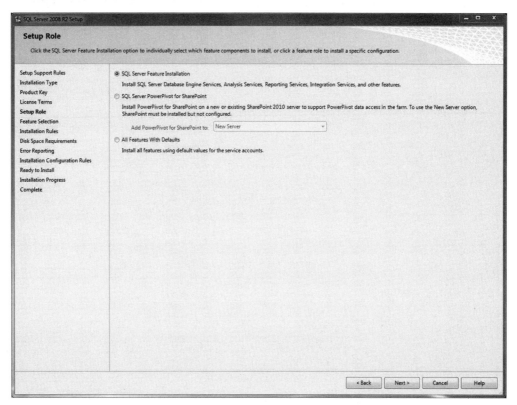

10. Now you see the **Feature Selection** screen. Make sure all are selected. Click **Next**.

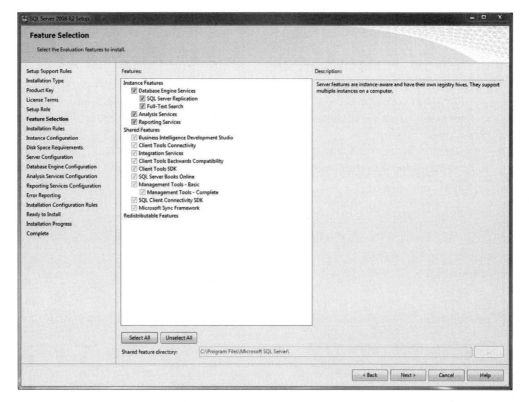

11. On the **Installation Rules** page, click **Show details** to see what happened. Click **Next**.

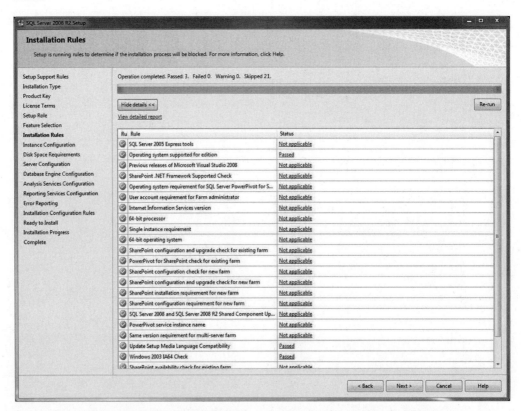

12. You then see the **Instance Configuration** screen. Note the Instance Root directory—you can change this to anything you want. Note also the Instance Path. You will need to understand this convention when locating your data files. Accept the defaults. Click **Next**.

13. Setup next checks **Disk Space Requirements**. If you place all files on your system disk, setup needs 5,485 MB. If you try to load SQL Server anywhere other than your operating system spindle, setup still wants more than 3.1 GB on the system disk—and doesn't give it back after loading SQL Server. Click **Next**.

14. Now for the **Server Configuration**. For classroom purposes change all service owners to **local system**. Change SQL Agent service to start automatically. Click **Next**.

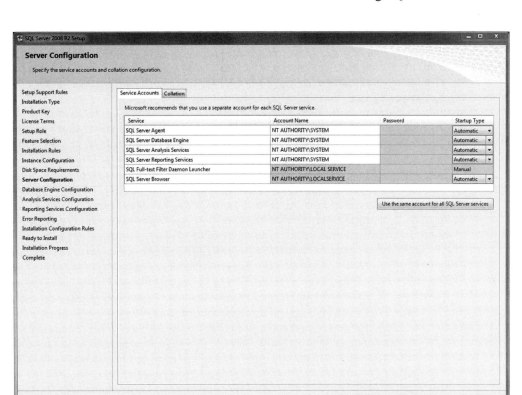

15. The **Database Engine Configuration** appears. Be sure your login appears.
     Accept the defaults and click **Next**.

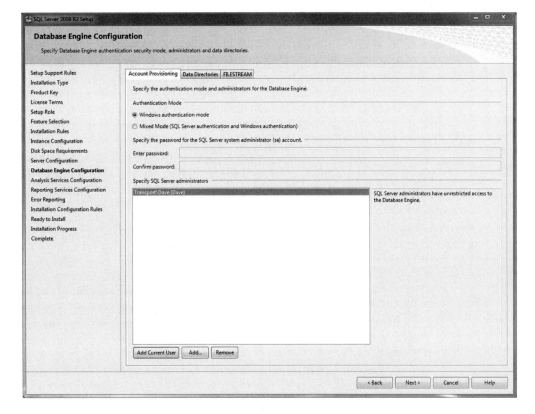

16. Now it's time for **Analysis Server Configuration**. Click the **Add Current User** button and click **Next**.

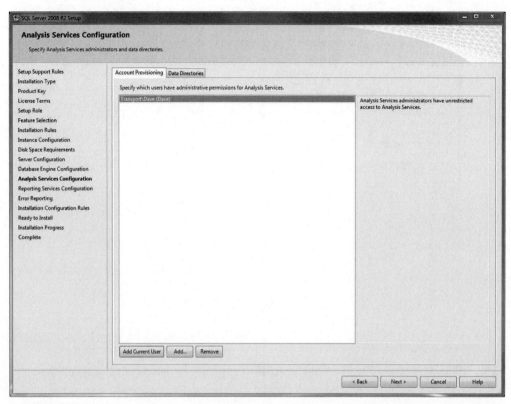

17. Check the Reporting Services Configuration page. Make sure **Install the native mode default configuration** is selected and click **Next**.

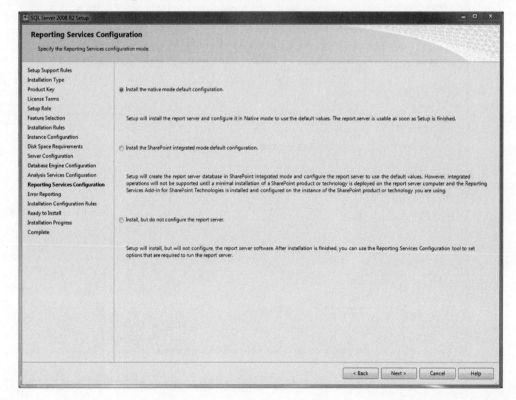

18.   On the **Error Reporting** screen, accept the defaults (do not send Windows and SQL Server Error Reports to Microsoft). Click **Next**.

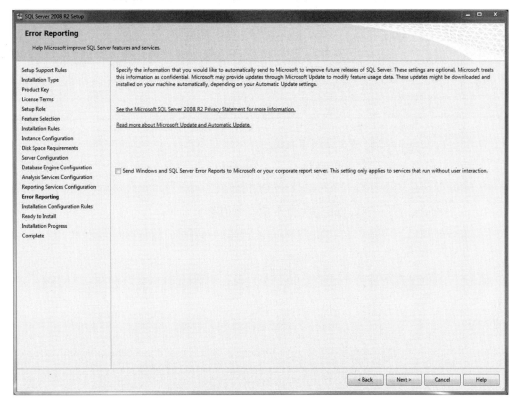

19.   Now for the **Installation Configuration Rules**. Verify nothing failed. Click **Next**.

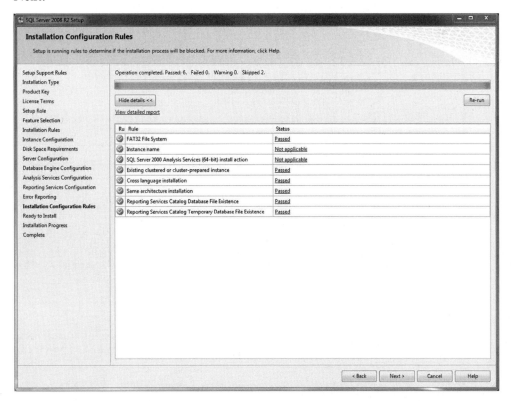

20. **Ready to Install**. Click **Install**.

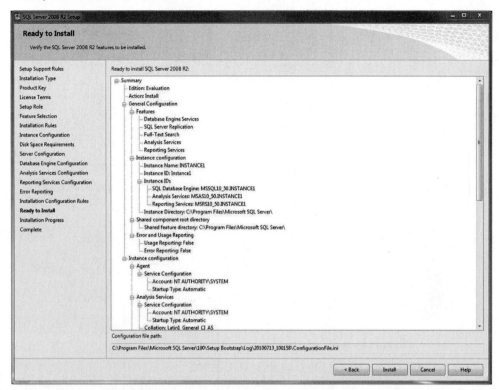

21. At long last, the **Installation Progress** screen appears. Setup reports activity. The DVD spins. The hard drive whirrs. Installation times vary; allow at least half an hour.

22. When setup **Complete**s, click **Close**.

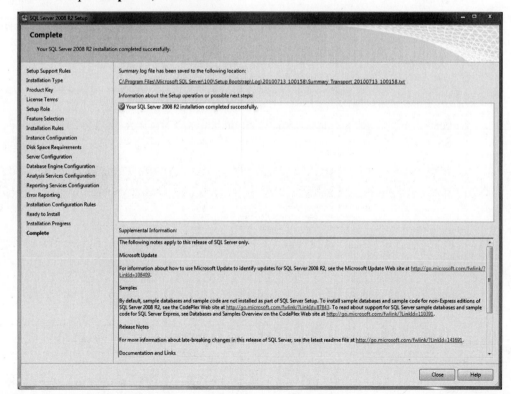

23.   Click **Start → All Programs → Microsoft SQL Server 2008 R2 → Configuration Tools → SQL Server Configuration Manager**. Expand **SQL Server Services**, right-click **SQL Server**, select **Properties**, choose the **FILESTREAM** tab and make sure *both* filestream options are selected.

24.   Visit http://SqlServerSamples.CodePlex.com. Download *and* run the samples (look for the second **here** in the first sentence).

25.   When complete, open **SQL Server Management Studio**, expand **Databases** and verify you have several different AdventureWorks databases. For most exercises you will use AdventureWorks because this works in both SQL Server 2005 and SQL Server 2008. You need AdventureWorks2008R2 to test filestreams. You use AdventureWorksDW with Analysis Servers, and AventureWorksLT is a lightweight database for faster processing in the classroom.

> **NOTE**
>
> *In subsequent loads (as when adding additional features) the product key requirement is skipped.*

■ PART C: Verifying Results

1.   Click **Start**.

2.   Click **All Programs**.

3.   Click **Microsoft SQL Server**.

4.   Click **Configuration Tools**.

5.   Click **SQL Server Configuration Manager**.

6.   Select **SQL Server Services,** and check the icons. If the icon next to SQL Server (MSSQLServer) service is green, then your installation is a success.

Exercise 2.2	Installing a Second Instance
Scenario	You are the database administrator (DBA) for a mid-sized company with offices in various cities throughout the United States and Canada. You know you need an instance of SQL Server for testing new service packs, new database schemas, and the like, but your company does not have the budget for new hardware at this time. The only way for you to have a test copy of SQL Server is to install a named instance.
Duration	This task should take less than one hour.
Setup	Again, all you need for this task is the machine you used in Exercise 2.1 and the same copy of SQL Server you used in Exercise 2.1.

Procedure	In this task, you will install a second instance of SQL Server on the same machine used in Exercise 2.1.
Equipment	See Setup.
Objective	To create a second instance of SQL Server on the same machine as the default instance.
Criteria for Completion	Check SQL Server Configuration Manager to see whether your services are running for the second instance.

■ PART A: Installing the Second Instance

Installing an instance of SQL Server 2008 follows the same sort of logic as creating the default instance. At the beginning you answer whether you want a default instance or a new instance. This time select **New installation or add features to an existing installation** and continue as with your first installation.

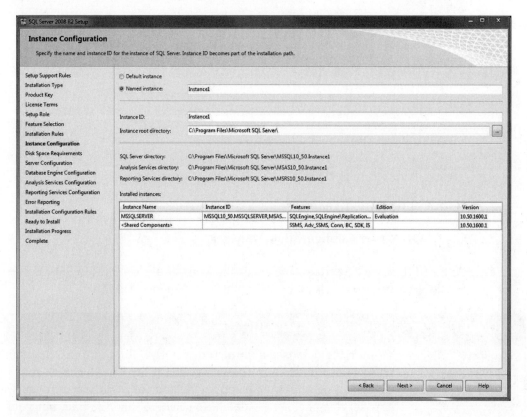

NOTE

The choice of an instance name should make business sense in your environment.

■ PART B: Verifying Results

1. Click **Start**.

2. Click **All Programs**.

3. Click **Microsoft SQL Server**.

4. Click **Configuration Tools**.

5. Click **SQL Server Configuration Manager**.

6. Select **SQL Server Services**, and check the icons. If the icon next to SQL Server (MSSQLServer) service is green for your new instance, then your installation is a success. If it is not green, refer to Lesson 29 of your textbook on troubleshooting techniques for guidance.

LAB 3
NAVIGATING SQL SERVER

This lab contains the following exercise and activity:

Exercise 3.1   Locating Information Using SQL Server Utilities

Exercise 3.1	Locating Information Using SQL Server Utilities
Scenario	You are new to SQL Server. You were hired as a trainee to be part of a new group providing support for a future installation of SQL Server at your new company. While getting ready for the new installation, architects are designing the databases, programmers are preparing code, and you are being given time to explore the RDBMS, the client tools, and the business requirements in preparation for the launch.
Duration	This task should take less than one hour.
Setup	This task requires little setup. All you need is access to a computer with SQL Server Enterprise Edition already loaded on it. You installed SQL Server in Exercise 2.1.
Procedure	In this task, you will verify that your computer meets the requirements for running SQL Server and then install the default instance.
Equipment	Although several editions of SQL Server exist, you will be working with the Enterprise Edition in this book because it has the widest range of available features. Use the computer on which you loaded SQL Server in Exercise 2.1.
Objective	To practice using the four main utilities provided with SQL Server.
Criteria for Completion	You have completed this task when you have answered all of the questions correctly.

■ PART A: Locating Information

1. What is the identity seed property for the FirstName column of the Person.Contact table in the AdventureWorks database?

   _____

2. How many different DBCC (Transact-SQL) statements does Microsoft supply with SQL Server?

   _____

3. How many default protocols are supplied by Microsoft for the SQL Server service?

   _____

4. Where do you add a new user to the SQLAgentOperatorRole?

   _____

5. What does the pipe symbol (|) mean in Transact-SQL?

   _____

6. What is your current configuration for remote connections?

   _____

7. How many database services are currently started? Do not use Windows Administrative Tools.

   _____

8. Where do you find the User Mapping configuration page?

   _____

9. What is stored in the Resource hidden database?

   _____

10. What is the easiest way to add a new user to the SysAdmin role?

    _____

11. How can you easily get a list of all blocking transactions for the AdventureWorks database?

    _____

12. What are the two keys defined for the Person.Address table in the AdventureWorks database?

   _____

13. What is the Microsoft Document Explorer and how to you install it?

   _____

14. Using Management Studio, what data type is returned when you use the Difference function?

   _____

15. Using Management Studio, what is the maximum length of the parameter you may pass to the sp_help system stored procedure in bytes?

   _____

LAB 4
WORKING WITH DATA TYPES

This lab contains the following exercises and activities:

Exercise 4.1   Creating a Data Type Using Object Explorer

Exercise 4.2   Using Date and Time Data Types

Exercise 4.3   Implementing a Sparse Column

Exercise 4.4   Using Page and Row Compression

Exercise 4.1	Creating a Data Type Using Object Explorer
Scenario	You have been tasked by your company to support the Enterprise planners and developers by creating needed objects in SQL Server. The Enterprise planners have completed their IDEF(0), IDEF(1X), and affinity analysis; the developers are designing the database table layouts (schema). Your job is to create needed objects. Your first task is to create a custom data type.
Duration	This task should take less than fifteen minutes.
Setup	This task requires little setup. All you need is access to a copy of SQL Server Enterprise Edition and a computer that meets the requirements to run it.
Procedure	Use SQL Server Management Studio's Object Explorer and included Query Editor to complete these tasks.
Equipment	Although several editions of SQL Server exist, you will be working with the Enterprise Edition.
Objective	To understand two methods of creating alias data types for use in table definitions and other development tasks.
Criteria for Completion	You have completed this task when check Object Explorer and find your new definitions recorded in system tables.

■ PART A: Creating an Alias Data Type Using Object Explorer

1.   Start **SQL Server Management Studio**. Connect to your default instance by making sure Database Engine, <YourServerName> and windows authentication are listed. Click **Connect**.

2.   If Object Explorer is not visible, click **Object Explorer** on the View menu.

3.   In Object Explorer, expand **Databases**, **AdventureWorks**, **Programmability**, and **Types**.

4.   Right-click **Types** and then click **New User-Defined Data Type**.

5.   Enter the following information:

   Schema: dbo
   Name: CountryCode
   Data type: Char
   Length: 2
   Allow NULLs: Selected

■ PART B: Creating an Alias Data Type Using Transact-SQL Code

1.   In SQL Server Management Studio, click the **New Query** button on the toolbar.

2.   In the new, blank query window, type the following Transact-SQL code:

```
USE AdventureWorks
CREATE TYPE dbo.EmailAddress
FROM varchar(6)
NULL;
```

3.   Click the **Execute** button on the toolbar or Press F5.

■ PART C: Verifying Results

1.   Right-click the User-defined data types folder in Object Explorer and then click Refresh.

2.   Verify that both CountryCode and EmailAddress have been added to the database.

Exercise 4.2	Using Date and Time Data Types
Scenario	SQL Server includes some new date-and-time-related data types and you want to use them but first you must understand how they differ from previous data types.
Duration	This task should take approximately 60 minutes.
Setup	For this task, you need access to the machine you installed SQL Server on in Exercise 2.1.
Procedure	In this task, you will develop various queries to explore how the data types can be used.
Equipment	See Setup.
Objective	To explore the uses and features of date and time data types.
Criteria for Completion	This task is complete when you understand the new data types.

■ PART A: Creating Some Date and Time Variables

1. Open **SQL Server Management Studio**. It does not matter which database is used in this exercise.

2. Open your **Query Editor**. You will be executing a series of queries in the steps that follow.

3. To use the system date and time, enter and execute the following code:

```
-- Code set 1
DECLARE @current_date date = GETDATE();
DECLARE @current_time time(7) = GETDATE();
DECLARE @current_datetime datetime = GETDATE();
SELECT @current_date AS 'Today',
@current_time AS 'Right Now',
@current_datetime AS 'Date & Time';
-- Now round the time value to whole seconds
DECLARE @short_current_time time(0) = @current_time;
SELECT @short_current_time, @current_time;
GO
```

> **NOTE**
>
> *Notice that you can set the precision for a time data type to any value from 0 through 7.*

4. To use fixed date and time values and specific parts of the data, enter and execute the following code:

```
-- Code set 2
-- Use the new date, time, and datetimeoffset data types
DECLARE @MyDate date = '07/13/2010';
DECLARE @MyTime time = '12:30:15';
DECLARE @MyDatetimeoffset datetimeoffset = '07/13/2010 12:30:15 -
8:00';
SELECT DATENAME(month, @MyDate) AS 'Month Name';
SELECT DATENAME(hour, @MyTime) As 'Hour Name';
SELECT CONVERT(VARCHAR(30), @MyDatetimeoffset) AS
'DATETIMEOFFSET';
GO
```

> **NOTE** *Notice that you can now include a time zone value using the datetimeoffset data type. The DATENAME function has existed in SQL Server for a while and can be used to extract various parts of a date or time value.*

5. Suppose your database contains employee work hours collected by a time clock. Can you calculate an amount of time worked? Enter and execute the following code to find out:

```
-- Code set 3
-- Calculate a time period with time data
DECLARE @starttime time = '09:00:00';
DECLARE @stoptime time = '17:00:00';
SELECT DATEDIFF(hour, @starttime, @stoptime) AS 'Work Hours';
GO
```

6. Suppose your desired date data includes historical dates from a few centuries ago. How far back in time can you go? Enter and execute the following code to test out a few dates:

```
-- Code set 4
-- Explore the datetime2 data type
DECLARE @mydatetime  datetime  = GETDATE();
DECLARE @mydatetime2 datetime2(7) = GETDATE();
SELECT @mydatetime, @mydatetime2;
SET @mydatetime = '1776/07/04';
SET @mydatetime2 = '1492/07/04';
SELECT @mydatetime, @mydatetime2;
GO
```

> **NOTE** *Notice that in the first select statement's results you have two values that are the same except that the datetime2 data type allows for more precision in fractions of a second. The two fixed dates in 1776 and 1492 worked as well.*

7. How far back in time can you go with date data? Enter and execute the following code to find out:

```
-- Code set 5
DECLARE @mydatetime  datetime  = GETDATE();
DECLARE @mydatetime2 datetime2(7) = GETDATE();
SELECT @mydatetime, @mydatetime2;
SET @mydatetime = '1492/07/04';
SET @mydatetime2 = '1492/07/04';
SELECT @mydatetime, @mydatetime2;
DECLARE @myolddate date;
SET @mydatetime2 = '0001/01/01'
SET @myolddate = @mydatetime2;
SELECT @mydatetime2, @myolddate;
GO
```

8. This code will fail because the basic datetime data type cannot handle years prior to 1753, and 1492 is much earlier than that. Change the code in some way to work around this problem and reexecute the code. You will then see that both the new date and datetime2 data types can store the date 0001/01/01, which is the earliest possible date for datetime2 data.

9. Now experiment with date data formatting. What date does the six-digit string 07/04/10 represent?

    July 4, 2010?

    April 7, 2010?

    October 4, 2007?

    April 10th in the year 0007?

    Enter and execute the following code to use DATEFORMAT. Experiment and change around the code to see other options:

```
-- Code set 6
-- Set date format to month, day, year.
SET DATEFORMAT mdy;
GO
DECLARE @ambiguous_date date = '07/04/10';
SELECT @ambiguous_date AS DateVar;
-- Returns: 2010-07-04
-- Set date format to year, day, month.
SET DATEFORMAT ydm;
GO
DECLARE @datevar datetimeoffset = '1710/04/07 12:30:15 -08:00';
SELECT @datevar AS DateVar;
GO
```

10. If a user enters a two-digit year value in a date such as 8/31/56—what century and 4-digit year will be used? 1956 or 2056? Enter and execute the following code to find out:

```
-- Code set 7
-- Experiments with Y2K dates and the century pivot value
SET DATEFORMAT mdy;
GO
```

```
DECLARE @nocentury49 datetime = '12/31/49'
DECLARE @nocentury50 date = '01/01/50'
DECLARE @withcentury date = '12/31/1949'
SELECT @nocentury49 AS 'W/O Century (49)',
@nocentury50 AS 'Without Century (50)',
@withcentury AS 'With Century (1949)'
SELECT DATEADD(dd, +1, @nocentury49) AS 'Increment 1 day',
 DATEADD(dd, -1, @nocentury50) AS 'Decrement 1 day'
DECLARE @test_AD_2_BC date = '01/01/2010'
SELECT DATEADD(yy, -2009, @test_AD_2_BC) AS 'Lowest Possible Date'
GO
```

Question 1	*What is the cutoff or pivot year?*

11. To determine the SQL Server pivot year setting, enter and execute the following code:

```
-- Code set 8
-- Determine the Pivot Year value
USE master;
GO
EXEC sp_configure 'show advanced option', '1';
RECONFIGURE
EXEC sp_configure 'two digit year cutoff';
SELECT value FROM sys.configurations WHERE name = 'two digit year cutoff'
GO
```

Exercise 4.3   Implementing a Sparse Column

Scenario	You want to add an email column to the existing Customers table. You have only a few email addresses initially so you want to use the sparse feature of SQL Server to reduce storage requirements.
Duration	This task should take approximately 30 minutes.
Setup	For this task, you need access to the machine you installed SQL Server on in Exercise 2.1 and the Sales database.
Procedure	In this task, you will set a column to be SPARSE in the Sales database.
Equipment	See Setup.
Objective	To see how to create a column using the SPARSE option.
Criteria for Completion	This task is complete when the column has a SPARSE attribute.

■ PART A: Creating a Temporary Database for the Table

1.   Open **SQL Server Management Studio**, and click on **New Query** to open a query window.

2.   Enter and execute the following code to create a dabase and table for the exercise:

```
CREATE DATABASE SalesDemo;
GO
USE salesdemo
GO
CREATE TABLE customers(
        CustID      int     NOT NULL,
        Fname       nvarchar(20),
        Lname       nvarchar(20),
        Address     nvarchar(20),
        City        nvarchar(20),
        State       nchar(2),
        Zip         nchar(5),
        Phone       nchar(10)
);
```

■ PART B: Creating a New Column in the Table

1.   Open **SQL Server Management Studio**, and in **Object Explorer**, expand **Databases** under your server.

2.   Select **SalesDemo** as the database.

3.   Insert some data into the table (feel free to add more data if you so desire):

```
USE salesdemo
GO
INSERT INTO customers VALUES (1, N'Jones', N'Jeremiah',
N'123 Maple St.', N'Boise', N'ID', N'87654', N'8015551212')
INSERT INTO customers VALUES (2, N'James', N'Jessie',
N'123 Maple St.', N'Stillwater', N'MN', N'55082', N'5025551212')
INSERT INTO customers VALUES (3, N'Cooper', N'D.B.',
N'c/o Postmaster', N'Ariel', N'WA', N'98603', null)
INSERT INTO customers VALUES (4, N'Brown', N'Paul',
N'4567 Green St.', N'Lexington', N'KY', N'40502', N'8595551234')
INSERT INTO customers VALUES (5, N'Medina', N'Jose',
N'789 Olive St.', N'Gila Bend', N'AZ', N'85337', N'5205551234')
INSERT INTO customers VALUES (6, N'Panther', N'Flora',
N'1234 Swamp Ln.', N'Panacea', N'FL', N'32346', N'8505551212')
INSERT INTO customers VALUES (7, N'Carter', N'Bill',
N'1 Peach Ave.', N'Macon', N'GA', N'31201', N'4781211212')
INSERT INTO customers VALUES (8, N'Washington', N'George',
N'3200 Mt. Vernon Hwy.', N'Mount Vernon', N'VA', N'22121',
N'7035550011')
```

4. Enter the following code to add a new column to the existing table. Note that the keyword SPARSE is included. This keyword will cause the new column to become a sparse column:

```
ALTER TABLE customers
ADD Emailaddress varchar(128)SPARSE NULL;
GO
```

5. Create a little bit of data for this new column:

```
UPDATE customers SET Emailaddress = 'pbrown@someisp.com'
WHERE CustID = 4;
```

6. Close the query window.

Question 2	What data will exist in the Emailaddress column for those table rows that existed prior to this change?

■ PART C: Verifying Results

1. In **Object Explorer**, expand the database name **SalesDemo** and then expand **Tables**.

2. Right-click **dbo.Customers**, select **Design**.

3. Select the new **Emailaddress** column from the **Design** window. Do this by clicking the left-most column. Once this is done you will see a black right arrow next to Emailaddress.

4. In the **Column Properties** tab, scroll down until you see the **Is Sparse** entry.

5. Ensure that the Is Sparse property is set to **Yes**.

6. To ensure that your modifications to the Customers table do not interfere with other exercises, you may wish to remove this new Emailaddress column. To do so, right-click the **Emailaddress** column name, select **Delete column** from the drop-down list. The column should now disappear. Make sure that you close the window and respond with Yes to the save changes pop-up window.

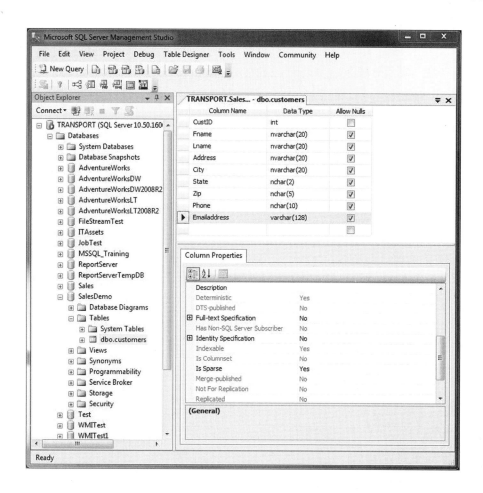

Exercise 4.4	Using Page and Row Compression
Scenario	To reduce the disk space used by a large table, you want to experiment with different compression options to see how much space can be saved.
Duration	This task should take approximately 30 minutes.
Setup	For this task, you need access to the machine you installed SQL Server on in Exercise 2.1 and the AdventureWorks database installed with the sample data.
Procedure	In this task, you will change the compression options for a table.
Equipment	See Setup.
Objective	To set the recovery model for the AdventureWorks database.
Criteria for Completion	This task is complete when the AdventureWorks database is configured to use the Full recovery model as outlined in the details of this task.

■ PART A: Viewing an Existing Table without Compression

1. Open **SQL Server Management Studio**, and in **Object Explorer**, expand **Databases** under your server.

2. Expand the **AdventureWorks** database and expand **Tables**.

3. Right-click **Production.TransactionHistoryArchive**, select **Storage** and then click **Manage Compression**.

4. The **Data Compression Wizard** window will open. Click **Next** to continue.

5. The **Select Compression Type** window will now show you that the current compression type is 'None.' Change this drop-down box to **Page** and click on the **Calculate** button. It may take a few seconds to perform the necessary calculations.

6. Note the newly displayed values for **Current space** and **Requested compressed space**.

7. Now change the **Compression type** drop-down box setting to **Row**.

8. Click on the **Calculate** button again and note the changed value under **Requested compressed space**.

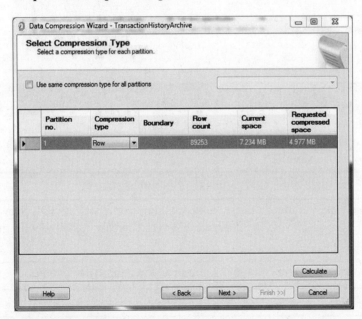

9. Click the **Cancel** button to exit out of the wizard without actually setting a compression type.

Question 3	*Which compression setting saves the most space? Is the space reduction meaningful?*

■ PART B: Adding PAGE or ROW Type Compression

1. Open **Management Studio**.

2. Open your **Query Editor**.

3. Run this code to create a new table:

```
USE SalesDemo
GO
CREATE TABLE MyNewTable(
CustomerID int    NOT NULL,
Notes        char(1000));
```

4. Now implement a compression type on this table. Choose one of the two commands listed here and run the code to set up compression on the table:

```
ALTER TABLE MyNewTable REBUILD WITH (DATA_COMPRESSION = PAGE);
ALTER TABLE MyNewTable REBUILD WITH (DATA_COMPRESSION = ROW);
```

■ PART C: Removing PAGE or ROW Type Compression

1. Run this code to remove all compression from this table:

```
ALTER TABLE MyNewTable REBUILD WITH (DATA_COMPRESSION = NONE);
```

2. Clean up the database by dropping this new table from the database:

```
DROP TABLE MyNewTable;
```

■ PART D: Sparse Columns and Compression

1. Try to implement either ROW or PAGE compression of the customers table in the sales database:

```
ALTER TABLE customers REBUILD WITH (DATA_COMPRESSION =
ROW);
```

2. A very strange and severe sounding error may occur. This is because the customers table may have a SPARSE column—Emailaddress. You cannot have both a SPARSE column and row/page compression. This column was added in a prior exercise. If you did not drop this column, then its presence as a SPARSE column will block the implementation of page or row compression. The reverse sequence of trying to add a SPARSE column to a compressed table will also generate an error.

3. Close the Query Window.

LAB 5
WORKING WITH DATABASES

This lab contains the following exercises and activities:

Exercise 5.1   Creating a Database

Exercise 5.2   Selecting and Setting a Recovery Model

Exercise 5.1	Creating a Database
Scenario	You are the DBA for a mid-sized company with offices in various cities throughout the United States and Canada. You have just installed a new instance of SQL Server, and now you need to create a database to hold data for your sales department.
Duration	This task should take approximately 30 minutes.
Setup	All you need for this task is access to the machine you installed SQL Server on in Exercise 2.1.
Procedure	In this task, you will create a database that will hold data for the sales department. You will use this database in later tasks for storing other database objects as well.
Equipment	See Setup.
Objective	To decide where to put the data and log files. Use these guidelines: • Data and log files should be on separate physical drives so that, in case of a disaster, you have a better chance of recovering all data. • Transaction logs are best placed on a RAID-1 array because this has the fastest sequential write speed together with redundancy. • Data files are best placed on a RAID-5 array because they have faster read speed than other RAID arrays together with redundancy.

	• If you have access to a RAID-10 array, you can place data and log files on it because it has all the advantages of RAID 1 and RAID 0.
Criteria for Completion	You have completed this task when you have a database named Sales that you can see in SQL Server Management Studio.

■ PART A: Calculating the Storage Requirements

1. Calculate the space used by a single row of the table.

    *   To do this, add the storage requirements for each data type in the table.
    *   Add the null bitmap using this formula: null_bitmap = 2 + ((number of columns + 7) ÷ 8).
    *   Calculate the space required for variable length columns using this formula: variable_datasize = 2 + (num_variable_columns × 2) + max_varchar_size.
    *   Calculate the total row size using this formula: Row_Size = Fixed_Data_Size + Variable_Data_Size + Null_Bitmap + Row_Header. The row header is always 4 bytes.

2. Calculate the number of rows that will fit on one page. Each page is 8,192 bytes with a header, so each page holds 8,096 bytes of data. Therefore, calculate the number of rows using this formula: 8096 ÷ (RowSize + 2).

3. Estimate the number of rows the table will hold. No formula exists to calculate this; you just need to have a good understanding of your data and user community.

4. Calculate the total number of pages that will be required to hold these rows. Use this formula: Total Number of Pages = Number of Rows in Table ÷ Number of Rows Per Page.

Question 1	Why bother with calculations? You can always allocate more disk storage, right?

■ PART B: Creating a Database Named Sales

1. Start **SQL Server Management Studio**.

2. Connect to your default instance of SQL Server.

3. Expand your **Databases** folder.

4. Right-click either the **Databases** folder in the console tree or the white space in the right pane, and choose **New Database** from the context menu.

5. You should now see the General tab of the Database properties sheet. Enter the database name **Sales**, and leave the owner as <default>.

6. In the Database files grid, in the Logical Name column, change the name of the Sales file to **Sales_Data**. Use the default location for the file, and make sure the initial size is 3.

7. Click the **ellipsis button** (the one with three periods) in the Autogrowth column for the Sales_Data file. In the dialog box that opens, check the Restricted File Growth (MB) radio button, and restrict the file growth to 20 MB. Click **OK**.

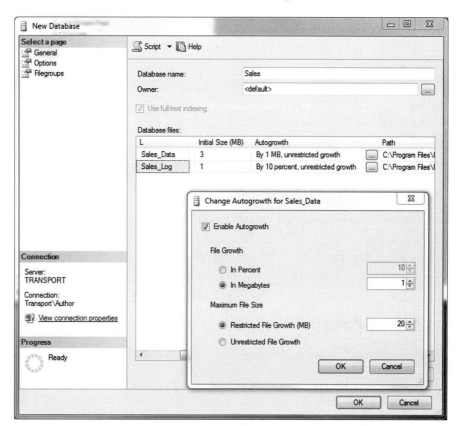

8. To add a secondary data file, click the **Add** button, and change the logical name of the new file to Sales_Data2. Here, too, use the default location for the file, and make sure the initial size is 3.

9. Restrict the file growth to a maximum of 20 MB for Sales_Data2 by clicking the **ellipsis** button in the Autogrowth column.

10. Leave all of the defaults for the Sales_Log file.

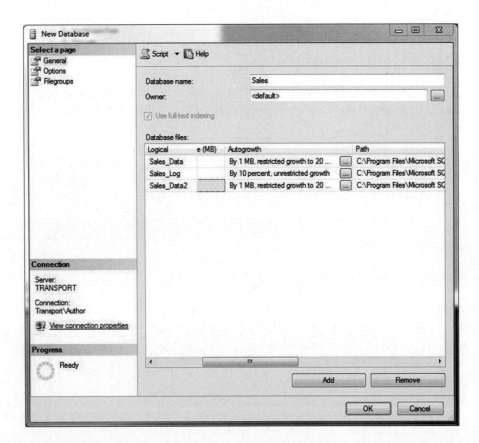

11. Click **OK** when you are finished. You should now have a new Sales database.

■ PART C: Verifying Results

1. In the Object Browser, click **Databases**.

2. Press **F5** or right-click database and choose **Refresh**.

3. Verify that your new database named Sales now appears.

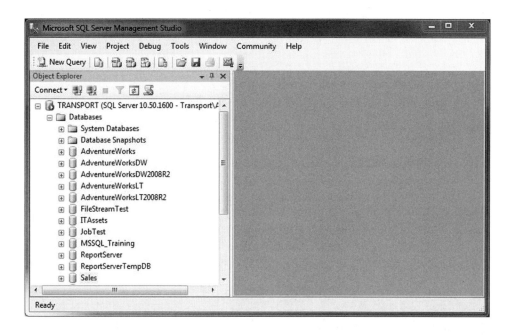

Exercise 5.2	Selecting and Setting a Recovery Model
Scenario	You have created a new database on your SQL Server, and you need to make sure it is being backed up as quickly and efficiently as possible. You know that, to ensure this, you need to configure the database to use the correct recovery model, so you decide to set the recovery model for the new database.
Duration	This task should take approximately 15 minutes.
Setup	For this task, you need access to the machine you installed SQL Server on in Exercise 2.1 and the AdventureWorks database installed with the sample data.
Procedure	In this task, you will configure the AdventureWorks database to use the Full recovery model.
Equipment	See Setup.
Objective	To set the recovery model for the AdventureWorks database.
Criteria for Completion	This task is complete when the AdventureWorks database is configured to use the Full recovery model as outlined in the details of this task.

■ PART A: Setting the Recovery Model

1. Open **SQL Server Management Studio**, and in Object Explorer, expand **Databases** under your server.

2. Right-click **AdventureWorks**, and click **Properties**.

3.   On the Options page, select **Full** from the Recovery model drop-down list.

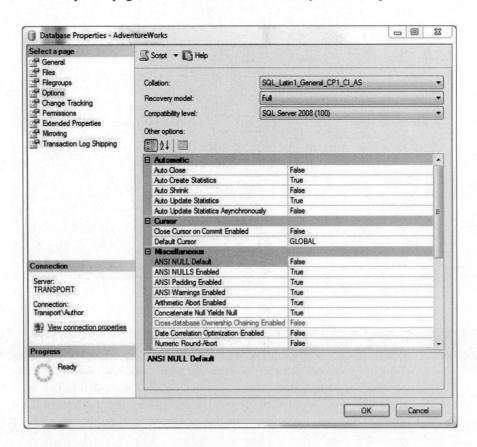

4.   Click **OK** to configure the model.

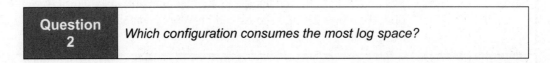

Question 2	*Which configuration consumes the most log space?*

■ PART B: Verifying Results

1.   Open **Management Studio**.

2.   Open your **Query Editor**.

3.   Run this code:

```
SELECT DATABASEPROPERTYEX('AdventureWorks', 'Recovery')
```

LAB 6
WORKING WITH
TABLES

This lab contains the following exercise and activity:

Exercise 6.1   Creating Tables

Exercise 6.1	Creating Tables
Scenario	You have just created a database for your sales department, and now you need to create some tables to hold customer, product, and order data.
Duration	This task should take approximately 30 minutes.
Setup	All you need for this task is access to the machine you installed SQL Server on in Exercise 2.1 and the Sales database you created in Exercise 5.1.
Caveats	Remember that this is just an exercise. In the real world, you would probably have multiple tables for each of these categories. For example, you would have an OrderHeader table and an Order Details table to store multiple line items for a single order. You are creating a single table for each category in this task only for the sake of simplicity.
Procedure	In this task, you will create three tables in your Sales database: • A Products table • A Customers table • An Orders table
Equipment	See Setup.
Objective	To create three tables based on the criteria shown in tables 6-1, 6-2, and 6-3.
Criteria for Completion	You have completed this task when you have the Products, Customers, and Orders tables in your database with the columns defined in the exercise.

Table 6-1
Products table attributes

Field Name	Data Type	Contains
ProdID	Int, Identity	A unique ID number for each product that can be referenced in other tables to avoid data duplication
Description	Nvarchar(100)	A brief text description of the product
InStock	Int	The amount of product in stock

Table 6-2
Customers table attributes

Field Name	Data Type	Contains
CustID	Int, Identity	A unique number for each customer that can be referenced in other tables
Fname	Nvarchar(20)	The customer's first name
Lname	Nvarchar(20)	The customer's last name
Address	Nvarchar(50)	The customer's street address
City	Nvarchar(20)	The city where the customer lives
State	Nchar(2)	The state where the customer lives
Zip	Nchar(5)	The customer's ZIP code
Phone	Nchar(10)	The customer's phone number without hyphens or parentheses (to save space, those will be displayed but not stored)

Table 6-3
Orders table attributes

Field Name	Data Type	Contains
CustID	Int	References the customer number stored in the Customers table so you don't need to duplicate the customer information for each order placed
ProdID	Int	References the Products table so you don't need to duplicate product information
Qty	Int	The amount of product sold for an order
OrdDate	Smalldatetime	The date and time the order was placed

■ PART A: Creating the Products Table

1. Open **SQL Server Management Studio**. In Object Explorer, expand your server, and expand **Databases** and then **Sales**.

2. Right-click the **Tables** icon, and select **New Table** to open the table designer.

3. In the first row, under Column Name, enter **ProdID**.

4. Just to the right of that, under Data Type, select **Int**.

5. Make certain Allow Nulls isn't checked. The field can be completely void of data if this option is checked, and you don't want that to be the case here.

6. In the bottom half of the screen, under Column Properties, in the Table Designer section, expand **Identity Specification**, and change (Is Identity) to **Yes**.

7. Just under ProdID, in the second row under Column Name, enter **Description**.

8. Just to the right of that, under Data Type, enter **nvarchar(100)**.

9. Make certain **Allow Nulls** is *not* checked.

10. Under Column Name in the third row, enter **InStock**.

11. Under Data Type, select **Int**.

12. Uncheck **Allow Nulls**.

13. Click the **Save** button on the left side of the toolbar (it looks like a floppy disk).

14. In the Choose Name box that opens, enter **Products**, then click **OK**.

15. Close the table designer by clicking the **X** in the upper-right corner of the window.

■ PART B: Creating the Customers Table

1. Right-click the **Tables** icon, and select **New Table** to open the table designer.

2. In the first row, under Column Name, enter **CustID**.

3. Under Data Type, select **Int**.

4. Make certain **Allow Nulls** is *not* checked.

5. Under Column Properties, in the Table Designer section, expand Identity Specification, and change **(Is Identity)** to **Yes**.

6. Just under CustID, in the second row under Column Name, enter **Fname**.

7. Just to the right of that, under Data Type, enter **nvarchar(20)**.

8. Make certain **Allow Nulls** is *not* checked for Fname.

9. Using the parameters displayed earlier, fill in the information for the remaining columns. Allow nulls in any of these remaining fields. This will be important in future exercises.

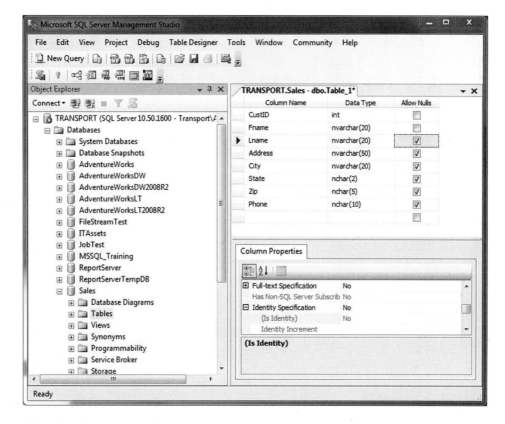

10. Click the **Save** button.

11. In the Choose Name box that opens, enter **Customers**, then click **OK**.

12. Close the table designer.

■ PART C: Creating the Orders Table

1. Right-click the **Tables** icon, and select **New Table** to open the table designer.

2. In the first row, under Column Name, enter **CustID**.

3. Under Data Type, select **Int**.

4. Make certain **Allow Nulls** is *not* checked.

5. This won't be an identity column like it was in the Customers table, so don't make any changes to the Identity Specification settings.

6. Just under CustID, in the second row under Column Name, enter **ProdID** with a data type of **int**. Don't change the Identity Specification settings. Don't allow null values.

7. Just below ProdID, create a field named **Qty** with a data type of **int** that doesn't allow nulls.

8. Create a column named **OrdDate** with a data type of **smalldatetime**. Don't allow null values.

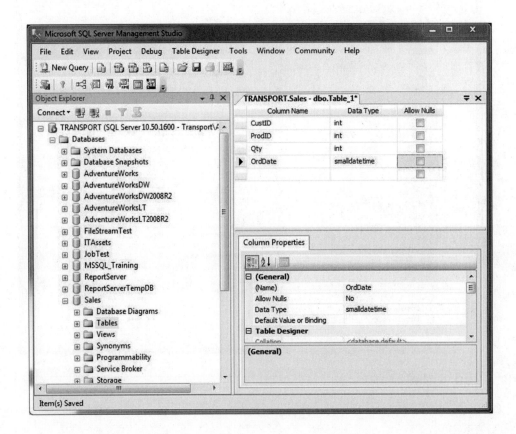

9. Click the **Save** button.

10. In the **Choose Name** box that opens, enter **Orders**, then click **OK**.

11. Close the table designer.

■ PART D: Verifying Results

Expand your Sales database in SQL Server Management Studio and then expand
Tables; you should see all three tables—dbo.Products, dbo.Customers, dbo.Orders.

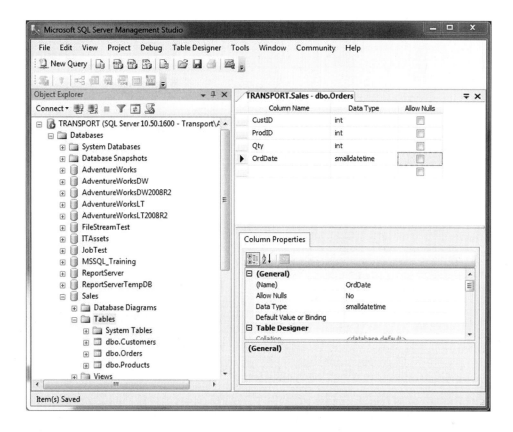

LAB 7
WORKING WITH VIEWS

This lab contains the following exercise and activity:

Exercise 7.1   Designing and Creating a View

Exercise 7.1	Designing and Creating a View
Scenario	You have a database that has been in use for some time and has a number of records in the Contacts table. Your users have asked you to break this data down for them by area code. You have decided that the easiest way to accomplish this goal is to create a view that displays only a subset of data from the table based on the area code.
Duration	This task should take approximately 15 minutes.
Setup	For this exercise, you need access to the machine you installed SQL Server on in Exercise 2.1 and the AdventureWorks database that is installed with the sample data.
Caveat	Realistically, views won't be this simplistic in the real world; this is just to keep the exercise simple.
Procedure	In this task, you will create a view based on the Person.Contact table in the AdventureWorks database. Specifically, you will create a view that displays only those customers in the 398 area code.
Equipment	See Setup.
Objective	To create the Contacts_in_398 view.
Criteria for Completion	This task is complete when you can query the Contacts_in_398 view and retrieve the correct results.

■ PART A: Designing and Creating a View

1. Open **SQL Server Management Studio** by selecting it from the Microsoft SQL Server group under Programs on your Start menu, and connect with Windows Authentication if requested.

2. In **Object Explorer**, expand your server, and then expand **Databases**, **AdventureWorks**. Right-click **Views**, and select **New View**.

3. In the **Add Table** dialog box, select **Contact (Person)**, and click **Add**.

4. Click **Close**, which opens the view designer.

5. In the Transact-SQL syntax editor text box, under the column grid, enter the following:

```
SELECT LastName, FirstName, Phone FROM Person.Contact
WHERE Phone LIKE '398%')
```

6. Click the **Execute** button (the red exclamation point) on the toolbar to test the query.

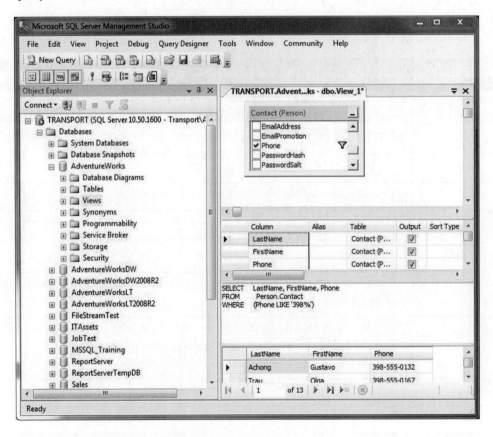

7. Choose **File**, Save View—**dbo.View_1**.

8. In the **Choose Name** dialog box, enter **Contacts_in_398**, and click **OK**.

9. To verify that the results are accurate, open a new query, and execute the code used to create the view:

```
USE AdventureWorks
SELECT lastname, firstname, phone
FROM Person.Contact WHERE phone LIKE '398%'
```

	How can you create a view of the Sales.Customers table to show the Lname, Fname, and Phone using Transact-SQL code?

■ PART B: Verifying Results

1. To test your view, execute this code:

```
USE AdventureWorks
SELECT * FROM dbo.Contacts_in_398
```

2. You should see only those contacts in the 398 area code—just as the previous select statement against the base table.

LAB 8
WORKING WITH CONSTRAINTS

This lab contains the following exercise and activity:

Exercise 8.1   Designing and Creating a Constraint

Exercise 8.1	Designing and Creating a Constraint
Scenario	You have just created tables in your new Sales database, one of which holds customer information. You want to make certain that users enter only valid ZIP codes in the Zip field of the Customers table, so you decide to create a constraint to restrict the data that can be entered in the field.
Duration	This task should take approximately 15 minutes.
Setup	For this exercise, you need access to the machine you installed SQL Server on in Exercise 2.1, the Sales database you created in Exercise 5.1, and the Customers table you created in Exercise 6.1.
Procedure	In this task, you will create a constraint on the Customers table to prevent users from entering invalid ZIP codes. Specifically, you will prevent users from entering letters; they can enter only numbers.
Equipment	See Setup.
Objective	To create a constraint on the Zip field of the Customers table.
Criteria for Completion	This task is complete when you have a constraint that prevents users from entering letters in the Zip field of the Customers table.

■ PART A: Designing and Creating a Constraint

1. In **Object Explorer**, expand the **Sales** database, and expand **Tables**, and then **dbo.Customers**.

2. Right-click **Constraints**, and click **New Constraint**.

3. In the **Check Constraints** dialog box, enter **CK_Zip** in the (Name) text box.

4. In the **Description** text box, enter **Check for valid zip codes**.

5. To create a constraint that will accept only five numbers that can be zero through nine, enter the following code in the Expression text box:

```
(zip like '[0-9][0-9][0-9][0-9][0-9]')
```

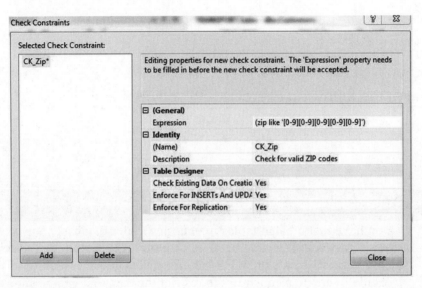

6. Click **Close**.

7. Click the **Save** button at the top left of the toolbar.

8. Close the table designer (which was opened when you started to create the constraint).

Question 1	*How can you force your users to always and only enter "NJ" for the state attribute?*

■ PART B: Verifying Results

1. In **SQL Server Management Studio**, click the **New Query** button.

2. Enter the following code in the query window:

```
USE Sales
INSERT Customers VALUES ('Greg', 'Scott', '111 Main',
'Provo', 'UT', '88102', '5045551212')
```

3. Click the Execute button just above the query window to execute the query, and notice the successful results.

4. To see the new record, click the New Query button, and execute the following code:

```
SELECT * FROM Customers
```

5. Notice that the record now exists with a CustID of 1 (because of the identity property discussed earlier, which automatically added the number for you).

6. To test the check constraint by adding characters in the Zip field, click the New Query button, and execute the following code (note the letters in the Zip field):

```
USE Sales
INSERT customers VALUES ('Amanda', 'Smith', '817 3rd',
'Chicago', 'IL', 'AAB1C', '8015551212')
```

7. Notice in the results pane that the query violated a constraint and so failed.

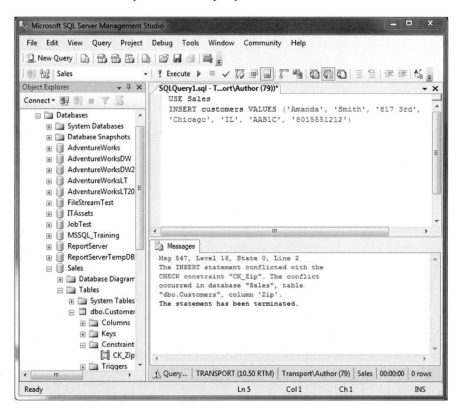

LAB 9
WORKING WITH STORED PROCEDURES

This lab contains the following exercise and activity:

Exercise 9.1   Designing and Creating a Stored Procedure

Exercise 9.1	Designing and Creating a Stored Procedure
Scenario	You have a database that has been in use for some time and has a number of records in the Products table. Your users frequently query the table for data based on the SellStartDate column. To speed up execution time and enhance ease of management, you have decided to create a stored procedure that accepts a date as an input parameter and returns a result set of the most frequently queried columns.
Duration	This task should take approximately 15 minutes.
Setup	For this task, you need access to the machine you installed SQL Server on in Exercise 2.1 and the AdventureWorks database that is installed with the sample data.
Procedure	In this task, you will create a stored procedure based on the Production.Product table in the AdventureWorks database. Specifically, you will create a stored procedure that returns product data based on an input parameter.
Equipment	See Setup.
Objective	To create the Production.Show_Products stored procedure.
Criteria for Completion	This task is complete when you can execute the Production.Show_Products stored procedure using an input parameter and have it return the correct results.

■ PART A: Designing and Creating a Stored Procedure

1. Open **SQL Server Management Studio**. In **Object Explorer**, expand your server, and then expand **Databases**, **AdventureWorks**, and **Programmability**.

2. Right-click the **Stored Procedures** folder icon, and select **New Stored Procedure** to open a new query window populated with a stored procedure template.

3. In the Transact-SQL syntax box, change the code to look like this:

```
CREATE PROCEDURE Production.Show_Products @Date datetime AS BEGIN
SELECT Name, Color, ListPrice, SellStartDate
FROM Production.Product
WHERE SellStartDate > @Date ORDER BY SellStartDate, Name
END
GO
```

> **NOTE** *Do not name your stored procedures with the sp_ prefix. If you do, it will slow processing in your database.*

4. Click the **Execute** button on the toolbar to create the procedure.

5. Close the query window.

■ PART B: Verifying Results

1. Execute the following code in a new query window to test your stored procedure:

```
USE AdventureWorks
EXEC Production.Show_Products '1/1/1998'
```

2.   You should see only those products that are available after January 1, 1998.

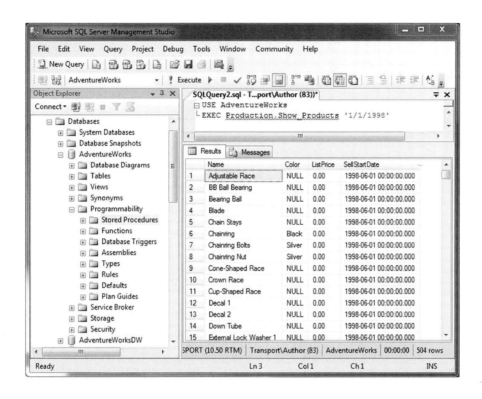

LAB 10
WORKING WITH FUNCTIONS

This lab contains the following exercise and activity:

Exercise 10.1   Designing and Creating a User-Defined Function

Exercise 10.1	Designing and Creating a User-Defined Function
Scenario	You have created a database for your sales department with a table that contains order information. Your sales manager wants to know the largest number of items for a given product on a single order. She wants to run this calculation every week, so you decide to create a user-defined function for ease of use and management.
Duration	This task should take approximately 15 minutes.
Setup	For this task, you need access to the machine you installed SQL Server on in Exercise 2.1, the Sales database you created in Exercise 5.1, and the Orders and Customers tables you created in Exercise 6.1.
Procedure	In this task, you will create a user-defined function that calculates the largest number of items for a given product on a single order. First you will add some orders to the database, and then you will create a function to calculate the sales; finally, you will verify the function.
Equipment	See Setup.
Objective	To place some orders in the Orders table so the function has some data to work with.
Criteria for Completion	This task is complete when you have created a function that tells you the largest amount of items for a specific product placed on a single order.

■ PART A: Inserting Data in the Orders Table

1. Open a new SQL Server query, and execute the following code to insert some new records in the **Orders** table:

```
USE Sales
GO
INSERT Orders VALUES (3,2,15,getdate( ))
GO
INSERT Orders VALUES (1,2,10,getdate( ))
GO
INSERT Orders VALUES (1,1,20,getdate( ))
GO
INSERT Orders VALUES (4,3,25,getdate( ))
GO
```

2. To verify that the new orders exist, enter and execute this code in a new query window:

```
USE Sales SELECT * FROM Orders
```

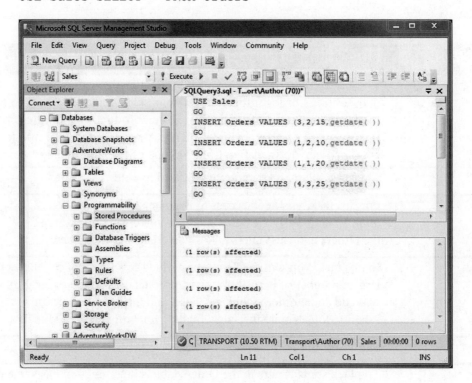

■ **PART B: Creating a User-Defined Function to Calculate the Largest Number of Items for a Given Product on a Single Order**

In **SQL Server Management Studio**, open a new query, and enter and execute the following code:

```
USE Sales
GO
CREATE FUNCTION ItemOrderCount (@ProductID int) RETURNS int
AS BEGIN
RETURN (SELECT MAX(Qty) FROM Orders WHERE ProdID = @ProductID)
END
```

> **NOTE** *The CREATE FUNCTION statement must be the first statement in a batch. GO separates the statements into separate batches.*

■ **PART C: Verifying Results**

1. Execute the following code:

```
USE Sales
GO
SELECT dbo.ItemOrderCount(1)
```

2. You should get a value of 20; this was the most items placed on a single order for product ID 1.

LAB 11
WORKING WITH SERVICE BROKER

This lab contains the following exercises and activities:

Exercise 11.1   Creating Service Broker Objects

Exercise 11.2   Setting a Priority in Service Broker

Exercise 11.1	Creating Service Broker Objects
Scenario	The Marketing Department at your company wants to send a welcome email message to new customers who register on the company's Web site. To minimize the impact to the site's scalability, the senior database developer has decided to implement this functionality through a service that will be invoked asynchronously when a new user registers.
Duration	This task should take approximately 60 minutes.
Setup	For this task, you need access to the machine you installed SQL Server on in Exercise 2.1 and the Sales database you created in Exercise 5.1.
Procedure	In this task, you will create the objects needed for a Service Broker instance and test it.
Equipment	See Setup.
Objective	To send an email asynchronously.
Criteria for Completion	This task is complete when you verify the email's creation.

■ PART A: Performing the Needed Procedures to Create Service Broker Objects

1. Click **Start**, point to **All Programs**, point to **Microsoft SQL Server**, and then click **SQL Server Management Studio.**

2. In the **Connect to Server** dialog box, specify the values in the following table, and then click Connect.

Property	Value
Server type	Database Engine
Server name	<YourComputerName>
Authentication	Windows Authentication

3. Start a new query editor session.

■ PART B: Enabling Service Broker in the Sales Database

1. Review the following code. Enter it into the **Query Editor:**

```
USE master;
GO
-- Enable Service Broker in the Sales database
ALTER DATABASE Sales SET ENABLE_BROKER;
```

2. Execute the code.

■ PART C: Creating a Master Key in the Sales Database

1. Review the following code. Enter it into the **Query Editor:**

```
-- Configure the Sales database
USE Sales
GO
IF NOT EXISTS (SELECT * FROM sys.symmetric_keys
WHERE name = '##MS_DatabaseMasterKey##')
CREATE MASTER KEY ENCRYPTION BY PASSWORD = 'Pa$$w0rd';
GO
```

2. Execute the code.

■ PART D: Creating a New Schema Named Email in the Sales Database

1. Review the following code. Enter it into the **Query Editor:**

```
CREATE SCHEMA Email
GO
```

2. Execute the code.

■ PART E: Creating a New Table Named Email.Emaillog in the Sales Database

1. Review the following code. Enter it into the **Query Editor:**

```
-- Create a table to log details of the customer emails sent
CREATE TABLE EMail.EmailLog
(Date datetime NOT NULL,
[Event] nvarchar(50) NOT NULL,
CustomerData xml)
GO
```

2. Execute the code.

■ PART F: Creating Service Broker Objects

1. Review the following code. Enter it into your **Query Editor**. Note that some syntax is case sensitive:

```
USE Sales
GO
-- Create message types that will be used to pass customer
-- data to the EmailService service
CREATE MESSAGE TYPE [//Training.com/EMail/CustomerDetails]
VALIDATION = WELL_FORMED_XML
GO
-- Create a contract that will be supported by the
-- EmailService service
CREATE CONTRACT [//Training.com/EMail/SendCustomerDetails]
([//Training.com/EMail/CustomerDetails] SENT BY INITIATOR)
GO
-- Create two queues that will be used by the EMailService service
CREATE QUEUE Email.NewCustomerQueue
WITH STATUS = ON
CREATE QUEUE EMail.NewCustomerEmailQueue
WITH STATUS = OFF
GO
-- Create a service which calls the EmailService to send
-- an e-mail message to a new customer
CREATE SERVICE [//Training.com/EMail/CustomerService]
ON QUEUE Email.NewCustomerQueue
-- Create the EmailService service which sends an e-mail
-- message to a new customer
CREATE SERVICE [//Training.com/EMail/EmailService]
ON QUEUE EMail.NewCustomerEmailQueue
([//Training.com/EMail/SendCustomerDetails])
```

2. Click the Execute button on the toolbar to execute the query.

3. In **Object Explorer**, expand **Databases**, **Sales**, and **Service Broker**, **Expand Message Types**, **Contracts**, **Queues**, and **Services**, and then show the various objects that you just created.

■ PART G: Preparing to Send and Receive Messages

1. Review the following code. Enter it into the **Query Editor:**

```
USE Sales
GO
-- Sends messages from the CustomerService service to the
-- EmailService service
CREATE PROCEDURE Email.uspEmailNewCustomer
@firstName nvarchar(50),
@lastName nvarchar(50),
@emailAddress nvarchar(50)
AS
BEGIN
SET NOCOUNT ON;
-- Create message body to pass to SendMail service.
DECLARE @message xml
SET @message = NCHAR(0xFEFF)
+ '<Customer>'
+ '<CustomerName>' + @firstName + ' ' + @lastName
+ '</CustomerName>'
+ '<EmailAddress>' + @emailAddress + '</EmailAddress>'
+ '</Customer>'
DECLARE @dialogHandle UNIQUEIDENTIFIER
BEGIN DIALOG @dialogHandle
FROM SERVICE [//Training.com/EMail/CustomerService]
TO SERVICE '//Training.com/EMail/EmailService'
ON CONTRACT [//Training.com/EMail/SendCustomerDetails];
SEND ON CONVERSATION @dialogHandle
MESSAGE TYPE [//Training.com/EMail/CustomerDetails] (@message)
END CONVERSATION @dialogHandle
END;
GO
--Processes messages received by the EmailService service
CREATE PROCEDURE EMail.uspSendCustomerEmail
AS
BEGIN
SET NOCOUNT ON;
DECLARE @conversation UNIQUEIDENTIFIER
DECLARE @msg NVARCHAR(MAX)
DECLARE @msgType NVARCHAR(256)
;RECEIVE TOP(1)
```

```
@conversation = conversation_handle,
@msgType = message_type_name,
@msg = message_body
FROM Sales.EMail.NewCustomerEmailQueue
IF (@@ROWCOUNT = 0) RETURN
IF (@msgType = '//Training.com/EMail/CustomerDetails')
BEGIN
-- Extract data from the message
DECLARE @emailAddress nvarchar(30)
DECLARE @hDoc int
EXECUTE sp_xml_preparedocument @hdoc OUTPUT, @msg
SELECT @emailAddress = EmailAddress
FROM OPENXML(@hDoc, 'Customer', 2)
WITH
(EmailAddress nvarchar(30))
EXECUTE sp_xml_removedocument @hDoc
-- Code to send the email would go here
-- Log the email
INSERT INTO Sales.EMail.EmailLog
(Date, [Event], CustomerData)
VALUES
(getdate( ), 'Email sent to ' + @emailAddress, @msg);
END
ELSE IF (@msgType = 'http://schemas.microsoft.com/SQL/
ServiceBroker/Error') OR
(@msgType = 'http://schemas.microsoft.com/SQL/ServiceBroker/
EndDialog')
END CONVERSATION @conversation
ELSE
BEGIN
END CONVERSATION @conversation
WITH ERROR = 500 DESCRIPTION = 'Invalid message type.';
INSERT INTO Sales.EMail.EmailLog (Date, [Event], CustomerData)
VALUES (getdate( ), 'Invalid message type', @msg);
END
END;
GO
ALTER QUEUE EMail.NewCustomerEmailQueue
WITH STATUS = ON,
ACTIVATION (
STATUS = ON,
PROCEDURE_NAME = Sales.EMail.uspSendCustomerEmail,
MAX_QUEUE_READERS = 5,
EXECUTE AS SELF)
```

2. Click the Execute button on the toolbar to execute the query.

■ **PART H: Send a Message**

Select and execute the following EXECUTE statement to send a message to the EmailService service:

```
EXECUTE Sales.Email.uspEmailNewCustomer
@firstName = 'Alice',
@lastName = 'Jones',
@emailAddress = 'Student@Training.com'
```

> **NOTE**
> In the real world you would need to configure your mailboxes (POP3 or SMTP server) to acknowledge the email address for Student and the training.com domain.

■ **PART I: Verifying Results**

Select and execute the following SELECT statement to show that the EmailService service has processed the message:

```
SELECT * FROM Sales.EMail.EmailLog
```

Exercise 11.2	Setting a Priority in Service Broker
Scenario	While it may be important to send an email message to new customers, it is not an urgent activity. Thus setting a low priority on the Service Broker process for customer emails is desired.
Duration	This task should take approximately 30 minutes.
Setup	For this task, you need access to the machine you installed SQL Server on in Exercise 2.1 and the Sales database containing the Service Broker objects created in Exercise 11.1.
Procedure	In this task, you will create the objects needed for using a priority with Service Broker.
Equipment	See Setup.
Objective	To set the priority for certain Service Broker contracts in the Sales database.
Criteria for Completion	This task is complete when the Service Broker contracts operate at a specified priority.

■ PART A: Set Up the Priority for Service Broker Contracts

1. Open **SQL Server Management Studio**, and in Object Explorer, expand **Databases** under your server.

2. Right-click **AdventureWorks**, and click **Properties**.

3. On the **Options** page, select **Full** from the **Recovery model** drop-down list.

    ```
    CREATE BROKER PRIORITY CustomerEmailPriority
    FOR CONVERSATION
    SET (CONTRACT_NAME = [//Training.com/EMail/SendCustomerDetails],
    LOCAL_SERVICE_NAME = [//Training.com/EMail/CustomerService],
    REMOTE_SERVICE_NAME = ANY,
    PRIORITY_LEVEL = 2);
    ```

4. Close the query window.

Question 1	*Which priorty value should be used? Does the value 2 set the priority to high or low?*

■ PART B: Verifying Results

1. In **SQL Server Management Studio** expand **Databases**, **Sales**, **Service Broker**, then **Broker Priorities**.

2. Look for a new priority named CustomerEmailPriority. Right-click on this priority entry and select **Properties**.

3. The Broker priority properties window will open. The Priority level will be shown. Verify that the value is 2.

4. Close the Broker priority properties window by clicking **OK**.

LAB 13
SETTING PERMISSIONS

This lab contains the following exercise and activity:

Exercise 13.1 Assigning Permissions

Exercise 13.1	Assigning Permissions
Scenario	You have just installed a new SQL Server for your company and want to make sure you fully understand how permissions work, so you have decided to test permissions on your test server before assigning them to users on production databases.
Duration	This task should take approximately 30 minutes.
Setup	For this task, you need access to the machine you installed SQL Server on in Exercise 2.1, the SmithB account you created in Exercise 2.1, and the AdventureWorks database.
Caveats	In a production environment, for ease of management, you will create custom roles and assign permissions to those roles. You will usually assign permissions to a specific user only when you want to deny a permission to that user.
Procedure	In this task, you will assign permissions to the SmithB user mapping. You will then change the permission state and test the effects of the change.
Equipment	See Setup.
Objective	To create assign and modify permissions for SmithB.
Criteria for Completion	This task is complete when you have successfully assigned the permissions as described in the PART A section.

■ PART A: Assigning Permissions

1. Open **SQL Server Management Studio**, expand your server, and then expand **Databases**, **AdventureWorks**, and **Security**.

2. Expand **Users**, right-click **SmithB**, and select **Properties**.

3. On the **Securables** page, click **Search** above the **Securables** list box, select the **Specific Objects** radio button, and click **OK**.

4. Click the **Objects Type** button, select **Tables**, and click **OK**.

5. Click **Browse**, select the **HumanResources.Department** check box, and click **OK** twice.

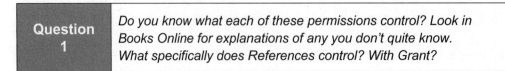

Question 1	Do you know what each of these permissions control? Look in Books Online for explanations of any you don't quite know. What specifically does References control? With Grant?

6. In the **Permissions** for **HumanResources.Department** list, select the **Grant** check box next to **Select**, and click **OK**.

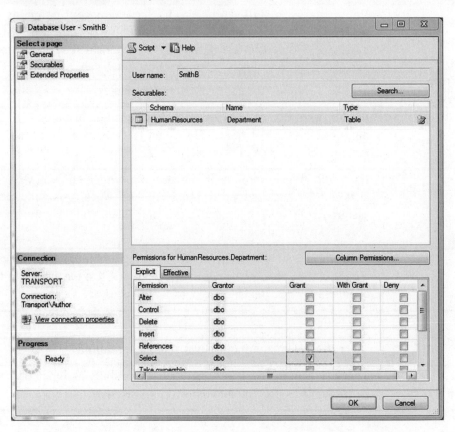

7. Open a new SQL Server query in **SQL Server Management Studio**.

8. On the **Query** menu, hover over **Connection**, and then click **Change Connection**.

9. Select SQL Server Authentication from the Authentication list box.

10. In the User Name box, enter **SmithB**; in the Password box, enter **Pa$$w0rd**, and click **Connect**.

11. Execute the following query:

```
USE AdventureWorks
SELECT * FROM HumanResources.Department
```

It's successful because SmithB has Select permission on the HumanResources.Department table.

12. Right-click **SmithB** under Users in the AdventureWorks database, and select **Properties**.

13. On the Securables page, click **Add** under the Securables list box, select the **Specific Objects** radio button, and click **OK**.

14. Click the **Objects Type** button, select **Tables**, and click **OK**.

15. Click **Browse**, select the HumanResources.Department check box, and click **OK** twice.

16. In the **Permissions** for **HumanResources.Department** list, uncheck the Grant check box next to Select (this revokes the permission), and click **OK**.

17. Return to the query window, and execute the query in Step 11. It fails because SmithB doesn't have explicit **Select** permission.

18. Right-click **SmithB** under **Users** in the **AdventureWorks** database, and select **Properties**.

19. Under **Role Membership**, deselect the check box next to the **db_denydatareader** role. Click **OK**.

20. Return to the query window, and rerun the query from Step 11. Now it fails because SmithB does not have the permission expressly applied and is not a member of a role that has this permission.

21. Right-click SmithB under Users in the AdventureWorks database, and select **Properties**.

22. On the **Securables** page, click **Add** under the Securables list box, select the **Specific Objects** radio button, and click **OK**.

23. Click the **Objects Type** button, select **Tables**, and click **OK**.

24. Click **Browse**, select the **HumanResources.Department** check box, and click **OK** twice.

25. In the **Permissions** for **HumanResources.Department** list, select the **Deny** check box next to Select, and click **OK**.

26. Return to the query window, and again run the query from Step 11. It fails this time because you've specifically denied SmithB access.

■ PART B: Verifying Results

1. In Management Studio, expand databases, **AdventureWorks**, **Tables**, **HumanResources.Department**.

2. Right click on **HumanResources.Department** and select **Properties**.

3. Click **Permissions**.

4. Confirm permissions are set as you wish them.

LAB 14
SETTING LOGINS AND ROLES

This lab contains the following exercises and activities:

Exercise 14.1   Creating a Windows Login

Exercise 14.2   Creating a Standard Login

Exercise 14.3   Assigning Logins to Fixed Server Roles

Exercise 14.4   Creating a Database User Mapping

Exercise 14.5   Assigning User Mappings to Fixed Database Roles

Exercise 14.6   Creating a Custom Database Role

Exercise 14.7   Creating an Application Role

Exercise 14.1	Creating a Windows Login
Scenario	You have just installed a new SQL Server at your company, and you need to make sure the right people have access. Some of these users will be using Windows accounts, so you have decided to create Windows logins in SQL Server for these users.
Duration	This task should take approximately 90 minutes.
Setup	For this task, you need access to the machine you installed SQL Server on in Exercise 2.1.
Caveat	You will need administrative access to the machine you will be using for this task, because you will be creating new groups and user accounts on the machine.

Procedure	In this task, you will create several Windows user and group accounts and then create Windows logins for these accounts in SQL Server.
Equipment	See Setup.
Objective	To create the Windows user and group accounts in Computer Management (or Active Directory Users and Computers if you are in a domain with Domain Admin rights).
Criteria for Completion	This task is complete when you have successfully created the Windows login accounts specified in the task.

■ PART A: Creating Users and Local Groups in Windows

1. Click **Start**, right-click **Computer**, and select **Manage**. Expand **Local Users and Groups**, click **Users**, and then select **Action, New User**.

> **NOTE**
> *If you are operating in a domain, open Active Directory Users and Computers.*

2. Create six new users with the criteria from Table 14-1.

Table 14-1
New Users

Username	Description	Password	Must Change	Never Expires
MorrisL	IT	Pa$$w0rd	Deselect	Select
RosmanD	Administration	Pa$$w0rd	Deselect	Select
JohnsonK	Accounting	Pa$$w0rd	Deselect	Select
JonesB	Accounting	Pa$$w0rd	Deselect	Select
ChenJ	Sales	Pa$$w0rd	Deselect	Select
SamuelsR	Sales	Pa$$w0rd	Deselect	Select

> **NOTE**
> *You're the DBA, right? Take advantage. Let the network administrator do all the user maintenance work. Specify the right number of groups and all you have to do is add the groups to SQL Server. Everything else is someone else's concern.*

3. While in **Computer Management**, create a **Local** group called **Accounting**.

4. Add the new users you just created whose **Description** value is **Accounting**.

5. While still in **Computer Management**, create a **Local** group named **Sales**.

6. Add all the users whose **Description** value is **Sales**.

7. Open Local Security Policy from the Administrative Tools group.

8. Expand **Local Policies**, and click **User Rights Assignment**.

9. Double-click the **Allow Log on Locally** right, and click **Add User or Group**.

10. Select the **Everyone** group, click **OK**, and then click **OK** again (on a production machine this is not a best practice; this is only for this exercise).

11. Close the **Local Policies** tool, and open **SQL Server Management Studio**.

■ PART B: Adding These Windows Accounts to SQL Server

1. Be sure you have SQL Server Management Studio open, expand your server, and then expand **Security** and then **Logins**.

2. Right-click **Logins**, and select **New Login**.

3. In the Login name box, enter **<YourComputerName>\Accounting** (the name of the first Local group created earlier).

4. Under Default database, select **AdventureWorks**.

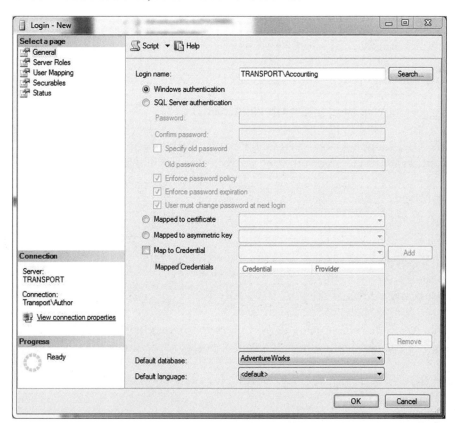

5. On the User Mapping page, select the **Map** check box next to AdventureWorks to give your user access to the default database.

6. Click **OK** to create the login.

7. Right-click **Logins**, and select **New Login**.

8. In the Login name box, enter **<YourComputerName>\Sales** (the name of the second Local group created earlier).

9. Under Default database, select **AdventureWorks**.

10. On the User Mapping page, select the **Map** check box next to AdventureWorks to give your user access to the default database.

11. Click **OK** to create the login.

12. Right-click **Logins**, and select **New Login**.

13. Enter **<YourComputerName>\RosmanD** in the Login Name field.

14. Under Default database, select **AdventureWorks**.

15. On the User Mapping page, select the **Permit** check box next to AdventureWorks to give your user access to the default database.

16. Click **OK** to create the login.

17. Right-click **Logins**, and select **New Login**.

18. Enter **<YourComputerName>\MorrisL** in the Login Name field.

19. Under Default database, select **AdventureWorks**.

20. On the User Mapping page, select the **Permit** check box next to **AdventureWorks** to give your user access to the default database.

21. Click **OK** to create the login.

■ PART C: Verifying Results

1. Log out of Windows, and log back in as **JonesB**.

2. Open a new SQL Server query in **SQL Server Management Studio**, and select **Windows Authentication** from the Authentication drop-down list.

3. Close **SQL Server Management Studio**, log out of Windows, and log back in as **RosmanD**.

4.   Open a new SQL Server query in **SQL Server Management Studio**, and select **Windows Authentication** from the Authentication drop-down list.

5.   Log off and back on as Administrator.

Exercise 14.2	Creating a Standard Login
Scenario	You have just installed a new SQL Server at your company, and you need to make sure the right people have access. Some of these users run Macintosh and Linux, and they do not have Windows accounts, so you must create Standard logins in SQL Server for these users.
Duration	This task should take approximately 30 minutes.
Setup	For this task, you need access to the machine you installed SQL Server on in Exercise 2.1.
Procedure	In this task, you will create two Standard logins in SQL Server.
Equipment	See Setup.
Objective	To create the Standard logins in SQL Server.
Criteria for Completion	This task is complete when you have successfully created the Standard login accounts specified in the task.

■ PART A: Creating a Standard Login

1.   Open **SQL Server Management Studio**, and expand your server by clicking the plus (+) sign next to the icon named after your server.

2.   Expand **Security**, and then expand **Logins**.

3.   Right-click **Logins**, and select **New Login**.

4.   Select the SQL Server Authentication radio button.

5.   In the **Name** box, enter **SmithB**.

6.   In the **Password** text box, enter Pa$$w0rd (remember, passwords are case sensitive).

7.   In the **Confirm password** text box, enter Pa$$w0rd again.

8.   Under **Default database**, select **AdventureWorks**.

9.   Uncheck the **User Must Change Password at Next Login** box. See figure on the next page.

NOTE	*The two additional checkmarks are new beginning with SQL Server 2005. They allow you to tie back to the operating system to enforce group policy settings as set for the enterprise network. Try setting Enforce password expiration without checking Enforce password policy.*

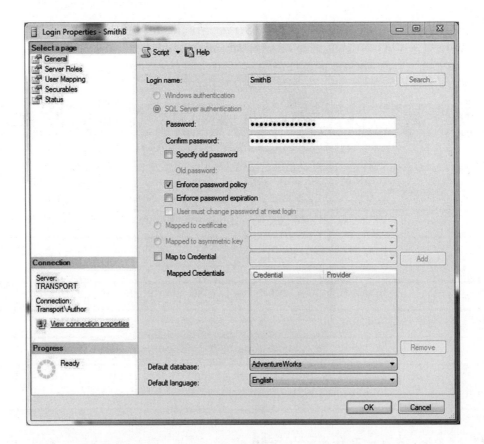

10. On the **User Mapping** page, select the **Map** check box next to **AdventureWorks** to give your user access to the default database.

11. Click **OK** to create your new login.

12. Right-click **Logins**, and select **New Login**.

13. Select the **SQL Server authentication** radio button.

14. In the **Name** box, enter **GibsonH**.

15. In the **Password** text box, enter Pa$$w0rd.

16. In the **Confirm password** text box, enter Pa$$w0rd.

17. Under **Default database**, select **AdventureWorks**.

18. Uncheck the **User Must Change Password at Next Login** box.

19. Do not select the **Permit** check box next to **AdventureWorks** on the **User Mapping** page. You'll create a database user account later in this phase.

20. Click **OK** to create your new login.

■ PART B: Verifying Results

1. To test the SmithB login, click the **New Query** button in **SQL Server Management Studio**.

2. On the **Query** menu, hover over **Connection**, and then click **Change Connection**.

3. In the dialog box that opens, select **SQL Server Authentication** from the Authentication drop-down list.

4. In the **Login** name box, enter **SmithB**.

5. In the Password box, enter **Pa$$w0rd**.

6. Click **Connect** to connect to **AdventureWorks**.

Exercise 14.3	Assigning Logins to Fixed Server Roles
Scenario	You have just created several new logins on your SQL Server so your users can access the system. You need to ensure that these accounts have the right amount of administrative access, so you have decided to assign two of these logins to fixed server roles.
Duration	This task should take approximately 15 minutes.
Setup	For this task, you need access to the machine you installed SQL Server on in Exercise 2.1 and the logins you created in Exercises 14.1 and 14.2.
Procedure	In this task, you will assign two of the logins you created to fixed server roles to limit their administrative access.
Equipment	See Setup.
Objective	To assign the logins to fixed server roles.
Criteria for Completion	This task is complete when you have successfully added MorrisL to the sysadmins fixed server role and GibsonH to the serveradmin fixed server role.

■ PART A: Assigning Logins to Fixed Server Roles

1. Open **SQL Server Management Studio** by selecting it from the SQL Server group under Programs on the Start menu, expand **Security**, and expand **Server Roles**.

Question 1	*What is the difference between groups in Windows Server and roles in SQL Server?*

2. Double-click the **Sysadmin** server role to open its properties.

3. Click **Add**, click **Browse**, select the check box next to <YourComputerName>\MorrisL, click **OK**, and then **OK** again.

4. MorrisL should now appear in the Role Members list.

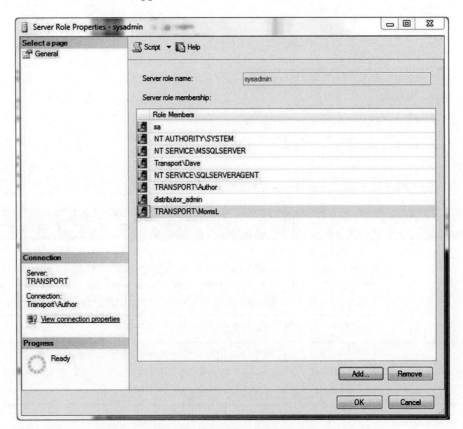

5. Click **OK** to exit the **Server Role Properties** dialog box.

6. Double-click **Serveradmin Server Role Properties**.

7. Click **Add**, enter **GibsonH**, and click **OK**.

8. Click **OK** to exit the **Server Role Properties** dialog box.

■ PART B: Verifying Results

1. Connect to **Management Studio**, expand **Security**, expand **Server** roles.

2. Verify that **MorrisL** is a member of the **Sysadmin** server role and that **GibsonH** is a member of the **Serveradmin** role.

3. **MorrisL** should show up in the sysadmin Role Members list.

4. **GibsonH** should show up in the serveradmin Role Members list.

Exercise 14.4	Creating a Database User Mapping
Scenario	You have just created several new logins on your SQL Server so your users can access the system. You didn't create user mappings for all the logins, though, so you need to create a user mapping for GibsonH to access the AdventureWorks database.
Duration	This task should take approximately 15 minutes.
Setup	For this task, you need access to the machine you installed SQL Server on in Exercise 2.1 and the GibsonH login you created in Exercise 14.2.
Procedure	In this task, you will create a user mapping for GibsonH to access the AdventureWorks database.
Equipment	See Setup.
Objective	To create a user mapping for GibsonH in AdventureWorks.
Criteria for Completion	This task is complete when you have successfully created a user mapping for GibsonH in the AdventureWorks database.

■ PART A: Registering a User with a Database

> **NOTE**
>
> When a user exists in SQL Server the only access to a database is through the Public role. If you remove that user from the Public role, he or she has no access to any database. If users must do more than what's allowed by the Public role, you must add them to all databases needed to support their business needs.

1. Open **SQL Server Management Studio**, and expand **<your server>**.

2. Expand **Databases** by clicking the plus (**+**) sign next to the icon.

3. Expand the **AdventureWorks** database.

4. Expand **Security**, and click the **Users** icon.

5. Right-click **Users**, and select **New User**.

6. Click the **ellipsis button** next to the Login name box, and click **Browse**. View all the available names; note that only logins you've already created are available.

7. Select the check box next to GibsonH, and click **OK** twice.

8. Enter **GibsonH** in the Login name box and **dbo** in the Default schema box.

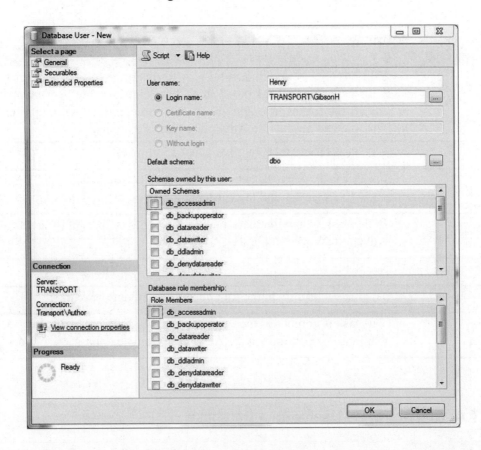

9. Click **OK** to create the GibsonH database user account.

■ PART B: Verifying Results

1. In **SQL Server Management Studio** migrate to the **AdventureWorks** database, expand **Security** and then **Users**.

2. Validate that GibsonH is now listed.

Exercise 14.5	Assigning User Mappings to Fixed Database Roles
Scenario	You have just created several new logins on your SQL Server and created user mappings for them in the AdventureWorks database. You now need to make sure these users have only the necessary permissions, so you need to add some of them to fixed database roles.
Duration	This task should take approximately 15 minutes.
Setup	For this task, you need access to the machine you installed SQL Server on in Exercise 2.1, the GibsonH and SmithB logins you created in Exercise 14.2, the SmithB user mapping you created in Exercise 14.2, and the GibsonH user mapping you created in Exercise 14.4.
Procedure	In this task, you will add the SmithB user mapping to the db_denydatawriter fixed database role and the GibsonH user mapping to the db_denydatareader fixed database role.
Equipment	See Setup.
Objective	To add these user mappings to the fixed database roles.
Criteria for Completion	This task is complete when you have successfully added the SmithB user mapping to the db_ denydatawriter fixed database role and the GibsonH user mapping to the db_denydatareader fixed database role.

■ PART A: Assigning a User to a Database Role

1. Open **SQL Server Management Studio**, expand your server, and then expand **Databases** and then **AdventureWorks**.

2. Expand **Security**, then **Roles**, and then **Database Roles**.

3. Right-click **db_denydatawriter**, and select **Properties**.

4. Click **Add**.

5. Enter **SmithB** in the **Enter Object Names to Select** box, and click **OK**.

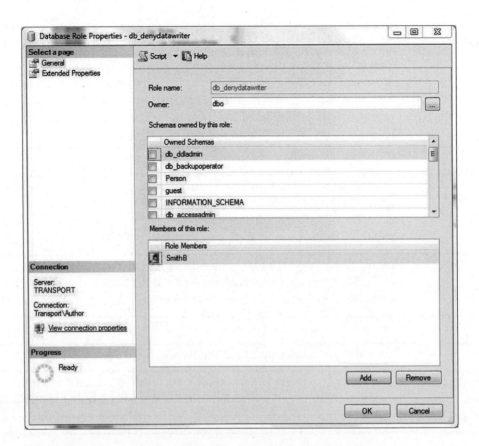

6. Click **OK** again to return to SQL Server Management Studio.

7. Right-click **db_denydatareader,** and select **Properties.**

8. Click **Add**.

9. Enter **GibsonH** in the **Enter Object Names to Select** box, and click **OK**. Then click **OK** again.

Question 2	*Which is easier, adding a user to a database role or assigning the user permissions?*

■ PART B: Verifying Results

1. Open a new SQL Server query in **SQL Server Management Studio**.

2. On the Query menu, hover over **Connection**, and then click **Change Connection**.

3. Select **SQL Server Authentication** from the Authentication list box.

4. In the **User Name** box, enter **SmithB**; in the **Password** box, enter **Pa$$w0rd**, and click **Connect**.

5. Enter and execute the following query, which tries to update information in the HumanResources.Department table (it fails because SmithB is a member of the db_denydatawriter role):

```
INSERT INTO HumanResources.Department (DepartmentID, Name,
GroupName,
ModifiedDate) values (200, 'Test','TestGroup',GetDate( ))
```

6.   On the Query menu, hover over **Connection**, and then click **Change Connection**.

7.   Select **SQL Server Authentication** from the **Authentication** list box.

8.   In the **User Name** box, enter **GibsonH**; in the **Password** box, enter **Pa$$w0rd**, and click **Connect**.

9.   Enter and execute the following query, which tries to read data from the HumanResources.Department table (it fails because GibsonH is a member of the db_ denydatareader role):

```
SELECT DepartmentID, Name, GroupName, ModifiedDate
FROM HumanResources.Department
```

10.   Close the query window.

Exercise 14.6	Creating a Custom Database Role
Scenario	You have just created several new logins on your SQL Server and created user mappings for them in the AdventureWorks database. You have added some of these users to fixed database roles, but other users require combinations of permissions that none of the fixed database roles offers. To assign the appropriate permissions to these users, you decide to create a custom database role.
Duration	This task should take approximately 15 minutes.
Setup	For this task, you need access to the machine you installed SQL Server on in Exercise 2.1, the AdventureWorks database, and the RosmanD login you created in Exercise 14.1.
Caveats	In the real world, you would not create a custom database role for just one user, and you would grant more than a single permission.
Procedure	In this task, you will create a custom database role that grants the members permission to select data from the HumanResources.Department table in the AdventureWorks database. You will then add the RosmanD user mapping to the new custom database role.
Equipment	See Setup.
Objective	To create a new custom database role and add users to it.
Criteria for Completion	This task is complete when you have successfully created a new custom database role, assigned permissions, and added the RosmanD user mapping to the new role.

■ PART A: Creating a Custom Database Role

1. Open **SQL Server Management Studio**, expand your server, and then expand **Databases** and then **AdventureWorks**.

2. Expand **Security** and then **Roles**.

3. Right-click **Database Roles**, and select **New Database Role**.

4. In the **Role name** box, enter **SelectOnly**, and enter **dbo** in the **Owner** box.

5. Add <YourServerName>\MorrisL to the **Role Members** list.

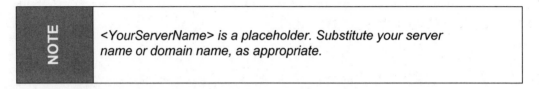

NOTE

<YourServerName> is a placeholder. Substitute your server name or domain name, as appropriate.

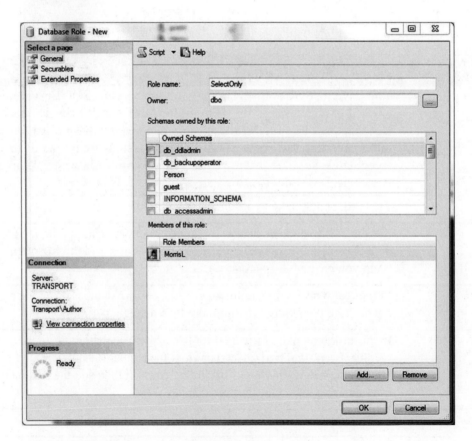

6. On the **Securables** page, click **Search** above the **Securables** list box, select the **Specific Objects** radio button, and click **OK**.

7. Click the **Objects Type** button, select **Tables**, and click **OK**.

8. Click **Browse**, select the **HumanResources.Department** check box, click **OK**, and then click **OK** again.

9. In the **Explicit Permissions** for **HumanResources.Department** list, check the **Grant** check box next to **Select**.

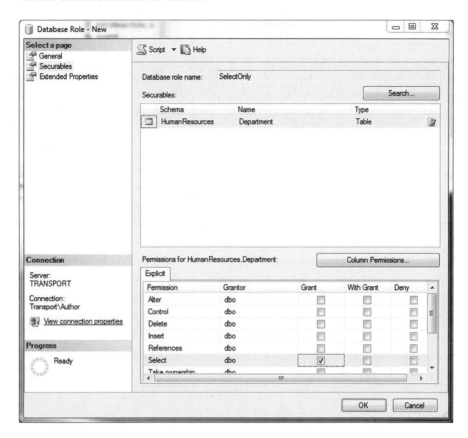

10. Click **OK** to create the role and return to **SQL Server Management Studio**.

■ PART B: Verifying Results

1. Close all programs, log out of Windows, and log back in as **MorrisL**.

2. Open a new SQL Server query in **SQL Server Management Studio**, and connect using **Windows Authentication**.

3. Notice that the following query succeeds because MorrisL is a member of the new SelectOnly role:

```
USE AdventureWorks
SELECT * FROM HumanResources.Department
```

4. Now notice the failure of the next query because MorrisL is a member of a role that is allowed to select only:

```
INSERT INTO HumanResources.Department (DepartmentID, [Name],
GroupName, ModifiedDate) values (200, 'Test','TestGroup',
GetDate( ))
```

5. Close all programs, log out of Windows, and log back in as yourself.

Exercise 14.7	Creating an Application Role
Scenario	Your company has written a custom application for manipulating data in one of your databases. This application has taken hundreds of staff hours and has cost hundreds of thousands of dollars, so management has insisted employees use this custom application to access the database and nothing else. You have decided the best way to accomplish this goal is to create an application role, which your developers can hard code into their application.
Duration	This task should take approximately 15 minutes.
Setup	For this task, you need access to the machine you installed SQL Server on in Exercise 2.1 and the AdventureWorks database.
Procedure	In this task, you will create an application role that grants the members permission to select data from the HumanResources.Department table in the AdventureWorks database.
Equipment	See Setup.
Objective	To create an application role and assign permissions to it.
Criteria for Completion	This task is complete when you have successfully created a new application role and assigned permissions.

■ **PART A: Creating an Application Role**

1. Open **SQL Server Management Studio**, and expand **Databases**, **AdventureWorks**, **Security**, **Roles**, and then **Application Roles**.

2. Right-click **Application Roles**, and select **New Application Role**.

3. In the **Role name** box, enter **EntAppRole**.

4. Enter **dbo** in the **Default schema** box.

5.   In the **Password** and **Confirm password** boxes, enter **Pa$$w0rd**.

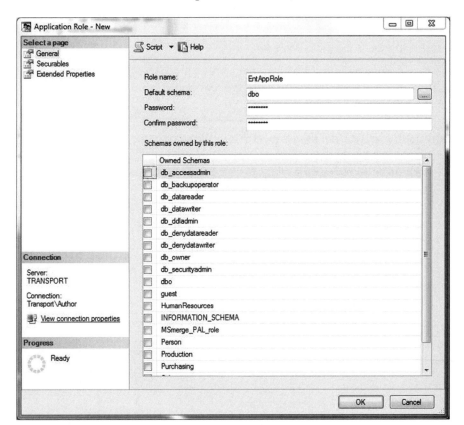

6.   On the **Securables** page, click **Search** above the **Securables** list box, select the **Specific Objects** radio button, and click **OK**.

7.   Click the **Objects Type** button, select **Tables**, and click **OK**.

8.   Click **Browse**, select the **HumanResources.Department** check box, click **OK**, and then click **OK** again.

9.   In the **Permissions** for **HumanResources.Department** list, select the **Grant** check box next to **Select**, and click **OK** to create the role.

■ PART B: Verifying Results

1.   Open a new SQL Server query in **SQL Server Management Studio**.

2.   On the Query menu, hover over **Connection**, and click **Change Connection**.

3.   Connect using **SQL Authentication** with **GibsonH** as the username and **Pa$$w0rd** as the password.

4. Enter and execute the following query:

    ```
    USE AdventureWorks
    SELECT * FROM HumanResources.Department
    ```
    Notice that it fails because GibsonH has been denied Select permissions because of membership in the db_denydatareader database role (assigned in Exercise 14.5).

5. To activate the application role, execute the following query:

    ```
    sp_setapprole @rolename='EntAppRole', @password='Pa$$w0rd'
    ```

6. Clear the query window, and execute the following query. Notice that the query is successful this time. This is because SQL Server now sees you as EntAppRole, which has Select permission.

    ```
    SELECT * FROM HumanResources.Department
    ```

7. Close the query window.

LAB 15
SETTING ENCRYPTED CONNECTIONS

This lab contains the following exercises and activities:

Exercise 15.1   Configuring Encrypted Connections

Exercise 15.2   Using TDE to Encrypt a Database

Exercise 15.3   Implementing Column Encryption

Exercise 15.1	Configuring Encrypted Connections
Scenario	You have just installed a new SQL Server for your company and created a database that holds e-commerce data. For your customers' convenience, your company has decided to store credit card information so users do not have to enter it every time they place an order on your site. You know you need to use the highest level of security possible, so you have decided to configure SQL Server to require encrypted connections.
Duration	This task should take approximately 30 minutes.
Setup	For this task, you need access to the machine you installed SQL Server on in Exercise 2.1.
Caveats	In production, you should not use a self-signed certificate. You are using one in this task for simplicity's sake.
Procedure	In this task, you will configure SQL Server to use encrypted connections using a self-signed certificate.
Equipment	See Setup.
Objective	To configure the server to force clients to use encrypted connections.
Criteria for Completion	This task is complete when you can connect to SQL Server using an encrypted connection.

■ PART A: Configuring Encrypted Connections

1. In SQL Server Configuration Manager, expand **SQL Server Network Configuration**, right-click **Protocols** for **<server instance>**, and then select **Properties**.

2. In the **Protocols for <instance name> Properties** dialog box, on the **Flags** tab, change **Force Encryption** to **Yes**.

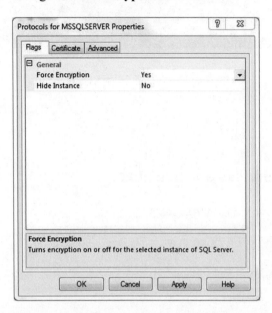

3. Click **OK** twice to close the warning dialog box that opens.

4. Restart the SQL Server service.

5. Again, right-click **Protocols** for **<server instance>**, and then select **Properties**.

6. In the **Protocols for <instance name> Properties** dialog box, on the Certificate tab, select the desired certificate (in this case the self-signed certificate) from the Certificate drop-down list, and then click **OK**.

7. Click **OK** to close the warning dialog box that opens.

8. Restart the SQL Server service. Next, you need to configure the clients to request encrypted connections to the server.

■ PART B: Configuring Clients to Request Encrypted Connections

1. In **SQL Server Configuration Manager**, right-click **SQL Native Client Configuration**, and select **Properties**.

2. On the **Flags** tab, in the **Force Protocol Encryption** box, select **Yes**, and then click **OK** to close the dialog box.

3. Restart the SQL Server service.

■ PART C: Verifying Results

1. Open a new SQL Server query in **SQL Server Management Studio**.

2. On the Query menu, hover over **Connection**, and then click **Change Connection**.

3. Select **Windows Authentication** from the **Authentication** list box.

4. Click the **Options** button, and check the **Encrypt Connection** box.

5. Click **Connect** to make the connection.

Question 1	What does it mean to secure a "connection"? Is this the same as configuring IPSEC on the server?

Exercise 15.2	Using TDE to Encrypt a Database
Scenario	You have a database on your SQL Server, and you need to make sure that the contents are secure, so you decide to set it up to use Transparent Data Encryption.
Duration	This task should take approximately 30 minutes.
Setup	For this task, you need access to the machine you installed SQL Server on in Exercise 2.1 and the Sales database created earlier.
Procedure	In this task, you will configure the Sales database to use Transparent Data Encryption.
Equipment	See Setup.
Objective	To set up Transparent Data Encryption.
Criteria for Completion	This task is complete when the Sales database is configured to use Transparent Data Encryption as outlined in the details of this task.

■ **PART A: Setting Up the Requirements for Transparent Data Encryption**

1. Open **SQL Server Management Studio** and connect using Windows authentication.

2. Open a **New Query**.

3. Enter and execute the following commands to create a master key and a certificate. Note that these steps use the master database even though the database to be encrypted is a different database:

```
USE master
GO
CREATE MASTER KEY ENCRYPTION BY PASSWORD = 'Wiley';
GO
CREATE CERTIFICATE labcert15
WITH SUBJECT = 'Exercise 15.2 TDE Certificate',
START_DATE = '01/01/2010',
EXPIRY_DATE = '2021-12-31';
GO
```

4. Now once the previous commands are successful, enter and execute the next commands, which will perform a backup of these crucial data elements:

```
BACKUP SERVICE MASTER KEY TO FILE = 'C:\practice\servmstrkey'
ENCRYPTION BY PASSWORD = 'ultrasecret';
GO
```

```
BACKUP CERTIFICATE labcert15 TO FILE = 'C:\practice\
myservercert.cer'
WITH PRIVATE KEY (FILE = 'C:\practice\myprivkey',
ENCRYPTION BY PASSWORD = 'SeCrEtCeRt');
GO
```

5. Now once the previous backup commands are successful, enter and execute the next commands. Note that here you are using the actual database to be encrypted:

```
USE sales
GO
-- Create the TDE key for the database
CREATE DATABASE ENCRYPTION KEY
WITH ALGORITHM = AES_128
ENCRYPTION BY SERVER CERTIFICATE labcert15;
GO
-- Implement TDE
ALTER DATABASE sales
SET ENCRYPTION ON
GO
```

6. You are finished. Close the Query window.

■ PART B: Verifying Results

1. In Object Explorer, expand **Databases**.

2. Right click on **Sales** and select **Properties**.

3. On the Database Properties window, select **Options** in the left-hand column.

4. Scroll down and look underneath the **State** heading. Locate the **Encryption Enabled** row and verify that it is set to True.

5. Close the Properties window.

> **NOTE**
>
> *Transparent Data Encryption is . . . transparent! You do not see the encryption because you are not someone trying to access the data on a backup tape or other media. Normal access is transparent to you and other authorized users.*

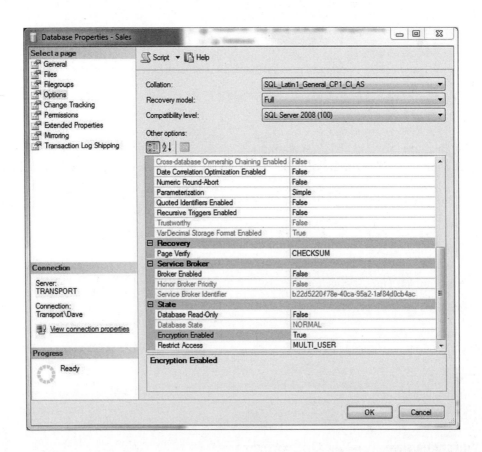

Exercise 15.3	Implementing Column Encryption
Scenario	You have a database containing data that you want to ensure is kept highly secure. You want to encrypt a specific column of data so that access to the data does not actually allow someone to read the data.
Duration	This task should take approximately 45 minutes.
Setup	For this task, you need access to the machine you installed SQL Server on in Exercise 2.1 and the Sales database created in a prior exercise.
Procedure	In this task, you will set up the keys required for encryption, back up these keys, and implement column encryption.
Equipment	See Setup.
Objective	To create a column of data that is encrypted.
Criteria for Completion	This task is complete when the CreditCard column is encrypted.

■ **PART A: Create the Key Structure**

1. Open SQL Server Management Studio, and in Object Explorer, expand Databases under your server.

2. Right-click **Sales,** and click **Properties.**

3. Enter and execute this code to add the new columns CreditCard, ExpireCode, and EncryptedCreditCard to the existing Customers table:

```
USE sales
GO
ALTER TABLE customers
ADD CreditCard char(16);
ALTER TABLE customers
ADD ExpireCode char(4);
-- Create a column in which to store the encrypted data.
ALTER TABLE Customers
      ADD EncryptedCreditCard varbinary(128);
GO
```

4. You are now in the Sales database so enter and execute this code to create the database master key and back up the database master key to a file:

```
CREATE MASTER KEY ENCRYPTION BY PASSWORD = 'verybigsecret'
OPEN MASTER KEY
DECRYPTION BY PASSWORD = 'verybigsecret'
BACKUP MASTER KEY TO FILE = 'C:\practice\mastkeybu123'
ENCRYPTION BY PASSWORD ='BACKUPkeyPass'
GO
```

5. In order to encrypt some data you must first have some data. So enter credit card data into the new CreditCard and ExpireCode columns using code something like the following:

```
-- Create some credit card data
UPDATE customers SET CreditCard = '5121123412346789', ExpireCode
= '0611'
WHERE CustID = 2;
UPDATE customers SET CreditCard = '4121454512346789', ExpireCode
= '0813'
WHERE CustID = 4;
UPDATE customers SET CreditCard = '6011223312340321', ExpireCode
= '0215'
WHERE CustID = 7;
GO
```

6. Create a certificate and from that, a symmetric key using this code:

```
-- Create a certificate
CREATE CERTIFICATE salescert
WITH SUBJECT = 'Customer Credit Card Encryption';
GO
-- Create a symmetric key using the certificate
CREATE SYMMETRIC KEY mysymkey
WITH ALGORITHM = AES_256
ENCRYPTION BY CERTIFICATE salescert
```

7. Now using the symmetric key that you just created, perform the encryption:

```
-- Open the symmetric key with which to encrypt the data.
OPEN SYMMETRIC KEY mysymkey
DECRYPTION BY CERTIFICATE salescert;
-- Encrypt the value in column CreditCard with symmetric
-- key mysymkey. Save the result in column EncryptedCreditCard.
UPDATE Customers
SET EncryptedCreditCard = EncryptByKey(Key_GUID('mysymkey'),
CreditCard);
GO
```

In this exercise the encrypted result is stored in the column EncryptedCreditCard while the original card number is still stored in the CreditCard column. In a production environment, you would delete this column and encrypt the credit card number as it was entered by a user.

■ PART B: Verifying Results

1. Continue as you did in the earlier steps and enter and execute the following code:

```
-- Verify the encryption.
-- First, open the symmetric key with which to decrypt the data.
OPEN SYMMETRIC KEY MySymKey
DECRYPTION BY CERTIFICATE SalesCert;
-- Now list the original credit card #, the encrypted card #, and
-- the decrypted ciphertext. If the decryption worked,
-- the original and the decrypted numbers will match.
SELECT CreditCard, EncryptedCreditCard
AS 'Encrypted Credit Card',
CONVERT(char(16), DecryptByKey(EncryptedCreditCard))
AS 'Decrypted Credit Card'
FROM Customers
WHERE CreditCard is NOT NULL;
GO
```

2. In order to ensure that future exercises in the following lessons work properly, you should now DROP the new columns of data from the Customers table. Enter and execute the following code to drop these columns:

```
-- Drop the columns used in this exercise
USE sales
GO
ALTER TABLE customers DROP COLUMN CreditCard;
ALTER TABLE customers DROP COLUMN ExpireCode;
ALTER TABLE customers DROP COLUMN EncryptedCreditCard;
```

LAB 16
BACKING UP AND RESTORING DATA

This lab contains the following exercises and activities:

Exercise 16.1	Creating a Backup Device
Scenario	You need to start backing up the databases you have created on your new SQL Server. Before you can start backing them up, though, you realize you need a place to store the backups, so you decide to create a backup device for storing backups.
Duration	This task should take approximately 15 minutes.
Setup	For this task, you need access to the machine you installed SQL Server on in Exercise 2.1.
Procedure	In this task, you will create a backup device.

Equipment	See Setup.
Objective	To create a backup device.
Criteria for Completion	This task is complete when you have created a new backup device.

■ PART A: Creating a Backup Device

1.   Open **SQL Server Management**. Expand your server, and then expand **Server Objects**.

2.   Right-click **Backup Devices** in Object Explorer, and select **New Backup Device**.

3.   In the Device name box of the Backup Device dialog box, enter **AdvWorks**. Notice that the filename and path are filled in for you; change it to C:\Practice and make sure you have enough free space on the drive SQL Server has selected.

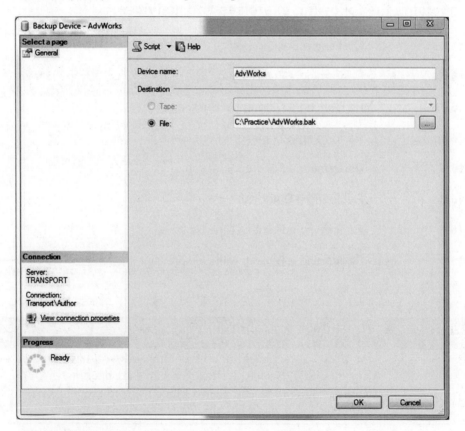

4.   Click **OK** to create the device.

Question 1	*What is the advantage of creating a backup device as opposed to specifying the full path name in a script?*

■ PART B: Verifying Results

In Object Explorer, under **Server Objects**, **Backup Devices**, verify that your new device is listed.

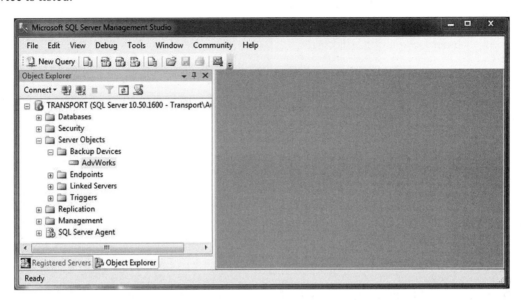

Exercise 16.2	Performing a Full Backup
Scenario	You need to start backing up the databases you have created on your new SQL Server. You know you need a full backup before you can start using differential or transaction log backups, so you decide to create a baseline by performing a full backup.
Duration	This task should take approximately 15 minutes.
Setup	For this task, you need access to the machine you installed SQL Server on in Exercise 2.1, the AdventureWorks database installed with the sample data, and the AdvWorks backup device you created in Exercise 16.1.
Procedure	In this task, you will perform a full backup on the AdventureWorks database.
Equipment	See Setup.
Objective	To perform a full backup of the AdventureWorks database.
Criteria for Completion	This task is complete when you have a full backup of the AdventureWorks database stored in the AdvWorks backup device.

■ PART A: Performing a Full Backup

1. Open **SQL Server Management Studio**, expand **Databases**, right-click **AdventureWorks**, point to Tasks, and click **Back Up**.

2. In the Backup dialog box, make sure **AdventureWorks** is the selected database to back up and make sure Backup Type is **Full**.

3. Leave the default name in the Name box. In the **Description** box, enter **Full Backup of AdventureWorks**.

4. Under **Destination**, a disk device may already be listed. If so, select the device, and click **Remove**.

5. Under Destination, click **Add**.

6. In the **Select Backup Destination** box, click the **Backup Device** radio button, select **AdvWorks**, and click **OK**.

7. You should now have a backup device listed under Destination.

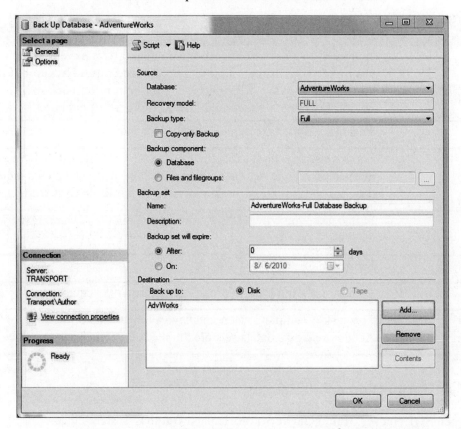

8. Switch to the **Options** page. On the **Options** page, select **Overwrite All Existing Backup Sets**. This option initializes a new device or overwrites an existing one.

9. Place a check mark next to **Verify Backup When Finished** to check the actual database against the backup copy, and be sure they match after the backup is complete.

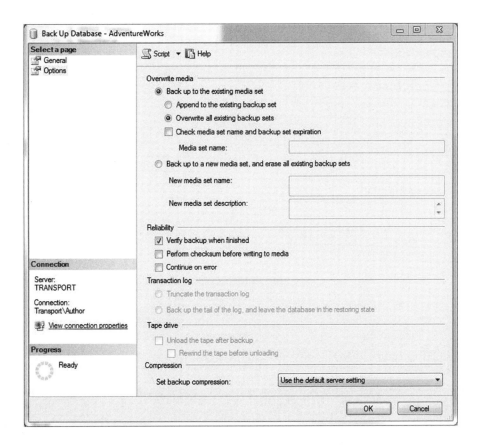

10. Click **OK** to start the backup.

11. When the backup is complete, you will get a notification; click **OK** to close it.

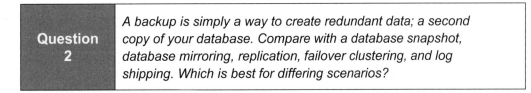

Question 2	*A backup is simply a way to create redundant data; a second copy of your database. Compare with a database snapshot, database mirroring, replication, failover clustering, and log shipping. Which is best for differing scenarios?*

■ PART B: Verifying Results

1. To verify the backup, you can look at the contents of the backup device by expanding Backup Devices under Server Objects in Object Explorer.

2. Right-click **AdvWorks**, and select **Properties**.

3. On the Media Contents page under Backup sets, you should see the full backup of AdventureWorks.

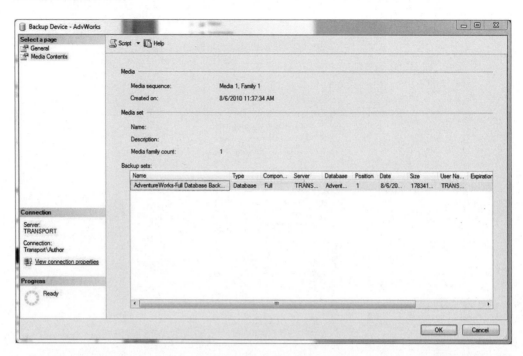

4. Click **OK** to return to **SQL Server Management Studio**.

Exercise 16.3	Performing a Differential Backup
Scenario	You have started performing full backups of your databases on a regular basis, and you have noticed that, as the database grows, the backup gets slower. You know you need to speed up the backup process, so you decide to incorporate differential backups into your backup scheme.
Duration	This task should take approximately 15 minutes.
Setup	For this task, you need access to the machine you installed SQL Server on in Exercise 2.1, the AdventureWorks database installed with the sample data, and the AdvWorks backup device you created in Exercise 16.1.
Procedure	In this task, you will perform a differential backup on the AdventureWorks database.
Equipment	See Setup.
Objective	To perform a differential backup of the AdventureWorks database.
Criteria for Completion	This task is complete when you have a differential backup of the AdventureWorks database stored in the AdvWorks backup device.

■ PART A: Performing a Differential Backup

1. Open **SQL Server Management Studio**. Expand your server, and then expand Databases.

2. Right-click **AdventureWorks**, point to **Tasks**, and select **Back Up**.

3. In the Back Up dialog box, make sure **AdventureWorks** is the selected database to back up and that **Backup Type** is **Differential**.

4. Leave the default name in the Name box. In the Description box, enter **Differential Backup of AdventureWorks**.

5. Under **Destination**, make sure the **AdvWorks** device is listed.

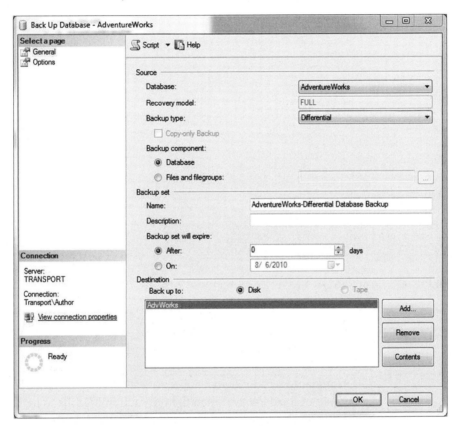

6. On the **Options** page, make sure **Append to the Existing Backup Set** is selected so you don't overwrite your existing full backup. Also, select **Verify Backup When Finished**.

7. Click **OK** to start the backup.

Question 3	*Database management is all about trade-offs. If you back up slowly you can restore quickly. A differential backup goes quickly but at the expense having having a full backup and potentially multiple differential backups to process. Which is best?*

■ **PART B: Verifying Results**

1. To verify the backup, you can look at the contents of the backup device, so expand **Backup Devices** under Server Objects in Object Explorer.

2. Right-click **AdvWorks**, and select **Properties**.

3. On the **Media Contents** page under Backup sets, you should see the differential backup of AdventureWorks.

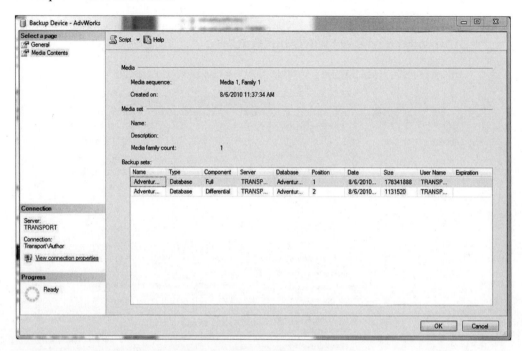

4. Click **OK** to return to **SQL Server Management Studio**.

Exercise 16.4	Performing a Transaction Log Backup
Scenario	You have started performing full and differential backups of your databases on a regular basis. You know that if you do not start performing transaction log backups, your users will eventually get locked out of the database when the transaction log fills to capacity. You also want the extra safety measure of having transaction log backups in place, so you decide to start performing transaction log backups.
Duration	This task should take approximately 15 minutes.
Setup	For this task, you need access to the machine you installed SQL Server on in Exercise 2.1, the AdventureWorks database installed with the sample data, and the AdvWorks backup device you created in Exercise 16.1. Also, the AdventureWorks database must be set to use the Full recovery model as outlined in Exercise 5.2.
Procedure	In this task, you will perform a transaction log backup on the AdventureWorks database.

Equipment	See Setup.
Objective	To perform a transaction log backup of the AdventureWorks database.
Criteria for Completion	This task is complete when you have a transaction log backup of the AdventureWorks database stored in the AdvWorks backup device.

■ PART A: Performing a Transaction Log Backup

1. Open **SQL Server Management Studio**. Expand your server, and then expand **Databases**.

2. Right-click **AdventureWorks**, point to **Tasks**, and select **Back Up**.

3. In the **Back Up Database** dialog box, make sure **AdventureWorks** is the selected database to back up and **Backup Type** is **Transaction Log**.

4. Leave the default name in the Name box. In the Description box, enter **Transaction Log Backup of AdventureWorks**.

5. Under **Destination**, make sure the **AdvWorks** device is listed.

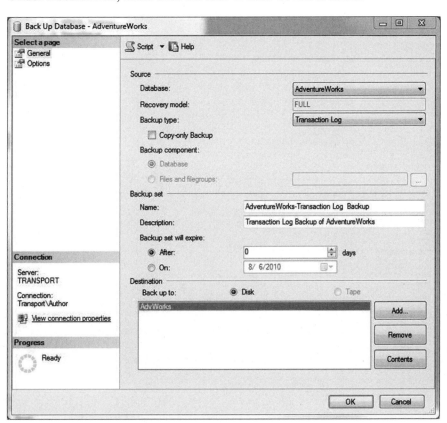

6. On the **Options** page, make sure **Append to the Existing Backup Set** is selected so you don't overwrite your existing full backup.

7. On the **Options** page, select **Verify Backup When Finished**.

8. Click **OK** to start the backup.

9. When the backup is complete, you will get a notification; click **OK** to close it.

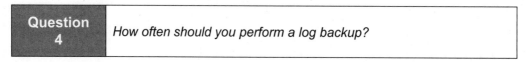

Question 4	*How often should you perform a log backup?*

■ PART B: Verifying Results

1. To verify the backup, you can look at the contents of the backup device, so expand **Backup Devices** under Server Objects in Object Explorer.

2. Right-click **AdvWorks**, and select **Properties**.

3. On the **Media Contents** page under Backup sets, you should see the transaction log backup of **AdventureWorks**.

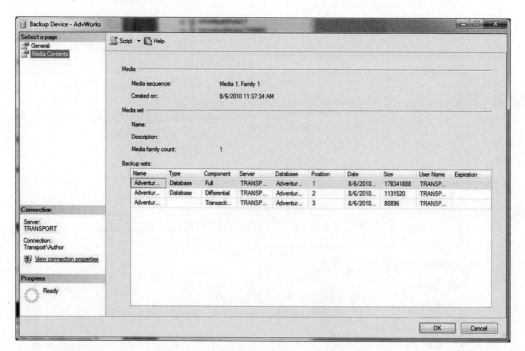

4. Click **OK** to return to **SQL Server Management Studio**.

Exercise 16.5	Performing a Filegroup Backup
Scenario	The database you created for your sales department has grown very large—so large that it does not fit on a single disk anymore. To accommodate this growth and enhance performance, you have decided to spread the Sales database across multiple disks using a filegroup. You know that performing a filegroup backup is the fastest backup method for large databases, so you have decided to start performing filegroup backups on Sales after you create the filegroup.
Duration	This task should take approximately 30 minutes.
Setup	For this task, you need access to the machine you installed SQL Server on in Exercise 2.1, the Sales database you created in Exercise 5.1, and the AdvWorks backup device you created in Exercise 16.1.
Caveat	In a production environment, you would not ordinarily add a new data file to a filegroup on the same disk as the Primary filegroup. The new filegroup would be on a separate disk.
Procedure	In this task, you will create a filegroup for the Sales database, add a table to the new filegroup, and perform a filegroup backup on Sales.
Equipment	See Setup.
Objective	To add a filegroup to the Sales database.
Criteria for Completion	This task is complete when you have added a new filegroup to the Sales database, added a table named Employees to the new filegroup, and performed a filegroup backup stored in the AdvWorks backup device.

■ PART A: Creating a Second Filegroup

1. Open **SQL Server Management Studio**. Expand your server, and then expand **Databases**.

2. Right-click the **Sales** database, and select **Properties**.

3. On the **Filegroups** page, click the **Add** button. In the **Name** text box, enter **Secondary**.

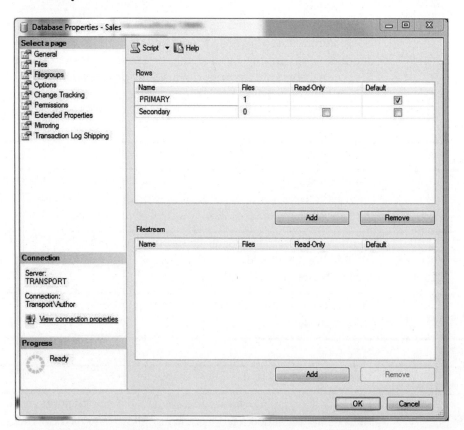

4. On the **Files** page, click the **Add** button, and enter this information:

- Name: Sales_Data3

- File Type: Data

- Filegroup: Secondary

- Initial Size: 3

5.   Click **OK** to create the new file on the Secondary filegroup.

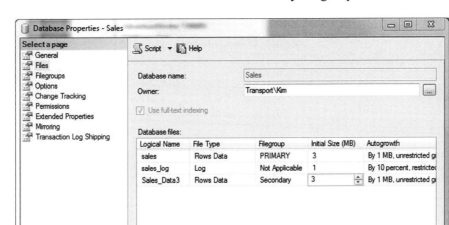

6.   Now, to add a table to the new filegroup, expand **Sales** in Object Explorer, right-click **Tables**, and select **New Table**.

7.   Under Column Name in the first row, enter **Emp_Name**.

8.   Next to **Emp_Name**, select **varchar** as the data type. Leave the default length of 50.

9.   Just below Emp_Name in the second row, enter **Emp_Number** as the column name with a type of **varchar.** Leave the default length of 50.

10.   Select **View Properties Window**.

11. Expand the **Regular Data Space Specification** section, and change the **Filegroup or Partition Scheme Name** setting to **Secondary**.

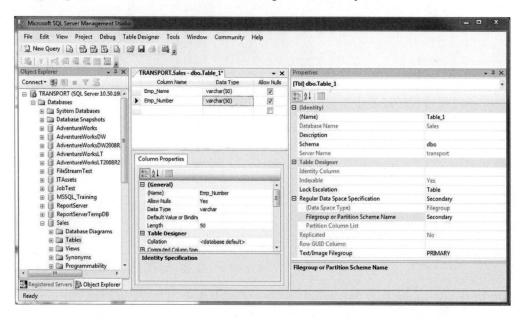

12. Click the **Save** button (it looks like a floppy disk on the toolbar) to create the new table. Name it **Employees**.

13. Close the table designer by clicking the **X** in the upper-right corner of the window.

14. Now, to add some data to the new table, open a new query, and execute the following code (note that the second value is arbitrary):

```
USE Sales
GO
INSERT Employees VALUES('Tim Hsu', 'VA1765FR')
INSERT Employees VALUES('Sue Hernandez', 'FQ9187GL')
```

15. Close the query window.

Question 5	List four advantages to having multiple filegroups.

■ PART B: Performing a Filegroup Backup

1. Right-click the **Sales** database in Object Explorer, point to **Tasks**, and select **Back Up**.

2. In the **Backup** dialog box, make sure **Sales** is the selected database to back up and **Backup Type** is **Full**.

3. Under Backup component, select **Files and Filegroups**.

4. In the **Select Files and Filegroups** dialog box, check the box next to **Secondary**, and click **OK** (notice that the box next to Sales_Data3 is automatically checked).

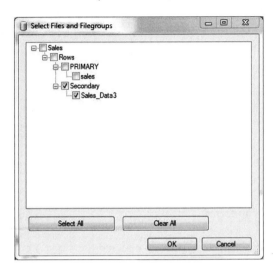

5. Leave the default name in the **Name** box. In the **Description** box, enter **Filegroup Backup of Sales**.

6. Under **Destination**, make sure the **AdvWorks** device is the only one listed.

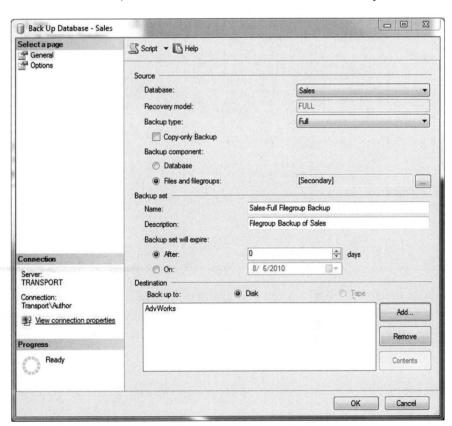

7. On the **Options** page, make sure **Append to the Existing Backup Set** is selected so you don't overwrite your existing backups.

8. On the **Options** page, select **Verify Backup When Finished**.

9. Click **OK** to start the backup.

10. When the backup is complete, you will get a notification; click **OK** to close it.

■ PART C: Verifying Results

1. To verify the backup, you can look at the contents of the backup device, so expand **Backup Devices** under Server Objects in Object Explorer.

2. Right-click **AdvWorks**, and select **Properties**.

3. On the **Media Contents** page under Backup sets, you should see the filegroup backup of **Sales**.

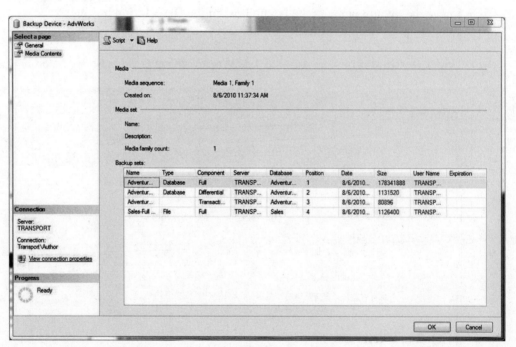

4. Click **OK** to return to **SQL Server Management Studio**.

Exercise 16.6	Restoring a Database
Scenario	You have been performing full, differential, and transaction log backups on your databases for some time. Everything was working just fine until this morning; when you came in this morning, the users are complaining that they can't access the database. You try to open the Management Studio but can't; it just won't expand. You know instantly that the database is down and needs to be restored, so you have decided to start the restore process.
Duration	This task should take approximately 30 minutes.
Setup	For this task, you need access to the machine you installed SQL Server on in Exercise 2.1, the AdventureWorks database installed with the sample data, the AdvWorks backup device you created in Exercise 16.1, the full backup you created in Exercise 16.2, the differential backup you created in Exercise 16.3, and the transaction log backup you created in Exercise 16.4.
Procedure	In this task, you will simulate a downed database by renaming critical files for the AdventureWorks database, and then you will restore the database. You will need to stop all the SQL Server services because while they're running, all the databases are considered open files—you will not be able to work with them outside SQL Server.
Equipment	See Setup.
Objective	To simulate a downed database.
Criteria for Completion	This task is complete when you have taken the AdventureWorks database down and restored it from backup, bringing it back to a usable state.

■ **PART A: Retaining Your Original Data**

1. Open **SQL Server Configuration Manager** from the Start menu.

2. In the left pane, select **SQL Server Services**.

3. Right-click **SQL Server (MSSQLSERVER)** in the right pane, and click **Stop**. You'll be asked whether you want to stop the SQL Server Agent service as well; click **Yes**.

4. Find the file **AdventureWorks_Data.mdf**. The default path is C:\Program Files\Microsft SQL Server\<InstanceName>\MSSQL\DATA.

5. Rename the file **AdventureWorks_Data.old**.

6. Find the file **AdventureWorks_Log.ldf**, and rename it **AdventureWorks_Log.old**.

7. From **SQL Server Configuration Manager**, restart the **SQL Server Agent** and **SQL Server services**.

8. Open **SQL Server Management Studio**, and expand **Databases** under your server name. AdventureWorks cannot be expanded and has no summary; it is now inaccessible.

■ PART B: Restoring the Database

1. Right-click **Databases**, and select **Restore Database**.

2. In the **Restore Database** dialog box, select **AdventureWorks** from the **To Database** drop-down list box.

3. Under Source for Restore, select **From Device**. Click the **ellipsis (…)** button next to the text box to select a device.

4. In the Specify Backup dialog box, select **Backup Device** from the Backup Media drop-down list box, and click **Add**.

5. In the Specify Backup dialog box, select **AdvWorks**, and click **OK**.

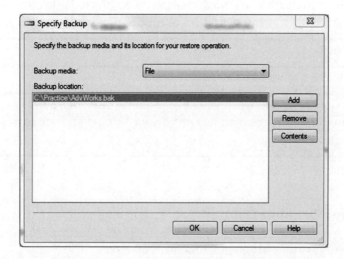

6. Click **OK** to close the Specify Backup dialog box.

7.   Under **Select the Backup Sets to Restore**, check all three backups (full, differential, and transaction log). Doing so returns the database to the most recent state.

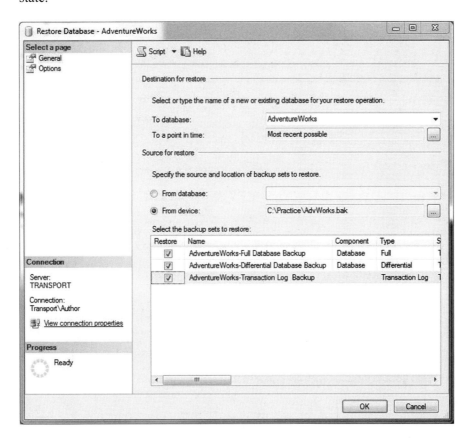

8.   On the **Options** page, make sure the **RESTORE WITH RECOVERY** option is selected, because you have no more backups to restore.

> **NOTE**
>
> *When a disaster occurs what do you do first? Back up the tail log. Restore each backup file in the correct order with NORECOVERY until the last file when you use WITH RECOVERY. Again, remember to use WITH RECOVERY on only the last media set.*

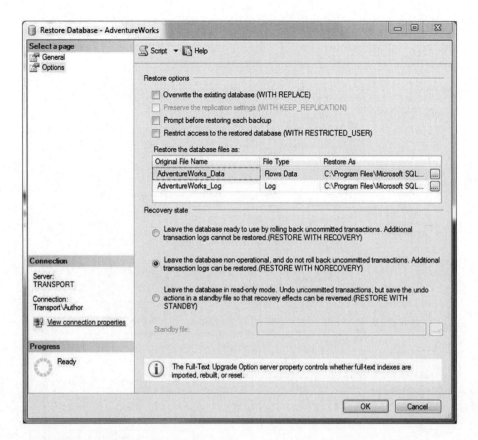

9.   Click **OK** to begin the restore process.

10.   Click **OK** in the dialog box that opens after the restore is complete.

■ PART C: Verifying Results

1.   In **SQL Server Management Studio**, right-click **Databases**, and click **Refresh**.

2.   Expand **Databases**, and you should see **AdventureWorks** is back to normal.

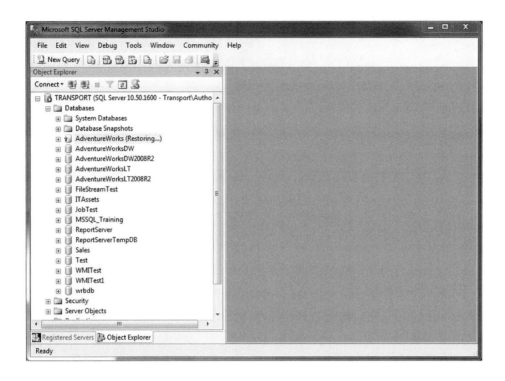

Exercise 16.7	Performing a Point-in-Time Restore
Scenario	It is the end of the month, which is the time when your accounting department performs all its month-end transactions to close the books and bring everything into balance. This has been an especially busy month for your company, so your accounting department has brought in some contract workers to assist with the month-end closeout. One of the contract workers is not familiar with your systems and accidentally enters some incorrect data into the system. Fortunately, your accounting manager caught it early and needs your help to remove the corrupt data from the database. You have decided that the best way to accomplish this task is to perform a point-in-time restore.
Duration	This task should take approximately 30 minutes.
Setup	For this task, you need access to the machine you installed SQL Server on in Exercise 2.1, the AdventureWorks database installed with the sample data, and the AdvWorks backup device you created in Exercise 16.1.
Procedure	In this task, you will update the HumanResources.Shift table of the AdventureWorks database, wait for two minutes, and update it again. You will then perform a transaction log backup of the database and a subsequent point-in-time restore.
Equipment	See Setup.
Objective	To restore your database to a previous known condition.
Criteria for Completion	This task is complete when you have created two new records in the HumanResources.Shift table of the AdventureWorks database and performed a point-in-time restore to eliminate the most recent update.

■ PART A: Adding Some Records

1. You need to add a record that will survive the restore. Open a new SQL Server query in **SQL Server Management Studio** by clicking the **New Query** button on the toolbar.

2. To create a new record, enter and execute the following code:

```
USE AdventureWorks
GO
INSERT HumanResources.Shift(Name, StartTime, EndTime, ModifiedDate)
VALUES('Test Shift 1', getdate( ) + 1, getdate( )+ 2,
getdate( ))
```

3. Note the time right now.

4. Wait two minutes, clear the query window, and then enter a new record using the following code:

```
USE AdventureWorks
GO
INSERT HumanResources.Shift(Name, StartTime, EndTime, ModifiedDate)
VALUES('Test Shift 2', getdate( )+1, getdate( )+ 2,
getdate( ))
```

5. To see both records, clear the query window, and enter and execute the following code:

```
USE AdventureWorks
GO
SELECT * FROM HumanResources.Shift
```

6. Close all open queries.

■ PART B: Performing a Transaction Log Backup

1. To perform a point-in-time restore, you must perform a transaction log backup. In Object Explorer, right-click **AdventureWorks**, point to **Tasks**, and select **Back Up**.

2. In the Back Up dialog box, make sure **AdventureWorks** is the selected database to back up and Backup Type is **Transaction Log.**

3. Leave the default name in the Name box. In the Description box, enter **Point-in-time Backup of AdventureWorks**.

4.   Under Destination, make sure the **AdvWorks** device is listed.

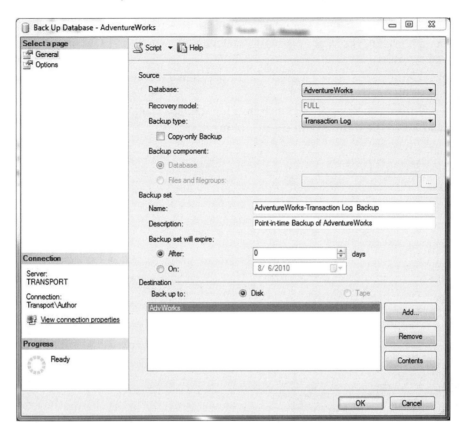

5.   On the **Options** page, make sure **Append to the Existing Backup Set** is selected so you don't overwrite your existing full backup.

6.   On the **Options** page, select **Verify Backup When Finished**.

7.   Click **OK** to start the backup.

8.   Click **OK** to close the dialog box that opens when the backup is complete.

9.   Now you have to back up the tail of the log, which is all the transactions in the log that have not been backed up or recorded to the data file yet. In **Object Explorer**, right-click **AdventureWorks**, point to **Tasks**, and select **Back Up**.

10.   In the **Back Up** dialog box, make sure **AdventureWorks** is the selected database to back up and **Backup Type** is **Transaction Log**.

11.   Leave the default name in the Name box. In the Description box, enter **Tail Backup of AdventureWorks**.

12.   Under **Destination**, make sure the **AdvWorks** device is listed.

13.   On the **Options** page, make sure **Append to the Existing Backup Set** is selected so you don't overwrite your existing full backup.

14.   On the **Options** page, select **Verify Backup When Finished**.

15.   On the **Options** page, under **Transaction log**, choose **Back up the tail of the log, and leave the database in the restoring state**.

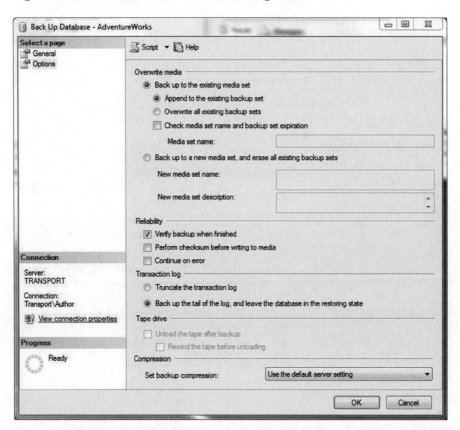

16.   Click **OK** to start the backup.

17.   Click **OK** to close the dialog box that opens when the backup is complete.

■ PART C: Performing a Point-in-Time Restore

1.   Open **SQL Server Management Studio**. Expand your server, and then expand **Databases**.

2.   Right-click **AdventureWorks**, point to **Tasks**, move to **Restore**, and select **Database**.

3.   Click the **ellipsis button** next to the **To a Point in Time** text box.

4.   In the **Point in Time Restore** dialog box, enter the time from Step 3 of Part A,
      Click on the **Options** tab, select **Overwrite the Existing Database**, and click
      OK.

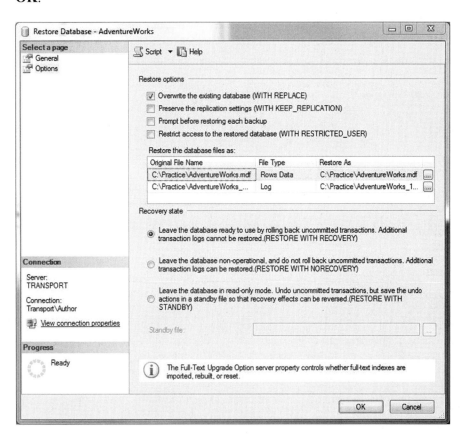

5. Make sure you're restoring from the **AdvWorks** device, select all the available backups in the device, and click **OK** to perform the restore.

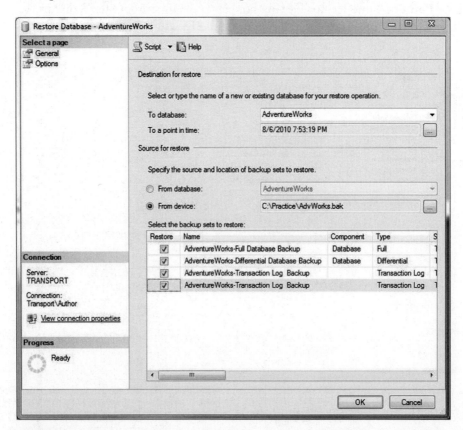

6. Click **OK** to close the dialog box that opens when the restore is complete.

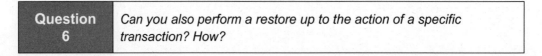

Question 6	Can you also perform a restore up to the action of a specific transaction? How?

■ PART D: Verifying Results

1. Open a new SQL Server Query in **SQL Server Management Studio**, and enter and execute the following code:

```
USE AdventureWorks
GO
SELECT * FROM HumanResources.Shift
```

2. Notice that Test Shift 2 is no longer there, but Test Shift 1 remains.

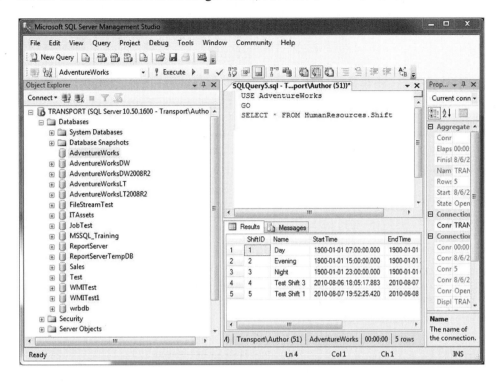

Exercise 16.8	Performing a Backup with Compression
Scenario	You want to reduce the storage space required for backups.
Duration	This task should take approximately 15 minutes.
Setup	For this task, you need access to the machine you installed SQL Server on in Exercise 2.1 and the AdventureWorks database installed with the sample data.
Caveat	This task uses the AdvWorks backup device configured in Exercise 16.1.
Procedure	In this task, you will configure the AdventureWorks database to use Backup Compression.
Equipment	See Setup.
Objective	To set the AdventureWorks database to use Backup Compression.
Criteria for Completion	This task is complete when the AdventureWorks database is configured to use Backup Compression as outlined in the details of this task.

■ **PART A: Setup Backup Compression**

1. Open **SQL Server Management Studio**, and in **Object Explorer**, right-click on the server instance name and select **Properties** from the drop-down menu.

2. The Server Properties window will open. Select the **Database Settings** page from the left-hand menu.

3. On the Database Settings page, look for the check box labeled **Compress backup**. Ensure that this box is *not* checked. In this exercise, we want to have the default backup compression setting turned off. Click **OK**.

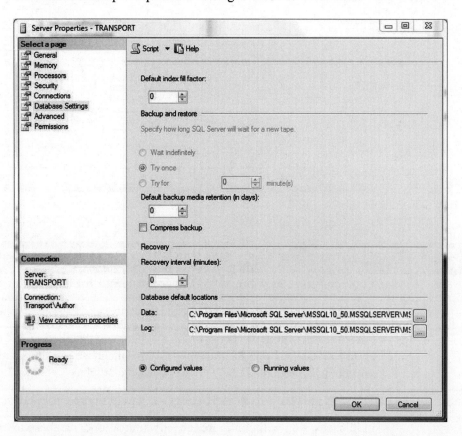

4. Enter and execute this code to perform a Full backup with compression.

```
USE AdventureWorks
GO
BACKUP DATABASE AdventureWorks TO AdvWorks
WITH COMPRESSION,
DESCRIPTION = 'Full B/U with compression',
NAME = 'AdvWorks FULL w/Comp.',
STATS = 5,
MEDIADESCRIPTION = 'LAB 16.8',
FORMAT
```

5. Close the Query window.

Question 7	*If the server instance setting had been checked for Compress backup and the WITH COMPRESSION option in the BACKUP command had not be specified, would compression have occured?*

■ PART B: Verifying Results

1. In Object Explorer, expand **Server Objects** and then expand **Backup Devices**.

2. Right click on the backup device **AdvWorks** and select **Properties**.

3. The Backup Device Properties window will open. Select the **Media Contents** page.

4. Check the entries listed under Backup sets. You may have to drag the divider to the right to see the full contents of the Name column. Look for an entry that matches the NAME value in the previous script. Note the value listed in the size column. This value might not be much different than other Full backups as the AdventureWorks database is not a large database.

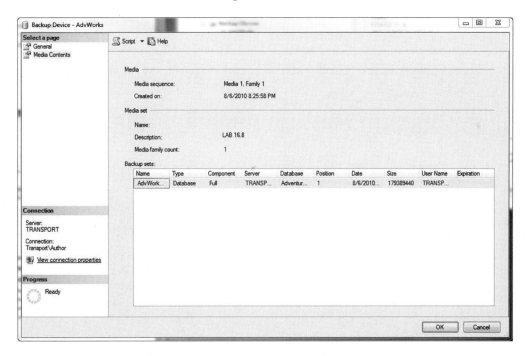

LAB 17
WORKING WITH ENDPOINTS

This lab contains the following exercise and activity:

Exercise 17.1   Understanding Endpoints

Exercise 17.1	Understanding Endpoints
Scenario	Your boss asked you to review endpoints. You checked Books Online and discovered there are four types: SOAP, TSQL, SERVICE_BROKER, and DATABASE_MIRRORING. You want to learn the syntax differences between them.
Duration	This task should take approximately 15 minutes.
Setup	For this task, you need access to the machine you installed SQL Server on in Exercise 2.1 and Books Online.
Procedure	Review the syntax differences between the four endpoint types using examples you find in Books Online and the snippets in this exercise.
Equipment	See Setup.
Objective	To understand endpoints.
Criteria for Completion	This task is complete when you have understood the requirements, purpose, and permissions for endpoints.

> **NOTE** *Currently there are no Transact-SQL <language_specific_ arguments>.*

■ PART A: Creating Endpoints for Service Broker

Review the following code for syntax requirements but do not execute.

```
USE Master
GO
CREATE ENDPOINT BrokerEndpoint
STATE = STARTED
AS TCP ( LISTENER_PORT = 4037 )
FOR SERVICE_BROKER ( AUTHENTICATION = WINDOWS );
GO
```

■ PART B: Creating Endpoints for Database Mirroring

Review the following code for syntax requirements but do not execute.

```
-- Endpoint for intital principal server instance which is the only
-- server instance running on the first host.
CREATE ENDPOINT EndPointMirroring
STATE = STARTED
AS TCP (LISTENER_PORT = 7022)
FOR DATABASE_MIRRORING (ROLE = PARTNER)
GO
-- Endpoint for intital principal server instance which is the only
-- server instance running on the second host.
CREATE ENDPOINT EndPointMirroring
STATE = STARTED
AS TCP (LISTENER_PORT = 7022)
FOR DATABASE_MIRRORING (ROLE = PARTNER)
GO
-- Endpoint for intital principal server instance which is the
only server instance running on the third host.
CREATE ENDPOINT EndPointMirroring
STATE = STARTED
AS TCP (LISTENER_PORT = 7022)
FOR DATABASE_MIRRORING (ROLE = WITNESS)
GO
```

■ PART C: Creating HTTP Endpoints

Review the following code for syntax requirements but do not execute.

```
USE Sales
GO
CREATE ENDPOINT Sql_Endpoint
STATE = STARTED
AS HTTP (
   PATH = '/SQL',
   AUTHENTICATION = (INTEGRATED),
   PORTS = (CLEAR),
   SITE = '<YourServerName>')
FOR SOAP (
   WEBMETHOD 'GetSqlInfo'
   -- Note that GetSqlInfo is an existing stored procedure or
   user
   -- defined function. The WEBMETHOD line can be repeated for as
   -- many procedures or functions you wish to expose.
   (name = 'master.dbo.sp_msver',
   ( SCHEMA = STANDARD ),
   -- You may also specify the schema as a parameter with the
   name,
   -- like this: ( name = 'AdventureWorks.dbo.ProductList',
   -- SCHEMA = STANDARD ),
   WEBMETHOD 'DayAsNumber'
   (name = 'master.sys.fn_MSDayAsNumber'),
   WSDL = DEFAULT,
   SCHEMA = STANDARD,
   DATABASE = 'master'
   NAMESPACE = 'http://Training.Com/');
GO
```

■ PART D: Creating Endpoints for Network Protocols

Look up "Network Protocols" and "TDS Endpoints" in Books Online. Examine the definition of an endpoint for a tabular data stream. Note especially that additional endpoints can be created.

■ PART E: Managing Permissions on Endpoints

Review the following code for syntax requirements but do not execute.

```
USE Master
GO
GRANT CONNECT ON ENDPOINT::Sql_Endpoint to RSmith;
-- Other permissions include: ALTER, CONTROL, TAKE OWNERSHIP, and
-- VIEW DEFINITION
GO
```

LAB 19
WORKING WITH TRIGGERS

This lab contains the following exercises and activities:

Exercise 19.1	Designing and Creating an Insert Trigger
Scenario	You have created a database for your sales department that contains information about orders customers have placed. The sales manager needs to know what is in stock at all times, so she would like to have the quantity of an item that is in stock decremented automatically when a user places an order. You have decided that the best way to accomplish this is by using a trigger on the Orders table.
Duration	This task should take approximately 30 minutes.
Setup	For this task, you need access to the machine you installed SQL Server on in Exercise 2.1, the Sales database you created in Exercise 5.1, and the Products table you created in Exercise 6.1.
Caveats	When executing a trigger, SQL Server uses two special tables: inserted and deleted. The inserted table holds new records that are about to be added to the table, and the deleted table holds records that are about to be removed. You will be using the inserted table in this task.
Procedure	In this task, you will create a trigger that automatically decrements the InStock quantity in the Products table when a user places an order.

Equipment	See Setup.
Objective	To add some data to the Customers and Products tables.
Criteria for Completion	This task is complete when you have a trigger that automatically updates the InStock column of the Products table whenever a record is inserted in the Orders table.

■ PART A: Designing and Creating an Insert Trigger

1. Open **SQL Server Management Studio** by selecting it from the Microsoft SQL Server group in Programs on the Start menu, and log in using either Windows Authentication or SQL Server Authentication.

2. Open a new SQL Server query window, and enter and execute the following code to populate the Customers table with customer information:

```
USE Sales
INSERT customers VALUES ('Andrea', 'Elliott', '111 Main', 'Oakland',
'CA', '94312', '7605551212')
INSERT customers VALUES ('Tom', 'Smith', '609 Georgia', 'Fresno',
'CA', '33045', '5105551212')
INSERT customers VALUES ('Janice', 'Thomas', '806 Star', 'Phoenix',
'AZ', '85202', '6021112222')
```

3. To populate the Products table with product and inventory information, enter, and execute the following code:

```
INSERT Products VALUES (1, 'Giant Wheel of Brie', 200)
INSERT Products VALUES (2, 'Wool Blankets', 545)
INSERT Products VALUES (3, 'Espresso Beans', 1527)
INSERT Products VALUES (4, 'Notepads', 2098)
```

4. Close the query window.

■ PART B: Creating the New Invupdate Trigger

1. In **Object Explorer**, expand your server, and then expand **Databases**, **Sales**, **Tables** and then **dbo.Orders**.

2. Right-click the **Triggers** folder, and select **New Trigger**.

> **NOTE**
>
> *As you noticed in the last exercise and as you see now, you must understand Transact-SQL statements even when using the graphical user interface.*

3. In the Transact-SQL syntax box, enter and execute the following code to create the trigger:

```
CREATE TRIGGER dbo.InvUpdate ON dbo.Orders FOR INSERT
AS BEGIN
UPDATE p
SET p.instock = (p.instock - i.qty)
FROM Products p JOIN inserted i ON p.prodid = i.prodid
END
GO
```

4. Close the query window.

■ PART C: Verifying Results

1. Open a new SQL Server query, and execute the following code to verify the InStock quantity for item 1 (it should be 200):

```
USE Sales
SELECT prodid, instock FROM Products
```

2. To cause the INSERT trigger to fire, you need to insert a new record in the Orders table. To do this, open a new query window, and enter and execute the following code, which assumes you're selling 15 quantities of product 1 to customer ID 1 on today's date. GETDATE( ) is used to return today's date:

```
USE Sales
INSERT Orders VALUES (1, 1, 15, getdate( ))
```

3. To verify that the INSERT trigger fired and removed 15 from the InStock column of the Products table, click the New Query button, and enter and execute the following code:

```
USE Sales
SELECT prodid, instock FROM Products
```

4. Notice that the exact quantity you sold customer 1 (15) was subtracted from the total InStock quantity of product ID 1. You now have 185 instead of 200.

5. Close the query windows.

Exercise 19.2	Designing and Creating a Delete Trigger
Scenario	You have created a database for your sales department that contains information about orders customers have placed. One of your biggest customers is in Arizona, and they have recently had to stop placing regular orders with you, which makes them look inactive. Your sales manager is concerned that someone new may accidentally delete important information about this customer, and she has asked you to prevent that from happening. You have decided that the best way to accomplish this is by using a trigger on the Customers table.
Duration	This task should take approximately 15 minutes.
Setup	For this task, you need access to the machine you installed SQL Server on in Exercise 2.1, the Sales database you created in Exercise 5.1, and the Customers table you created in Exercise 6.1.
Caveat	When executing a trigger, SQL Server uses two special tables named inserted and deleted. The inserted table holds new records that are about to be added to the table, and the deleted table holds records that are about to be removed. You will be using the deleted table in this task.
Procedure	In this task, you will create a DELETE trigger that prevents users from deleting customers based in Arizona.

Equipment	See Setup.
Objective	To create the new AZDel trigger.
Criteria for Completion	This task is complete when you have a trigger that prevents you from deleting customers who reside in Arizona.

■ PART A: Designing and Creating a Delete Trigger

1. In **Object Explorer**, expand your server, and then expand **Databases**, **Sales**, **Tables** and **dbo.Orders**.

2. Right-click the **Triggers** folder, and select **New Trigger**.

3. In the Transact-SQL syntax box, enter and execute the following code to create the trigger:

```
CREATE TRIGGER dbo.AZDel ON dbo.Customers FOR DELETE AS BEGIN IF
(SELECT state FROM deleted) = 'AZ' BEGIN PRINT 'Cannot remove
customers from AZ' PRINT 'Transaction has been cancelled'
ROLLBACK END END

GO
```

> **NOTE**
> Triggers fire based on an insert and/or update and/or delete action.

4. Close the query window.

■ PART B: Verifying Results

1. Open a new SQL Server query, and execute the following code to verify you have customers from Arizona (for example, Janice Thomas should be in Arizona):

```
USE Sales
SELECT * FROM customers
```

2. To cause the DELETE trigger to fire, try to delete Janice from the Customers table. To do this, open a new query, and enter and execute the following code (you should see an error message upon execution):

```
USE Sales
DELETE from Customers WHERE Lname = 'Thomas'
```

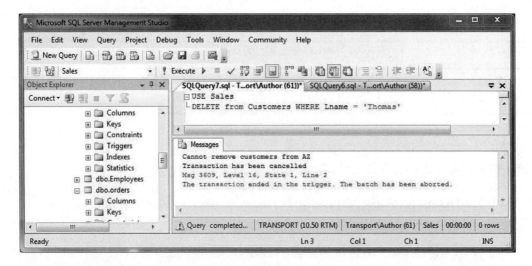

3. To verify that Janice has not been deleted, enter and execute the following code (you should still see Janice):

```
USE Sales
SELECT * FROM Customers
```

4. Close the query window.

Exercise 19.3	Designing and Creating an Update Trigger
Scenario	You have created a database for your sales department that contains product information. Some of the new sales personnel have accidentally oversold some product, and the sales manager has asked you for a technical means to prevent this in the future. You have decided to put a trigger in place that prevents users from selling any amount of product that will set the InStock column to a negative value. If they try to execute such a transaction, you have opted to use the RAISERROR( ) command to write an event to the Windows event log for tracking and reporting purposes.
Duration	This task should take approximately 30 minutes.
Setup	For this task, you need access to the machine you installed SQL Server on in Exercise 2.1, the Sales database you created in Exercise 5.1, and the Products table you created in Exercise 6.1.
Caveat	When executing a trigger, SQL Server uses two special tables named inserted and deleted. The inserted table holds new records that are about to be added to the table, and the deleted table holds records that are about to be removed. You will be using the inserted table in this task.
Procedure	In this task, you will create a trigger that prevents users from updating a record in the Products table if that update would set the InStock column to a negative amount. If they try to execute such a query, you will use the RAISERROR( ) command to write an event to the Windows event log.

Equipment	See Setup.
Objective	To create the new CheckStock trigger.
Criteria for Completion	This task is complete when you have a trigger that prevents you from entering a negative value in the InStock column of the Products table in the Sales database and also writes an event to the Windows event log if you try.

■ PART A: Designing and Creating an Update Trigger

1. Expand your server, and then expand **Databases**, **Sales**, **Tables** and then **dbo.Products**.

2. Right-click the **Triggers** folder, and select **New Trigger**.

3. In the Transact-SQL syntax box, enter and execute the following code to create the trigger:

```
CREATE TRIGGER dbo.CheckStock ON dbo.Products FOR UPDATE AS
BEGIN IF (SELECT InStock from inserted) < 0 BEGIN PRINT 'Cannot
oversell Products' PRINT 'Transaction has been cancelled'
ROLLBACK RAISERROR('Cannot oversell products', 10, 1) WITH LOG
END END
GO
```

4. Close the query window.

■ PART B: Verifying Results

1. Open a new SQL Server query, and execute the following code to verify the quantity in stock on available products (product ID 2 should have 545 in stock currently):

```
USE Sales
SELECT prodid, instock FROM Products
```

2. To cause the UPDATE trigger to fire, you'll try to sell 600 units of product ID 2 (wool blankets) to a customer. Open a new SQL Server query, and enter and execute the following code (you should see an error message upon execution):

```
USE Sales
GO
UPDATE Products SET InStock = (Instock - 600) WHERE prodid = 2
```

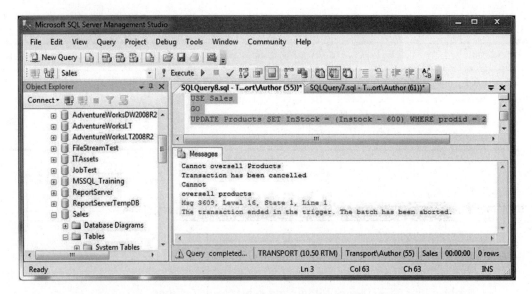

3. To verify that the transaction was disallowed and that you still have 545 wool blankets in stock, click the **New Query** button, and enter and execute the following code (you should still see 545 of product ID 2):

```
USE Sales
GO
SELECT prodid, instock FROM Products
```

4. Now, open **Event Viewer**, and look in the **Application** log for the event written by RAISERROR( ).

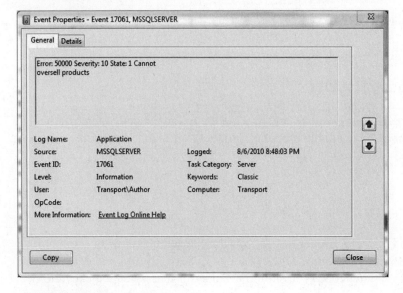

5. Close the query window.

Question 1	*Why use triggers? Why were they invented in the first place?*

Exercise 19.4	Designing and Creating an Instead Of Trigger
Scenario	You have created a database for your sales department with a table that contains customer information. Your sales manager has asked you to make it easier for sales representatives to find the customer data they need, so you have decided to create a view that displays only the necessary data. You need to make sure the sales representatives can insert new data through the view, and because the view does not show all the required columns, you need to create an INSTEAD OF trigger to modify the INSERT statement so that INSERT statements on the view will succeed.
Duration	This task should take approximately 30 minutes.
Setup	For this task, you need access to the machine you installed SQL Server on in Exercise 2.1, the Sales database you created in Exercise 5.1, and the Customers table you created in Exercise 6.1.
Procedure	In this task, you will create a view that shows only a subset of columns from the Customers table in the Sales database. Then you will create a trigger that intercepts an INSERT statement and modifies the statement so that all required columns are filled in.
Equipment	See Setup.
Objective	To create a view based on the Customers table that does not display the City field (which is a required field for an INSERT).
Criteria for Completion	This task is complete when you have an INSTEAD OF trigger that intercepts an INSERT statement on the PHX_Customers database and adds a value to insert into the City field.

■ PART A: Creating a View

1. In **SQL Server Management Studio**, open a new query, and enter and execute the following code:

    ```
    USE Sales
    GO
    CREATE VIEW PHX_Customers AS SELECT fname, lname, address, state, zip,
    phone FROM Customers WHERE City = 'Phoenix'
    ```

2. To verify that the view displays only the columns you want, click the **New Query** button, and enter and execute the following query:

    ```
    USE Sales
    SELECT * FROM PHX_Customers
    ```

3. Now you will try to insert a new customer through the view. Select New Query with Current Connection from the Query menu, and enter and execute the following code:

```
USE Sales
GO
INSERT PHX_Customers VALUES ('Timothy', 'Calunod', '123 Third',
'AZ', '85002', '6022221212')
```

■ PART B: Creating an Instead Of Trigger That Inserts the Missing Value for You When You Insert through the View

1. Expand your server, and then expand **Databases**, **Sales**, **Views** and then **dbo.PHX_Customers**.

2. Right-click the **Triggers** folder, and select **New Trigger**.

3. In the Transact-SQL syntax box, enter and execute the following code to create the trigger:

```
CREATE TRIGGER Add_City ON PHX_Customers INSTEAD OF INSERT AS
DECLARE
@FNAME VARCHAR(20), @LNAME VARCHAR(20), @ADDR VARCHAR(50), @CITY
VARCHAR(20), @STATE NCHAR(2), @ZIP CHAR(5), @PHONE CHAR(10)
SET @CITY = 'Phoenix'
SET @FNAME = (SELECT FNAME FROM INSERTED)
SET @LNAME = (SELECT LNAME FROM INSERTED)
SET @ADDR = (SELECT ADDRESS FROM INSERTED)
SET @STATE = (SELECT STATE FROM INSERTED)
SET @ZIP = (SELECT ZIP FROM INSERTED)
SET @PHONE = (SELECT PHONE FROM INSERTED)
INSERT CUSTOMERS VALUES(@FNAME, @LNAME, @ADDR, @CITY, @STATE, @ZIP,
@PHONE)
```

> **NOTE** *Caution that DDL triggers are always* after *triggers. DML triggers, as used here, can be either.*

■ **PART C: Verifying Results**

1. Enter and execute the same code from Step 3 in the previous series of steps:

    ```
    USE Sales
    INSERT PHX_Customers VALUES ('Timothy', 'Calunod', '123
    Third', 'AZ', '85002', '6052221212')
    ```

2. To check that the data was inserted into the Customers table and that the City
    column was populated, select New Query with Current Connection from the
    Query menu, and enter and execute the following query:

    ```
    USE Sales
    GO
    SELECT * FROM Customers
    ```

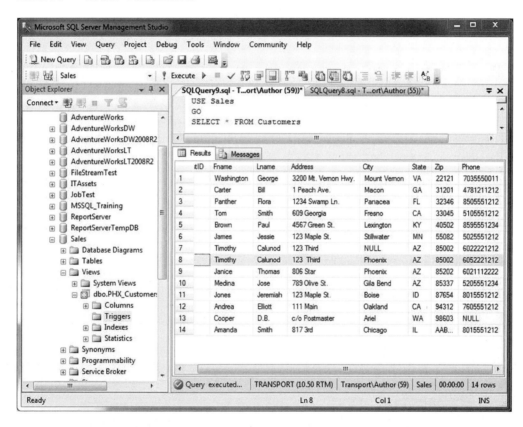

3. Close the query windows.

LAB 20
WORKING WITH REPLICATION

This lab contains the following exercises and activities:

Exercise 20.1	Choosing a Replication Type
Scenario	You work for a medium-sized company that has offices throughout the world. Many of the users in these offices need access to the data stored on SQL Server, and they need it as fast as possible. You know that the best way to get this data to the users is via replication; however, before you can configure replication, you need to figure out which type of replication to use.

Duration	This task should take approximately 15 minutes.
Setup	You don't need to perform any setup for this task because it all takes place on paper.
Procedure	In this task, you will read each scenario and decide on the proper replication type.
Equipment	The only equipment you need for this task is some paper and a pencil or pen.
Objective	To choose the correct replication type.
Criteria for Completion	This task is complete when you have chosen the correct replication type for each of the scenarios presented.

■ PART A: Choosing the Best Solution

> **NOTE**
>
> *Replication is yet another way to create redundant data in case disaster destroys one data center. Replication is also a method to reduce wide area networking costs in a distributed environment. Replication is overhead expensive. Do you have machines able to handle both the production needs and the replication needs? Consider both the dollar costs and user response time in choosing first whether you will use replication and second whether it represents the best solution*

1. One of your servers, located in New York City, contains a Sales database that needs to be replicated to your satellite offices in Berlin, London, and Moscow, which are connected via a T1 connection that consistently runs at 80 percent capacity. Your sales associates make changes to the database regularly throughout the day, but the users in the satellite offices do not need to see the changes immediately. Which type of replication should you use?

   a. Merge
   b. Transactional
   c. Snapshot
   d. Transactional with updating subscribers
   e. Snapshot with updating subscribers

2. Each branch office of your company has its own accounting department. The network connections between the branch offices are reliable, but they are consistently at 80 percent usage during the day. Each of your branch office accounting departments needs a copy of the main accounting database that they can update locally, and they need it to be as current as possible. Which replication type best suits your needs?

    a. Merge

    b. Transactional

    c. Snapshot

    d. Transactional with immediate updating subscribers

    e. Snapshot with updating subscribers

3.   Several of your company's sales offices are located throughout the country. Headquarters needs an up-to-date copy of the sales offices' databases. When they send new inventory to the sales offices, they want to update the database at headquarters and have the new data replicated to the respective sales offices. Which replication type should you use?

    a. Merge

    b. Transactional

    c. Snapshot

    d. Transactional with immediate updating subscribers

    e. Snapshot with updating subscribers

4.   The retail division of your company manages shops in various cities. Each shop maintains its own inventory database. The retail manager in Phoenix wants each of her four shops to be able to share inventory with each other so employees can pick up a part from another nearby store rather than waiting for a shipment from the manufacturer. To do this, employees at each shop should be able to update their local copy of the inventory database, decrement the other store's inventory, and then go pick up the part. This way, the other store won't sell its part because the part will have already been taken out of stock. Which replication type should you use to accomplish this?

    a. Merge

    b. Transactional

    c. Snapshot

    d. Transactional with updating subscribers

    e. Snapshot with updating subscribers

■ PART B: Verifying Results

1.   **Scenario 1:** The answer is B. Because the entire database does not change every day, you do not need to use the snapshot type. Also, the snapshot type would use a great deal more bandwidth than the transactional type. Because the subscribers do not need to update their copy of the data, you do not need the added complexity of merging or updating subscribers. Also, you do not have much network bandwidth to play with, and transactional replication uses the least amount of bandwidth.

2.   **Scenario 2:** The answer is D. Because the network is running close to capacity most of the time, it would not support snapshot replication. Because the users would be updating only their own data, merge replication would be overkill. Transactional with updating subscribers fits your needs because the network usage is lower than snapshot and still allows users to update local copies of the data.

3.   **Scenario 3:** The answer is D. Because individual offices need to be able to update their own inventory databases each time they make a sale and headquarters needs to be able to update the main database, you need to give the sales offices the capability to update. Merge replication would be overkill here because each sales office does not need to update other sales offices' data.

4.   **Scenario 4:** The answer is A. In this scenario, you do not have a central "main" database that each subscriber will update. All the stores must be able to update data for the other stores' data. The best way to accomplish this is through merge replication.

Exercise 20.2	Designing a Replication Topology
Scenario	You work for a medium-sized company that has offices throughout the world. Many of the users in these offices need access to the data stored on SQL Server, and they need it as fast as possible. You know that the best way to get this data to the users is via replication; however, before you can configure replication, you need to decide on a replication topology.
Duration	This task should take approximately 15 minutes.
Setup	You don't need to perform any setup for this task because it all takes place on paper.
Procedure	In this task, you will read each scenario and decide on the proper replication topology.
Equipment	The only equipment you need for this task is some paper and a pencil or pen.
Objective	To choose the correct replication topology.
Criteria for Completion	This task is complete when you have chosen the correct replication type for each of the scenarios presented.

■ PART A: Choosing the Correct Replication Topology

1.   One of your servers, located in New York City, contains a Sales database that needs to be replicated to your satellite offices in Berlin, London, and Moscow, which are connected via a T1 connection that consistently runs at 80 percent capacity. Your sales associates make changes to the database regularly throughout the day, but the users in the satellite offices do not need to see the

changes immediately. You have decided to use transactional replication. Which replication topology should you use?

a. Central subscriber/multiple publishers

b. Multiple publishers/multiple subscribers

c. Central publisher/central distributor

d. Remote distribution

2. Each branch office of your company has its own accounting department. The network connections between the branch offices are reliable, but they are consistently at 80 percent usage during the day. Each of your branch office accounting departments needs a copy of the main accounting database that they can update locally, and they need it to be as current as possible. You have decided to use transactional replication with immediate updating subscribers. Which replication topology best suits your needs?

a. Central subscriber/multiple publishers

b. Multiple publishers/multiple subscribers

c. Central publisher/central distributor

d. Remote distribution

3. Several of your company's sales offices are located throughout the country. Headquarters needs an up-to-date copy of the sales offices' databases. When they send new inventory to the sales offices, they want to update the database at headquarters and have the new data replicated to the respective sales offices. You have decided to use transactional replication with immediate updating subscribers. Which replication topology should you use?

a. Central subscriber/multiple publishers

b. Multiple publishers/multiple subscribers

c. Central publisher/central distributor

d. Remote distribution

4. The retail division of your company manages shops in various cities. Each shop maintains its own inventory database. The retail manager in Phoenix wants each of her four shops to be able to share inventory with each other so employees can pick up a part from another nearby store rather than waiting for a shipment from the manufacturer. To do this, employees at each shop should be able to update their local copy of the inventory database, decrement the other store's inventory, and then go pick up the part. This way, the other store won't sell its part because the part will have already been taken out of stock. You have decided to use merge replication. Which replication topology should you use?

a. Central subscriber/multiple publishers

b. Multiple publishers/multiple subscribers

c. Central publisher/central distributor

d. Remote distribution

■ PART B: Verifying Results

1. **Scenario 1:** The answer is D. The models that involve multiple publishers obviously won't work here because you have only one publisher. The remote distributor option can save long distance charges because instead of making several long-distance calls from New York to the satellites, you can place a distributor in London and let the distributor make less-expensive calls to the remaining satellites.

2. **Scenario 2:** Either answer C or answer D is acceptable here. Because you are using transactional replication with updating subscribers, you can use a central publisher at headquarters with each sales office being a subscriber.

3. **Scenario 3:** As with scenario 2, either answer C or answer D is acceptable. Because you are using transactional replication with updating subscribers, you can use a central publisher at headquarters with each sales office being a subscriber.

4. **Scenario 4:** The answer is B. Each store will publish its inventory database and subscribe to the other stores' inventory databases. This makes it the perfect scenario for a multiple publishers/multiple subscribers model.

Exercise 20.3	Configuring Replication
Scenario	You work for a medium-sized company that has offices throughout the world. Many of the users in these offices need access to the data stored on SQL Server, and they need it as fast as possible. You know that the best way to get this data to the users is via replication; however, before you can create publications and subscriptions, you must configure a distribution server.
Duration	This task should take approximately 30 minutes.
Setup	For this task, you need access to the machine you installed SQL Server on in Exercise 2.1.
Caveat	Make sure the SQL Server Agent is set to start automatically before starting this task.
Procedure	In this task, you will configure the default instance of SQL Server on your machine as a distribution server.
Equipment	See Setup.
Objective	To configure your default instance as a distribution server.
Criteria for Completion	This task is complete when you have configured your default instance of SQL Server to act as a distributor.

■ PART A: Configuring Replication

1. Open **SQL Server Management Studio**, and connect to your server.

2. Right-click **Replication**, and click **Configure Distribution**.

3. You are presented with a welcome screen; click **Next** to continue.

4. The **Distributor** screen appears. Select the server that will act as its own distributor option, and click **Next**.

5. If your SQL Server agent is not configured to start automatically, you may be presented with a screen asking you to configure the agent. Set it to start automatically, and click **Next**.

6.   You are now asked to specify the snapshot folder. A good reason to change this is if you are replicating over the Internet and need to specify a folder that is accessible via FTP. Accept the defaults, and click **Next**.

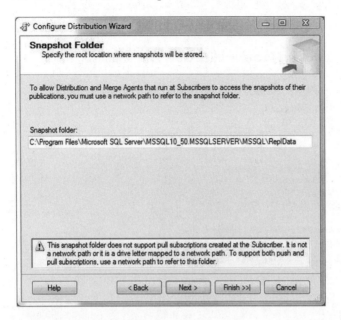

7.   The **Distribution Database** screen appears next. You can supply a name for the distribution database as well as location information for its database file and transaction log. Keep the defaults, and click **Next** to continue.

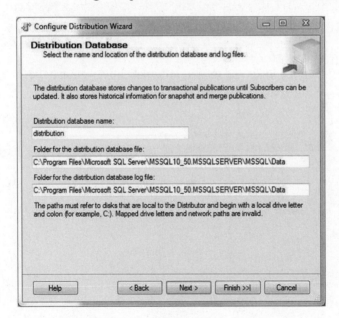

8. Now you are on the **Publishers** screen where you can choose which servers you want to configure as publishers. Clicking the **ellipsis (…)** button allows you to specify security credentials such as login ID and password, as well as the location of the snapshot folder. Be sure to place a check mark next to your local SQL Server system, and then click **Next** to continue.

9. On the **Wizard Actions** screen, you can have the wizard configure distribution, write a script to configure distribution that you can run later, or do both. Leave the **Configure distribution** box checked, and click **Next** to continue.

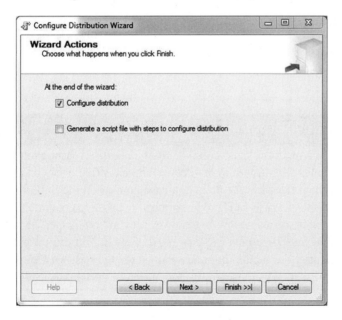

10. On the **Complete the Wizard** screen, review your selections, and click **Finish**.

11. When the wizard is finished, click **Close**.

Question 1	*The distributor can be anywhere; it does not need to be cohosted with the publisher. Also note the default folder for the distributor. What is it?*

■ PART B: Verifying Results

Right-click **Replication** in **Object Explorer**; you should see an option labeled **Distributor Properties**. When you click that option, you should see a dialog box confirming successful results.

Exercise 20.4	Creating a Transactional Publication
Scenario	You work for a medium-sized company that has offices throughout the world. The sales department in the Fresno branch office needs access to some of the data stored in the main database housed on the SQL Server at the corporate headquarters. They do not need the data immediately, so there is room for some latency; in addition, they are connected by a partial T1 that is at about 80 percent capacity, so there is little room for more traffic. Bearing these factors in mind, you decide the best way to get the data to the users in Fresno is to configure a transactional publication.
Duration	This task should take approximately 30 minutes.
Setup	For this task, you need access to the machine you installed SQL Server on in Exercise 2.1, the AdventureWorks database installed with the sample data, and the default instance of SQL Server you configured as a distributor in Exercise 20.3.

Caveat	If you have log shipping enabled on the AdventureWorks database, you will need to disable it. Here's how:
	1. Open **SQL Server Management Studio**, and connect to the default instance.
	2. Expand **Databases**, right-click **AdventureWorks**, point to **Tasks**, and click **Ship Transaction Logs**.
	3. Uncheck the box next to **Enable This as a Primary Database in a Log Shipping Configuration**.
	4. Click **Yes** on the subsequent dialog box, and then click **OK**.
	5. Click **Close** when the configuration is complete.
	6. Make sure SQL Server Agent service has started.
Procedure	In this task, you will create a transactional publication on your default instance of SQL Server on the Production.ProductCategory table in the AdventureWorks database.
Equipment	See Setup.
Objective	To create a transactional publication on the Production.ProductCategory table.
Criteria for Completion	This task is complete when you have created a transactional publication based on the Production.ProductCategory table in the AdventureWorks database on the default instance of SQL Server.

■ PART A: Creating a Transactional Publication

1. Open **SQL Server Management Studio**, and connect to your SQL Server.

2. Expand **Replication**, right-click **Local Publications**, and click **New Publication**. This brings you to the **New Publication Wizard** welcome screen.

3. Click **Next** to continue.

4. On the **Publication Database** screen, highlight **AdventureWorks**, and click **Next** to continue.

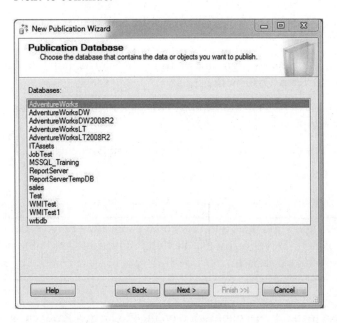

5. On the **Publication Type** screen, you can choose what type of publication to create. For this task, choose **Transactional Publication**, and click **Next** to continue.

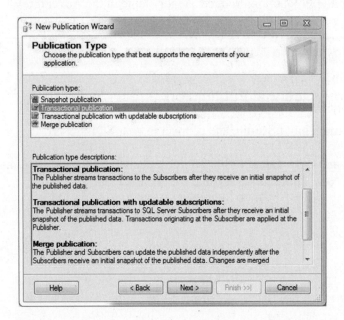

6. On the **Articles** screen, you can select what data and objects you want to replicate. Expand **Tables**, and check the **ProductCategory** box.

7. You can also set the properties for an article from this screen. Make sure **ProductCategory** is highlighted, click **Article Properties**, and then click **Set Properties of Highlighted Table Article**.

8. In the **Destination Object** section, change the destination object name to
    ReplicatedCategory, change the destination object owner to **dbo**, and click **OK**.

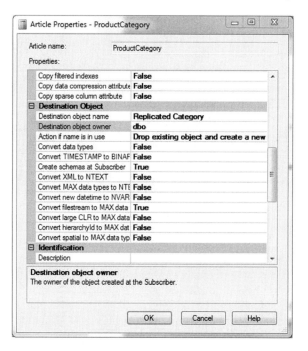

9. Back at the **Articles** screen, click **Next** to continue.

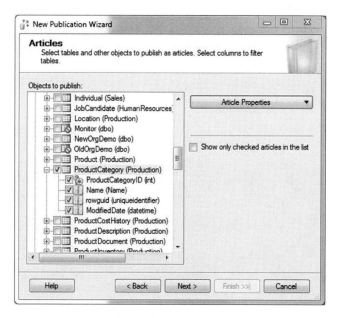

10. On the next screen, you can filter the data that is replicated. You do not want to filter the data in this case, so click **Next** to continue.

11. On the **Snapshot Agent** screen, check the box to create a snapshot immediately, and click **Next**.

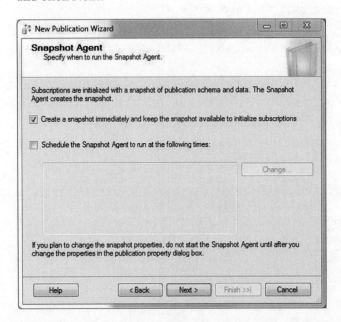

12. On the **Agent Security** screen, you are asked how the agents should log in and access data. To set this for the snapshot agent, click the **Security Settings** button next to Snapshot Agent.

13. Ordinarily you would create an account for the agent to run under, but to make the task simpler, you will run the agent using the SQL Server Agent service account, so select the radio button for that option, and click **OK**.

14. Back at the **Agent Security** screen, click **Next** to continue.

15.   On the **Wizard Actions** screen, you can have the wizard create the publication, write a script to create the publication that you can run later, or do both. Leave the **Create the Publication** box checked, and click **Next** to continue.

16.   On the **Complete the Wizard** screen, you need to enter a name for the new publication, so enter **CategoryPub**, and click **Finish**.

17.   When the wizard is finished, click **Close**.

Question 2	*What are the differences between distributed transactions and transactional replication?*

■ PART B: Verifying Results

1. Open **SQL Server Management Studio**, connect to your SQL Server, and expand **Replication**. You should see the CategoryPub publication listed.

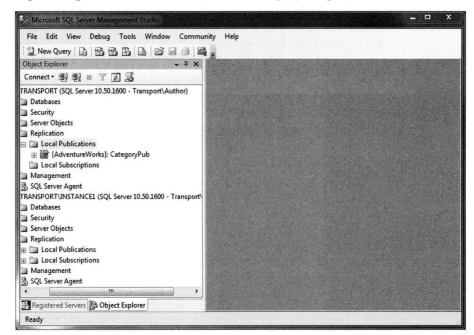

2. Right-click **CategoryPub**, and click **Properties**. The type should be Transactional.

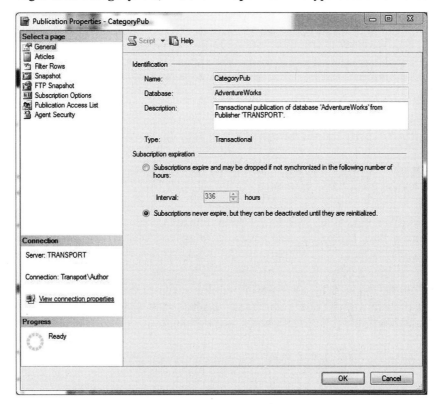

3. Click **OK**.

Exercise 20.5	Subscribing to a Transactional Publication
Scenario	You work for a medium-sized company that has offices throughout the world. The sales department in the Fresno branch office needs access to some of the data stored in the main database housed on the SQL Server at the corporate headquarters. They do not need the data immediately, so there is room for some latency; in addition, they are connected by a partial T1 that is at about 80 percent capacity, so there is little room for more traffic. You have already configured a transactional publication at headquarters; now you must create a subscription on the server in Fresno.
Duration	This task should take approximately 30 minutes.
Setup	For this task, you need access to the machine you installed SQL Server on in Exercise 2.1, the second instance of SQL Server installed in Exercise 2.2, the AdventureWorks database installed with the sample data, the default instance of SQL Server configured as a distributor in Exercise 20.3, and the transactional publication configured in Exercise 20.4.
Caveat	Make sure the SQL Server Agent service for the second instance is set to start automatically before starting this task.
Procedure	In this task, you will create a pull subscription to the transactional publication on your default instance of SQL Server.
Equipment	See Setup.
Objective	To create a pull subscription to the transactional publication on the default instance of SQL Server.
Criteria for Completion	This task is complete when replication is running properly.

■ PART A: Subscribing to a Transactional Publication

1. Open **SQL Server Management Studio**, and connect **Instance1** by selecting it from the Server Name drop-down list.

2. Expand **Replication**, right-click **Local Subscriptions**, and click **New Subscription**. This brings you to the New Subscription Wizard welcome screen. Click **Next** to continue.

3. On the **Publication** screen, select the default instance of your server from the Publisher drop-down list (if it is not listed, select Find SQL Server Publisher), select **CategoryPub** from the Databases and Publications list, and click **Next** to continue.

4. On the **Distribution Agent Location** screen, you are asked which machine should run the replication agents—at the distributor or at the subscriber. Because you want to create a pull subscription, select the **Run Each Agent at Its Subscriber** option, and click **Next**.

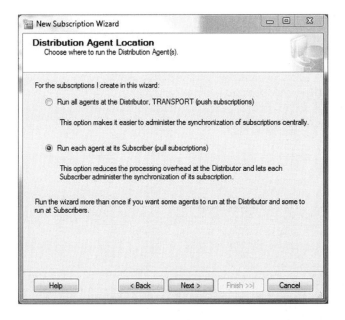

5. On the **Subscribers** screen, you can choose a subscriber for the publication. Check the box next to the second instance of your server.

6. Then the drop-down list is populated with all the available databases on the subscriber. Select **New Database** from the list to open the **New Database** dialog box.

7. Enter **TR_Test** in the Database name box, and click **OK**. Then click **Next**.

8. On the next screen you need to set the distribution agent security. To do so, click the **ellipsis (...)** button in the Subscription Properties list.

9. Ordinarily you would create an account for the agent to run under, but to make the task simpler, you will run the agent using the SQL Server Agent service account, so select the radio button for that option, and click **OK**.

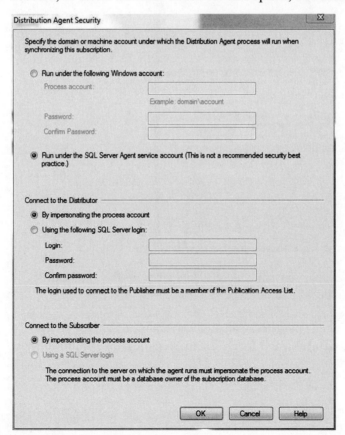

10.   Back at the **Distribution Agent Security** screen, click **Next** to continue.

11.   The next step is to set the synchronization schedule. Because you are using transactional replication, select **Run Continuously**, and click **Next** to continue.

12. On the next screen, you can tell SQL Server when to initialize the subscription, if at all. If you have already created the schema on the subscriber, then you do not need to initialize the subscription. In this case, you should select **Immediately** from the drop-down list, make sure the **Initialize** box is checked, and click **Next** to continue.

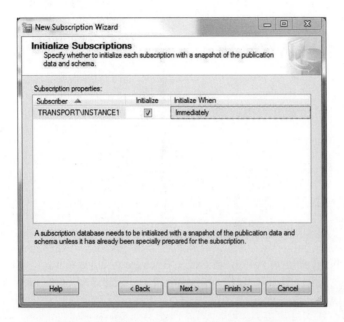

13. On the **Wizard Actions** screen, you can have the wizard create the subscription, write a script to create the subscription that you can run later, or do both. Leave the **Create the Subscription(s)** box checked, and click **Next** to continue.

14. On the **Complete the Wizard** screen, review your options, and click **Finish** to create the subscription.

15.   When the wizard is finished, click **Close**.

	You have unreliable and intermittant network connection to the publisher. Is transactional replication an acceptable replication solution?

■ PART B: Verifying Results

1.   You should have four records in the ReplicatedCategory table. To verify that, open a new query, connect to the second instance, and execute the following code:

```
USE TR_Test
GO
SELECT * FROM ReplicatedCategory
```

2.   Now add a new record to the ProductCategory table in the AdventureWorks database on the default instance. Open a new query, and from the Query menu, select **Connection and Change Connection**. Then connect to the default instance.

3.   Run the following code to add a new record:

```
USE AdventureWorks
GO
INSERT INTO Production.ProductCategory (Name)
VALUES('Tools')
```

4. You should get the message that one row was added. Give the server about a minute to replicate the transaction; then run the following query against the second instance:

```
USE TR_Test
GO
SELECT * FROM ReplicatedCategory
```

5. You should get five records. The last record should be the new Tools record.

Exercise 20.6	Creating a Snapshot Publication
Scenario	You work for a medium-sized company that has offices throughout the world. The sales department in the Tucson branch office needs access to one of the databases housed on the SQL Server at the corporate headquarters. They will use the data only for reporting purposes, so they will not be making updates to their local copy of the data. They need the data to be refreshed only once a day, so you can allow for a full day of latency. They are connected by a T1 circuit that is at about 75 percent capacity during peak hours, but off-hours it is at about 30 percent capacity, so the network has plenty of room during off-hours. Bearing these factors in mind, you decide that the best way to get the data to the users in Tucson is to configure a snapshot publication.
Duration	This task should take approximately 30 minutes.
Setup	For this task, you need access to the machine you installed SQL Server on in Exercise 2.1, the AdventureWorks database installed with the sample data, and the default instance of SQL Server you configured as a distributor in Exercise 20.3.
Caveat	If you have log shipping enabled on the AdventureWorks database, you will need to disable it. Here's how: 1. Open **SQL Server Management Studio**, and connect to the default instance. 2. Expand **Databases**, right-click **AdventureWorks**, point to **Tasks**, and click **Ship Transaction Logs**. 3. Uncheck the box next to **Enable This as a Primary Database in a Log Shipping Configuration**. 4. Click **Yes** in the subsequent dialog box, then click OK. 5. Click **Close** when the configuration is complete.
Procedure	In this task, you will create a snapshot publication on your default instance of SQL Server on the Person.AddressType table in the AdventureWorks database.
Equipment	See Setup.

Objective	To create a snapshot publication.
Criteria for Completion	This task is complete when you have created a snapshot publication based on the Person.AddressType table in the AdventureWorks database on the default instance of SQL Server.

■ PART A: Creating a Snapshot Publication

1. Open **SQL Server Management Studio**, and connect to the default instance of SQL Server.

2. Expand **Replication**, right-click **Local Publications**, and click **New Publication**. This brings you to the New Publication Wizard welcome screen.

3. Click **Next** to continue.

4. On the **Publication Database** screen, highlight **AdventureWorks**, and click **Next** to continue.

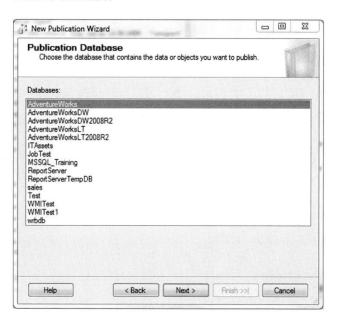

5. On the **Publication Type** screen, you can choose what type of publication to create. For this task, choose **Snapshot Publication**, and click **Next** to continue.

6. On the **Articles** screen, you can select what data and objects you want to replicate. Expand **Tables**, and check the **AddressType** box.

7. You can also set the properties for an article from this screen. Make sure AddressType is highlighted, click **Article Properties**, and then click **Set Properties of Highlighted Table Article**.

8. In the **Destination Object** section, change the destination object name to **ReplicatedType**, change the destination object owner to **dbo**, and click **OK**.

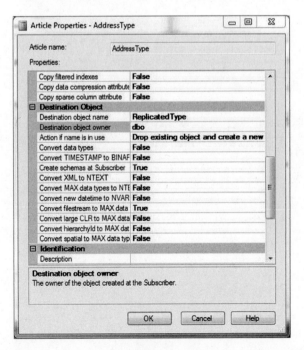

9.   Back at the **Articles** screen, click **Next** to continue.

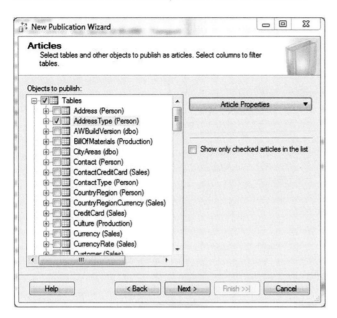

10. On the next screen, you can filter the data that is replicated. You do not want to filter the data in this case, so click **Next** to continue.

11. On the **Snapshot Agent** screen, check the box to create a snapshot immediately, and check the **Schedule the Snapshot** agent to run at the following times. Leave the default schedule of one hour, and click **Next**.

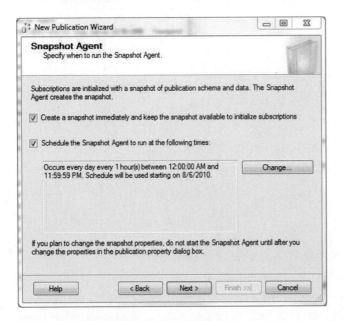

12. On the **Agent Security** screen, you are asked how the agents should log in and access data. To set this for the snapshot agent, click the **Security Settings** button next to **Snapshot Agent**.

13. Ordinarily you would create an account for the agent to run under, but to make the task simpler, you will run the agent using the SQL Server Agent service account, so select the radio button for that option, and click **OK**.

14.   Back at the **Agent Security** screen, click **Next** to continue.

15.   On the **Wizard Actions** screen, you can have the wizard create the publication, write a script to create the publication you can run later, or do both. Leave the **Create the Publication** box checked, and click **Next** to continue.

16. On the Complete the Wizard screen, you need to enter a name for the new publication, so enter **AddressTypePub**, and click **Finish**.

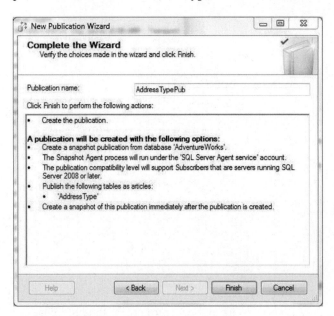

17. When the wizard is finished, click **Close**.

Question 4	You have a partial T1 connection and a very large database. Is this an acceptable solution? If you decide no, what are your alternatives while still using a replication scenario?

■ PART B: Verifying Results

1. Open **SQL Server Management Studio**, connect to your SQL Server, expand Replication, and then expand Local Publications. You should see the **AddressTypePub** publication listed.

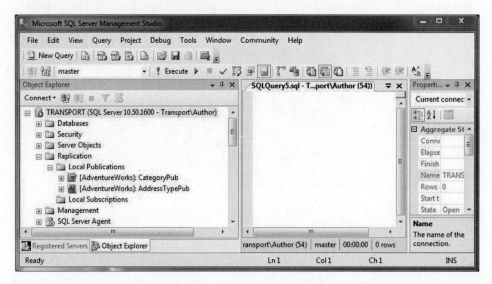

2.   Right-click **AddressTypePub**, and click **Properties**. The type should be Snapshot.

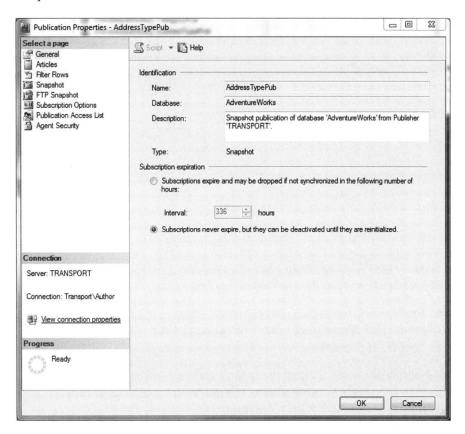

3.   Click **OK**.

Exercise 20.7	Subscribing to a Snapshot Publication
Scenario	You work for a medium-sized company that has offices throughout the world. The sales department in the Tucson branch office needs access to one of the databases housed on the SQL Server at the corporate headquarters. They will use the data for reporting purposes only, so they will not be making updates to their local copy of the data. They need the data to be refreshed only once a day, so you can allow for a full day of latency. They are connected by a partial T1 that is at about 75 percent capacity during peak hours, but off-hours it is at about 30 percent capacity, so the network has plenty of room during off-hours. You have already configured a snapshot publication at the headquarters; now you must create a subscription on the server in Tucson.
Duration	This task should take approximately 30 minutes.
Setup	For this task, you need access to the machine you installed SQL Server on in Exercise 2.1, the second instance of SQL Server installed in Exercise 2.2, the AdventureWorks database installed with the sample data, the default instance of SQL Server configured as a distributor in Exercise 20.3, and the snapshot publication configured in Exercise 20.6.

Caveat	Make sure the SQL Server Agent service for the second instance is set to start automatically before starting this task.
Procedure	In this task, you will create a pull subscription to the snapshot publication on your default instance of SQL Server.
Equipment	See Setup.
Objective	To create a pull subscription to the snapshot publication on the default instance of SQL Server.
Criteria for Completion	This task is complete when replication is running properly.

■ PART A: Subscribing to a Snapshot Publication

1. Open **SQL Server Management Studio**, and connect to the second instance by selecting it from the Server Name drop-down list.

2. Expand **Replication**, right-click **Local Subscriptions**, and click **New Subscription**. This brings you to the **New Subscription Wizard** welcome screen. Click **Next** to continue.

3. On the **Publication** screen, select the default instance of your server from the Publisher drop-down list, select **AddressTypePub** from the **Databases and Publications** list, and click **Next** to continue.

4. On the **Distribution Agent Location** screen, you are asked which machine should run the replication agents—at the distributor or at the subscriber. Because you want to create a pull subscription, select the **Run Each Agent at Its Subscriber** option, and click **Next**.

5.   On the **Subscribers** screen, you can choose a subscriber for the publication. Check the box next to the second instance of your server.

6.   Then the drop-down list is populated with all the available databases on the subscriber. Select **New Database** from the list to open the New Database dialog box.

7.   Enter **SR_Test** in the Database name box, click **OK**, and then click **Next**.

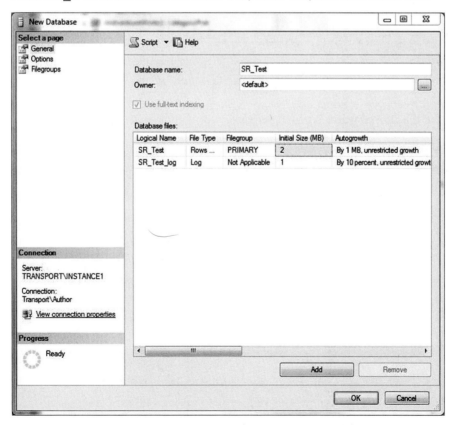

8. On the next screen you need to set the distribution agent security. To do so, click the **ellipsis (…)** button in the Subscription Properties list.

9. In a production environment you would create an account for the agent to run under, but to make the task simpler, you will run the agent using the SQL Server Agent service account, so select the radio button for that option, and click **OK**.

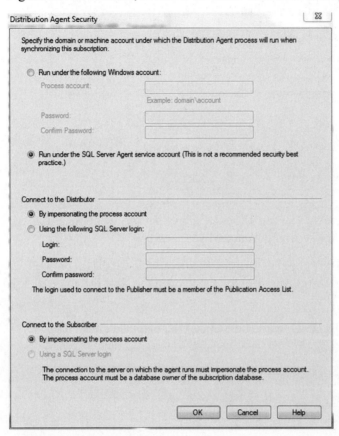

10. Back at the **Distribution Agent Security** screen, click **Next** to continue.

11.   The next step is to set the synchronization schedule, so select **Define Schedule**.

12.   In the New Job Schedule dialog box, under Frequency, set **Occurs** to **Daily**, and click **OK**.

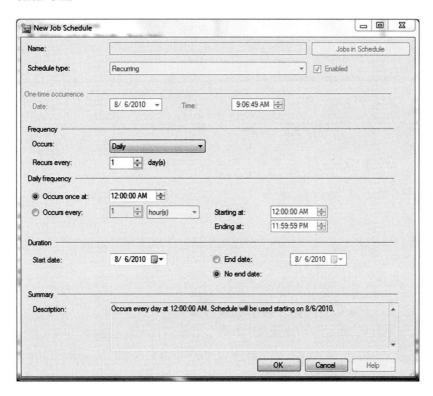

13.   Back at the **Synchronization Schedule** screen, click **Next**.

14. On the next screen, you can tell SQL Server when to initialize the subscription, if at all. If you have already created the schema (an empty copy of the database to be replicated) on the subscriber, then you do not need to initialize the subscription. In this case, you should select **Immediately** from the drop-down list, make sure the **Initialize** box is checked, and click **Next** to continue.

15. On the **Wizard Actions** screen, you can have the wizard create the subscription, write a script to create the subscription that you can run later, or do both. Leave the **Create the Subscription(s)** box checked, and click **Next** to continue.

16. On the **Complete the Wizard** screen, review your options, and click **Finish** to create the subscription.

17. When the wizard is finished, click **Close**.

■ **PART B: Verifying Results**

1. You should have several records in the **ReplicatedType** table. To verify that, open a new query, connect to the second instance, and execute the following code:

    ```
    USE SR_Test
    GO
    SELECT * FROM dbo.ReplicatedType
    ```

2. Now add a new record to the Person.AddressType table in the AdventureWorks database on the default instance. Open a new query, and from the Query menu, select **Connection and Change Connection**. Then connect to the default instance.

3. Run the following code to add a new record:

    ```
    USE AdventureWorks
    GO
    INSERT INTO Person.AddressType (Name) VALUES ('Tucson Office')
    ```

4. Now you could wait for 24 hours or so for this to replicate, but that is a bit too long, so you need to run replication manually. To start, expand your default instance server in **Object Explorer**.

5. Expand **SQL Agent**, and then expand **Jobs**.

6. Right-click the job whose name starts with **<YourServerName>** → **AdventureWorks** → **AddressType Pub-2**, click **Start Job at Step**, and select **Step 1**.

7. Click **Close** when the job is complete.

8. Next, expand your second instance in **Object Explorer**.

9. Expand **SQL Agent**, and then expand **Jobs**.

10. Right-click the job whose name starts with **<YourServerName>** → **AdventureWorks** → **AddressType Pub** → **<YourServerName>\INSTANCE**, and click **Start Job at Step**.

11. Click **Close** when the job is complete.

12. Run the following query against the second instance:

    ```
    USE SR_Test SELECT * FROM dbo.ReplicatedType
    ```

13. One of the records in the result set should be the new Tucson Office record.

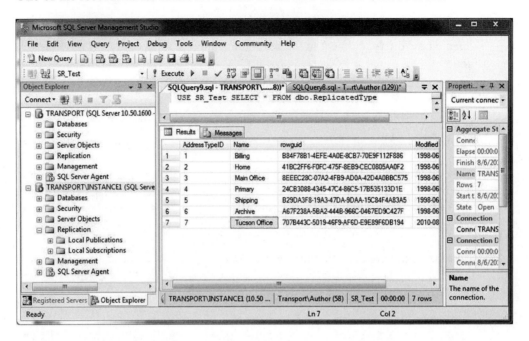

Exercise 20.8	Creating a Merge Publication
Scenario	You work for a medium-sized company that has offices throughout the world. The retail division of your company manages shops in various cities. Each shop maintains its own inventory database. The retail manager in Phoenix wants each of her four shops to be able to share inventory with each other so employees can pick up a part from another nearby store rather than wait for a shipment from the manufacturer. To do this, employees at each shop need to be able to update their local copy of the inventory database, decrement the other store's inventory, and then go pick up the part. This way, the other store won't sell its part because the part will have already been taken out of stock. To accomplish this goal, you have decided to create a merge publication.
Duration	This task should take approximately 30 minutes.
Setup	For this task, you need access to the machine you installed SQL Server on in Exercise 2.1, the AdventureWorks database installed with the sample data, and the default instance of SQL Server configured as a distributor, as shown in Exercise 20.3.
Caveat	If you have log shipping enabled on the AdventureWorks database, you will need to disable it. Here's how: 1. Open **SQL Server Management Studio**, and connect to the default instance. 2. Expand **Databases**, right-click **AdventureWorks**, point to **Tasks**, and click **Ship Transaction Logs**.

	3. Uncheck the box next to **Enable This as a Primary Database in a Log Shipping Configuration**. 4. Click **Yes** in the subsequent dialog box, and then click **OK**. 5. Click **Close** when the configuration is complete.
Procedure	In this task, you will create a merge publication on your default instance of SQL Server on the ProductionCulture table in the AdventureWorks database.
Equipment	See Setup.
Objective	To create a merge publication.
Criteria for Completion	This task is complete when you have created a merge publication based on the Production.Culture table in the AdventureWorks database on the default instance of SQL Server.

■ PART A: Creating a Merge Publication

1. Open **SQL Server Management Studio**, and connect to your SQL Server.

2. Expand **Replication**, right-click **Local Publications**, and click **New Publication**. This brings you to the **New Publication Wizard** welcome screen.

3. Click **Next** to continue.

4. On the **Publication Database** screen, highlight **AdventureWorks**, and click **Next** to continue.

5. On the **Publication Type** screen, you can choose what type of publication to create. For this task, choose **Merge Publication**, and click **Next** to continue.

6. On the next screen you are asked what version of SQL Server the subscribers are running. This is because different versions of SQL Server handle merge replication differently. In this case, check only **SQL Server 2008**, and click **Next**.

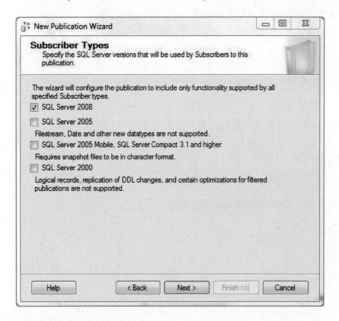

7. On the **Articles** screen, you can select what data and objects you want to replicate. Expand **Tables**, and check the **Culture** box.

8. You can also set the properties for an article from this screen. Make sure **Culture** is highlighted, click **Article Properties**, and then click **Set Properties of Highlighted Table Article**.

9.   Notice all of the defaults, but do not make any changes; click **OK**.

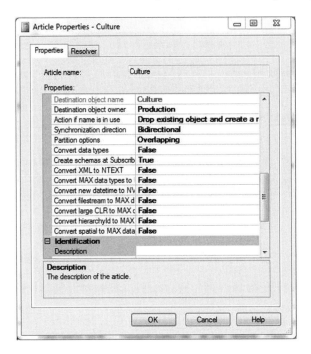

10.   Back at the **Articles** screen, click **Next** to continue.

11. On the next screen, you are reminded that a uniqueidentifier column will be added to the replicated table. Click **Next** to continue.

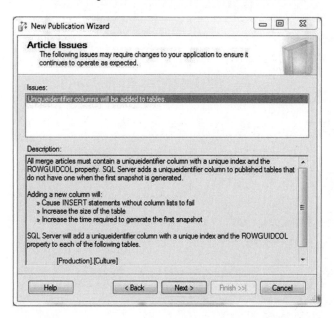

12. On the next screen, you can filter the data that is replicated. You do not want to filter the data in this case, so click **Next** to continue.

13. On the **Snapshot Agent** screen, check the box to create a snapshot immediately, and check the **Schedule the Snapshot** agent to run at the following times. Leave the default schedule, and click **Next**.

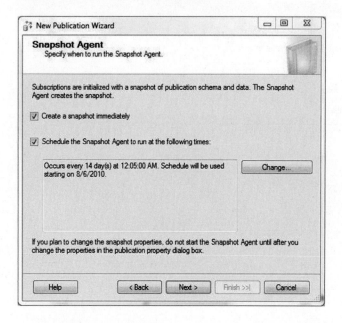

14. On the **Agent Security** screen, you are asked how the agents should log in and access data. To set this for the snapshot agent, click the **Security Settings** button next to Snapshot Agent.

15.   Ordinarily you would create an account for the agent to run under, but to make the task simpler, you will run the agent using the SQL Server Agent service account, so select the radio button for that option, and click **OK**.

16.   Back at the **Agent Security** screen, click **Next** to continue.

17.   On the **Wizard Actions** screen, you can have the wizard create the publication, write a script to create the publication that you can run later, or do both. Leave the **Create the Publication** box checked, and click **Next** to continue.

18. On the **Complete the Wizard** screen, you need to enter a name for the new publication, so enter **CulturePub**, and click **Finish**.

19. When the wizard is finished, click **Close**.

■ PART B: Verifying Results

1. Open **SQL Server Management Studio**, connect to your SQL Server, and expand **Replication**. You should see the **CulturePub** publication listed.

2. Right-click **CulturePub**, and click **Properties**. The type should be Merge.

3. Click **OK**.

Exercise 20.9	Subscribing to a Merge Publication
Scenario	You work for a medium-sized company that has offices throughout the world. The retail division of your company manages shops in various cities. Each shop maintains its own inventory database. The retail manager in Phoenix wants each of her four shops to be able to share inventory with each other so employees can pick up a part from another nearby store rather than wait for a shipment from the manufacturer. To do this, employees at each shop need to be able to update their local copy of the inventory database, decrement the other store's inventory, and then go pick up the part. This way, the other store won't sell its part because the part will have already been taken out of stock. You have already configured a merge publication to which you must now subscribe.
Duration	This task should take approximately 30 minutes.
Setup	For this task, you need access to the machine you installed SQL Server on in Exercise 2.1, the second instance of SQL Server installed in Exercise 2.2, the AdventureWorks database installed with the sample data, the default instance of SQL Server you configured as a distributor in Exercise 20.3, and the merge publication you configured in Exercise 20.8.
Caveat	Make sure the SQL Server Agent service for the second instance is set to start automatically before starting this task.
Procedure	In this task, you will create a pull subscription to the merge publication on your default instance of SQL Server.
Equipment	See Setup.
Objective	To subscribe to a merge publication.
Criteria for Completion	This task is complete when replication is running properly.

■ PART A: Subscribing to a Merge Publication

1. Open **SQL Server Management Studio**, and connect to the second instance by selecting it from the **Server Name** drop-down list.

2. Expand **Replication**, right-click **Local Subscriptions**, and click **New Subscription**. Click **Next** to continue. This brings you to the New Subscription Wizard welcome screen.

3. On the **Publication** screen, select the default instance of your server from the **Publisher** drop-down list. Select **CulturePub** from the Databases and Publications list, and click **Next** to continue.

4. On the **Merge Agent Location** screen, you are asked which machine should run the replication agents—at the distributor or at the subscriber. Because you want to create a pull subscription, select the **Run Each Agent at Its Subscriber** option, and click **Next**.

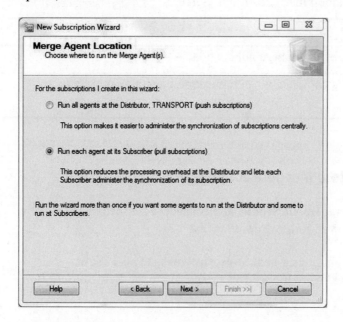

5. On the **Subscribers** screen, you can choose a subscriber for the publication. Check the box next to your server.

6. Then the drop-down list is populated with all the available databases on the subscriber. Select **New Database** from the list to open the New Database dialog box.

7. Enter **MR_Test** in the Database Name box, and click **OK**. Then click **Next**.

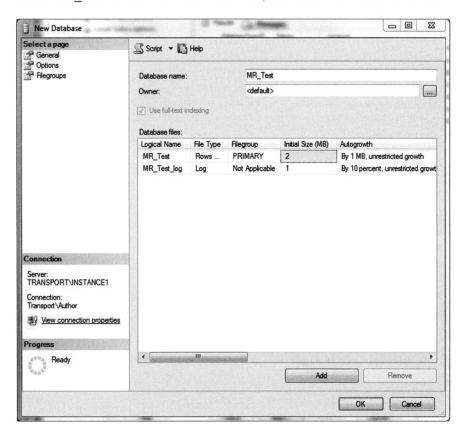

8. On the next screen you need to set the merge agent security. To do so, click the **ellipsis (...)** button in the **Subscription Properties** list.

9. Ordinarily you would create an account for the agent to run under, but to make the task simpler, you will run the agent using the SQL Server Agent service account, so select the radio button for that option, and click **OK**.

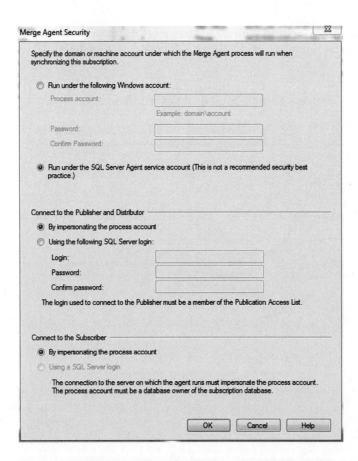

10.   Back at the **Merge Agent Security** screen, click **Next** to continue.

11.   The next step is to set the synchronization schedule, so select <**Define Schedule**>.

12.   In the **New Job Schedule** dialog box, make these changes:

   • Under Frequency, set **Occurs** to **Daily**

   • Under Daily Frequency, select **Occurs Every**, and set the interval to
   10 minutes.

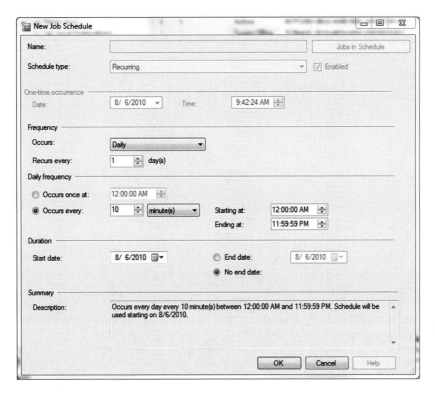

13.   Click **OK**.

14.   Back at the **Synchronization Schedule** screen, click **Next**.

15. On the next screen, you can tell SQL Server when to initialize the subscription, if at all. If you have already created the schema (an empty copy of the database to be replicated) on the subscriber, then you do not need to initialize the subscription. In this case, you should select **Immediately** from the drop-down list, make sure the **Initialize** box is checked, and click **Next** to continue.

16. The next screen shows you how conflicts will be resolved when they occur. In this case, select the defaults, and click **Next**.

17. On the **Wizard Actions** screen, you can have the wizard create the subscription, write a script to create the subscription that you can run later, or do both. Leave the **Create the Subscription(s)** box checked, and click **Next** to continue.

18. On the **Complete the Wizard** screen, review your options, and click **Finish** to create the subscription.

19. When the wizard is finished, click **Close**.

 Question 5 — *OK. You have transactional, snapshot, and merge as basic replication technologies and distributed transactions as a database engine technology. Which is best?*

■ PART B: Verifying Results

1. You should have several records in the Culture table. To verify that, open a new query, connect to the second instance, and execute the following code:

```
USE MR_Test
GO
SELECT * FROM Production.Culture
```

2. Now add a new record to the Production.Culture table in the AdventureWorks database on the default instance. Open a new query, and from the Query menu, select **Connection and Change Connection**. Then connect to the default instance.

3. Run the following code to add a new record:

```
USE AdventureWorks
GO
INSERT INTO Production.Culture (CultureID, Name)
VALUES('DE', 'German')
```

4. Wait about 10 minutes, and run the following query against the second instance:

```
USE MR_Test
GO
SELECT * FROM Production.Culture
```

5. One of the records in the result set should be the new DE record.

6. Now to test replication from the subscriber back to the publisher, run the following code on the second instance to add a new record:

```
USE MR_Test
GO
INSERT INTO Production.Culture (CultureID, Name)
VALUES('AL', 'Albanian')
```

7. Wait about 10 minutes, and run the following query against the default instance. You should see the new AL record:

```
USE AdventureWorks
GO
SELECT * FROM Production.Culture
```

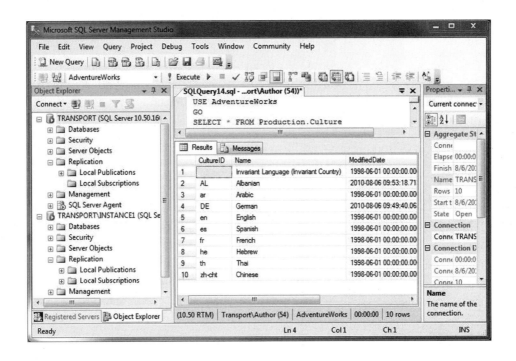

Exercise 20.10   Resolving Merge Conflicts

Scenario	You have created a merge publication and a corresponding subscription so employees at each of the four shops in Phoenix are able to share inventory with each other and automatically affect inventory. This has been working fine for some time, but recently two of the stores tried to get a part from a third store at the same time. This has caused a merge conflict that you need to resolve.
Duration	This task should take approximately 30 minutes.
Setup	For this task, you need access to the machine you installed SQL Server on in Exercise 2.1, the second instance of SQL Server installed in Exercise 2.2, the AdventureWorks database installed with the sample data, the default instance of SQL Server you configured as a distributor in Exercise 20.3, the merge publication you configured in Exercise 20.8, and a subscription to the merge publication you configured in Exercise 20.9.
Procedure	In this task, you will create and resolve a merge conflict.
Equipment	See Setup.
Objective	To create a merge conflict.
Criteria for Completion	This task is complete when you have successfully created and resolved a conflict in a merge publication.

■ PART A: Resolving Merge Conflicts

1. First you will update a record in the **Production.Culture** table in the **AdventureWorks** database on the default instance. Open a new query, and from the Query menu, select **Connection and Change Connection**. Then connect to the default instance.

2. Run the following (incorrect) code to update an existing record:

```
USE AdventureWorks
GO
UPDATE Production.Culture SET [Name] = 'Dutch'
WHERE CultureID = 'DE'
```

3. Now you will update the same record in the Production.Culture table in the MR_Test database on the second instance. Open a new query, and from the Query menu, and select **Connection and Change Connection**. Then connect to the second instance.

4. Run the following code to update an existing record:

```
USE MR_Test
GO
UPDATE Production.Culture SET [Name] = 'Danis'
WHERE CultureID = 'DE'
```

5. Wait about 10 minutes for the updates to apply before moving on to conflict resolution.

> **Question 6**
>
> *To make this work you must be able to define a business rule that has no exceptions. If New York and Atlanta each update a record but differently you can solve the problem if New York always, emphasis always, wins. How can you handle situations that cannot meet the "always" criterion?*

■ PART B: Viewing and Resolving Conflicts

1. In **Object Explorer**, expand **Replication**, **Publications**, right-click **the [AdventureWorks]: CulturePub** publication, and click **View Conflicts**.

2. In the **Select Conflict Table** dialog box, double-click the **Culture(1)** listing. The (1) denotes that there is one conflict.

3. In the **Microsoft Replication Conflict Viewer**, click the line under **Conflict Loser** in the top grid. This will change the data on the bottom to show you which record is the winner (currently displayed in all databases) and which is the loser (not shown to anyone).

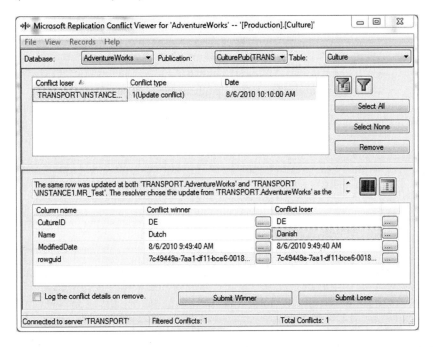

4. Click the **Submit Loser** button to accept the losing record and discard the winning record (that is, if Dutch is the winner, change it to Danish).

5. Click **OK** in the subsequent dialog box, and click **OK** again to exit the **Replication Conflict Viewer**.

■ **PART C: Verifying Results**

Confirm that there are no more conflicts listed in the dialog box.

Exercise 20.11	Monitoring Replication
Scenario	You have created several publications on your server at corporate headquarters, and you have created several subscriptions on servers throughout your enterprise. Many of these servers are scattered geographically, so it is difficult for you to go there in person to work with the subscriptions. To monitor and configure the publications and subscriptions remotely, you have decided to use Replication Monitor.
Duration	This task should take approximately 15 minutes.
Setup	For this task, you need access to the machine you installed SQL Server on in Exercise 2.1, the second instance of SQL Server installed in Exercise 2.2, the AdventureWorks database installed with the sample data, the default instance of SQL Server you configured as a distributor in Exercise 20.3, the transactional publication you configured in Exercise 20.4, and a subscription to the transactional publication you configured in Exercise 20.5.
Procedure	In this task, you will use the Replication Monitor to view replication status. You will insert a tracer record to monitor performance and set up a replication alert.
Equipment	See Setup.
Objective	To configure replication properties using the Replication Monitor.
Criteria for Completion	This task is complete when you have successfully viewed and configured replication properties using the Replication Monitor.

■ **PART A: Monitoring Replication**

1. Open **SQL Server Management Studio** on the distribution server, which is the default instance.

2. Right-click **Replication**, and select **Launch Replication Monitor**.

> **NOTE** *This is an executable that may be run separately from Management Studio. You can find it at …\Tools\Binn\sqlmonitor.exe.*

3.   Expand your server to view the publications available.

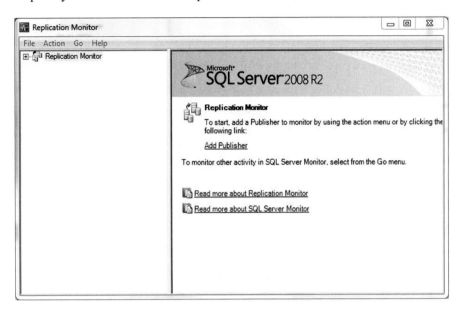

4.   Switch to the **Subscriptions Watch List** tab. From here you can view reports about the performance of all publications and subscriptions that this distributor handles.

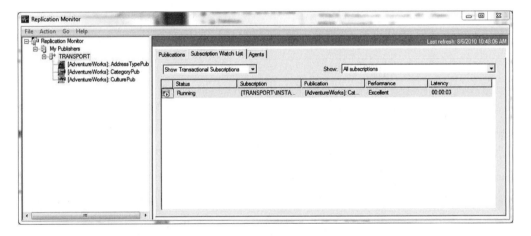

5.   Select the **CategoryPub** publication in the left pane.

6.   On the **All Subscriptions** tab, you can view reports about all the subscriptions for this particular publication.

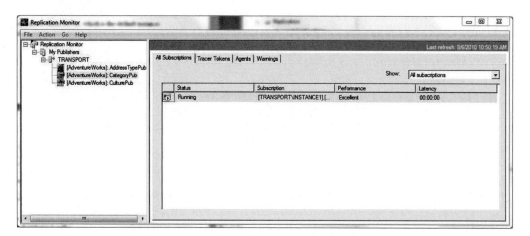

7. Switch to the **Tracer Tokens** tab. From here you can insert a special record called a tracer token that is used to measure performance for this subscription.

8. To test it, click the **Insert Tracer** button, and wait for the results.

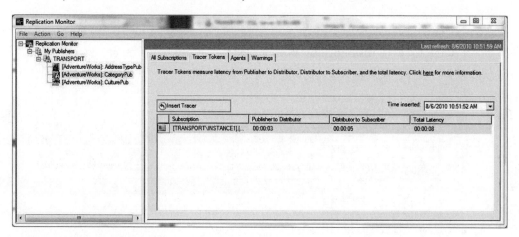

9. Switch to the **Warnings** tab. From here you can change settings for agents and configure replication alerts.

10. Click the **Configure Alerts** button, select **Replication: Agent Failure**, and click **Configure**.

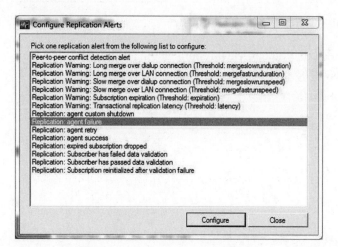

11.   Notice that this opens a new alert dialog box. Check the **Enable** box, and click
       OK to enable this alert.

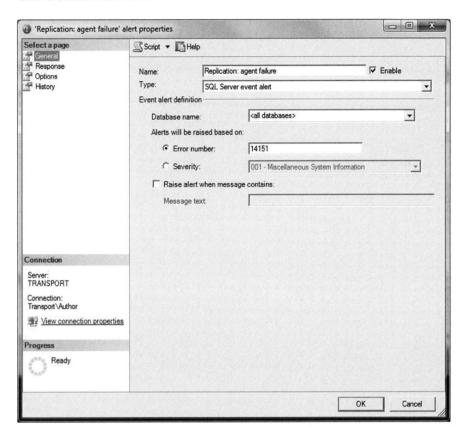

12.   Click **Close** to return to Replication Monitor.

13.   Close **Replication Monitor**.

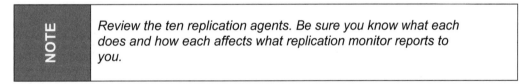

NOTE   *Review the ten replication agents. Be sure you know what each
        does and how each affects what replication monitor reports to
        you.*

■ PART B: Verifying Results

1.   Open **SQL Server Management Studio** on the distribution server, which is the
      default instance.

2.   In **Object Explorer**, expand your server, and then expand **SQL Server Agent**.

3.   Click **Alerts**, and you should see the **Replication: Agent Failure** alert in the
      right pane.

LAB 21
WORKING WITH INDEXES

This lab contains the following exercises and activities:

Exercise 21.1   Designing and Creating a Clustered Index

Exercise 21.2   Designing and Creating a Nonclustered Index

Exercise 21.3   Designing and Creating a Full-Text Index

Exercise 21.1	Designing and Creating a Clustered Index
Scenario	You have created a database for your sales department with a table that contains customer information. Your sales representatives have started complaining about slow access times. You know that the sales representatives look up customers based on their zip codes quite often, so you decide to create a clustered index on the Zip column of the Customers table to improve data access times.
Duration	This task should take approximately 15 minutes.
Setup	For this task, you need access to the machine you installed SQL Server on in Exercise 2.1, the Sales database you created in Exercise 5.1, and the Customers table you created in Exercise 6.1.
Caveat	Because this is just a test system and Customers is a small table with little data, you will not see a significant improvement in data access time.
Procedure	In this task, you will create a clustered index on the Customers table based on the Zip column.
Equipment	See Setup.

Objective	To create the new idx_cl_Zip clustered index.
Criteria for Completion	This task is complete when you have a clustered index on the Zip column of the Customers table in the Sales database.

■ PART A: Designing and Creating a Clustered Index

1. Open **SQL Server Management Studio**, and connect using Windows Authentication.

2. In **Object Explorer**, expand your server, and then expand **Databases**, **Sales**, **Tables**, and **dbo.Customers**.

3. Right-click **Indexes**, and select **New Index**.

4. In the **Index** name box, enter **idx_cl_Zip**.

5. Select **Clustered** for the index type.

6. Click the **Add** button next to the **Index Key Columns** grid.

7. Check the box next to the Zip column.

8.   Click **OK** to return to the New Index dialog box.

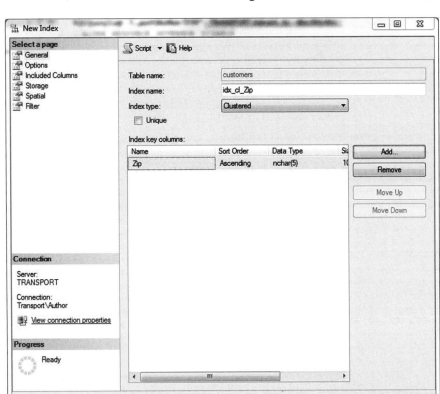

9.   Click **OK** to create the index.

Question 1	What happens when you try to create a second clustered index on a table? Try it on Customers.Lname.

■ PART B: Verifying Results

Expand **Databases**, **Sales**, **Tables**, **dbo.Customers**, **Indexes**, and you should see the idx_cl_Zip index listed.

Exercise 21.2	Designing and Creating a Nonclustered Index
Scenario	You have created a database for your sales department with a table that contains customer information. You want to make sure data access is as fast as possible. After some investigation, you have discovered that your sales representatives consistently search for customer information by searching for a last name. Because they search only for a single record at a time, you decide to create a nonclustered index on the Lname column of the Customers table to improve data access times.
Duration	This task should take approximately 15 minutes.

Setup	For this task, you need access to the machine you installed SQL Server on in Exercise 2.1, the Sales database you created in Exercise 5.1, and the Customers table you created in Exercise 6.1.
Caveat	Because this is just a test system and Customers is a small table with little data, you will not see a significant improvement in data access time.
Procedure	In this task, you will create a nonclustered index on the Customers table based on the Zip column.
Equipment	See Setup.
Objective	To create the new idx_ncl_Lname nonclustered index.
Criteria for Completion	This task is complete when you have a nonclustered index on the Lname column of the Customers table in the Sales database.

■ PART A: Designing and Creating a Nonclustered Index

1. Open **SQL Server Management Studio**, and connect using Windows Authentication.

2. In **Object Explorer**, expand your server, and then expand **Databases, Sales, Tables, dbo.Customers**.

3. Right-click **Indexes**, and select **New Index**.

4. In the **Index Name** box, enter **idx_ncl_Lname**.

5. Select **Nonclustered** for the index type.

6. Click the **Add** button next to the Index Key Columns grid.

7.   Check the box next to the Lname column.

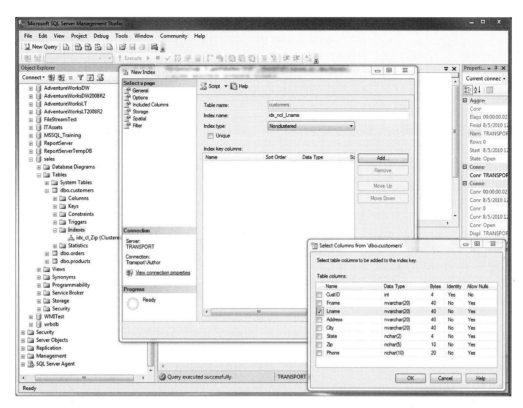

8.   Click **OK** to return to the New Index dialog box.

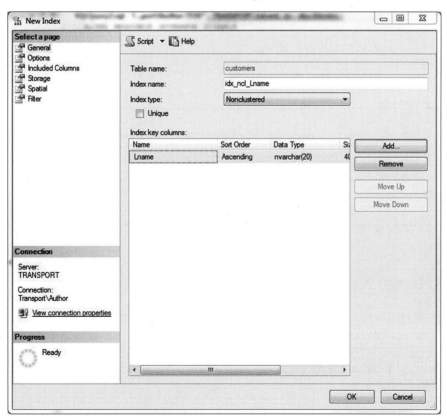

9. Click **OK** to create the index.

Question 2	*What happens when you try to create a second nonclustered index on a table? Try it on Customers.Fname.*

■ PART B: Verifying Results

Expand **Databases, Sales, Tables, dbo.Customers, Indexes,** and you should see the idx_ncl_Lname index listed.

Exercise 21.3	Designing and Creating a Full-Text Index
Scenario	One of the databases that your company has been using for some time contains a table that stores large documents. Your users have been using standard SELECT statements to access the documents in this table, but that method is proving too slow now that the table is starting to grow. You want to make sure users can query the table and get results as quickly and easily as possible, so you decide to create a full-text index on the table.
Duration	This task should take approximately 20 minutes.
Setup	For this task, you need access to the machine you installed SQL Server on in Exercise 2.1 and the AdventureWorks database that is installed with the sample data.
Procedure	In this task, you will create a full-text catalog and index on the Production.Document table of the AdventureWorks database.
Equipment	See Setup.
Objective	To create the new full-text catalog and index on the Production.Document table.
Criteria for Completion	This task is complete when you have a full-text index on the Production.Document table of the AdventureWorks database.

■ PART A: Designing and Creating a Full-Text Index

1. Open **SQL Server Management Studio,** and in **Object Explorer,** expand **Databases, AdventureWorks,** and **Tables.**

2. Right-click **Production.Document,** move to **Full-Text Index,** and click **Define Full-Text Index.**

3. On the first screen of the **Full-Text Indexing Wizard,** click **Next.**

4.   Each table on which you create a full-text index must already have a unique index (primary key) associated with it for the FullText Search service to work. In this instance, select the default **PK_Document_DocumentID** index, and click **Next**.

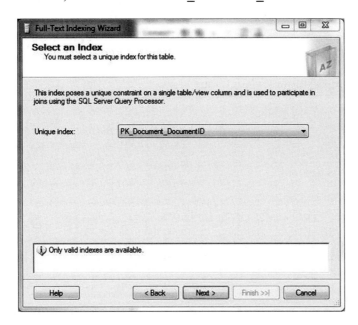

5.   On the next screen, you are asked which column you want to full-text index. DocumentSummary is the only nvarchar(max) column in the table, so it is the best candidate; select the box next to it, and click Next.

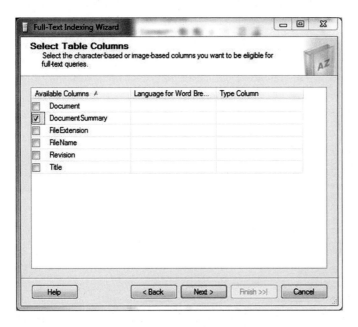

6.   On the next screen, you are asked when you want changes to the full-text index applied:

   • **Automatically** means the full-text index is updated with every change made to the table. This is the fastest, least-hassle way to keep full-text indexes up to date, but it can tax the server because it means the changes to the table and index take place all at once.

- **Manually** means changes to the underlying data are maintained, but you will have to schedule index population yourself. This is a slightly slower way to update the index, but it is not as taxing on the server because changes to the data are maintained but the index is not updated immediately.

- **Do Not Track Changes** means changes to the underlying data are not tracked. This is the least taxing, and slowest, way to update the full-text index. Changes are not maintained, so when the index is updated, the FullText Search service must read the entire table for changes before updating the index.

7. Choose **Automatically**, and click **Next**.

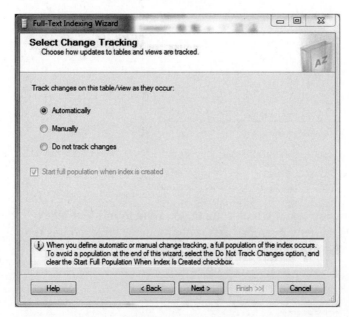

8. The next screen asks you to select a catalog. You'll need to create one here, because you don't have any available. In the Name field, enter **AdventureWorks Catalog.** You can also select a filegroup to place the catalog on; leave this as default, and click **Next.**

9. On the next screen, you are asked to create a schedule for automatically repopulating the full-text index. If your data is frequently updated, you will want to do this more often, maybe once a day. If it is read more often than it is changed, you should repopulate less frequently. You can schedule population for a single table or an entire catalog at a time. Here, you will set repopulation to happen just once for the entire catalog by clicking the **New Catalog Schedule** button.

10. On the **New Full-Text Indexing Catalog Schedule** Properties screen, enter **Populate AdventureWorks**, and click **OK**.

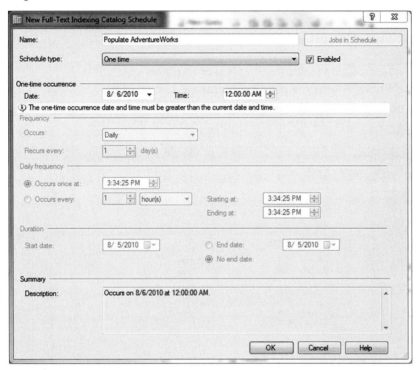

11. When you are taken back to the **Full-Text Indexing Wizard**, click **Next**.

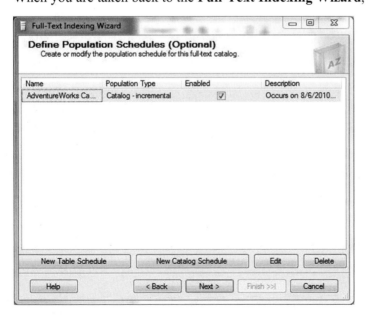

12.   On the final screen of the wizard, you are given a summary of the choices you
have made. Click **Finish** to create the index.

> **NOTE**
>
> *If you work for ABC Corporation, it does no good to include ABC
> and words like "the" and "and" and "it" as each will have too many
> hits to be useful. Include these kinds of terms in the Noise Words
> file or as Stopwords in the Stoplist to exclude them.*

■ PART B: Verifying Results

1.   To see your new catalog and index, in **Object Explorer** expand
AdventureWorks, **Storage**, **Full-Text Catalogs**.

2.   Double-click the **AdventureWorks** catalog to open its properties.

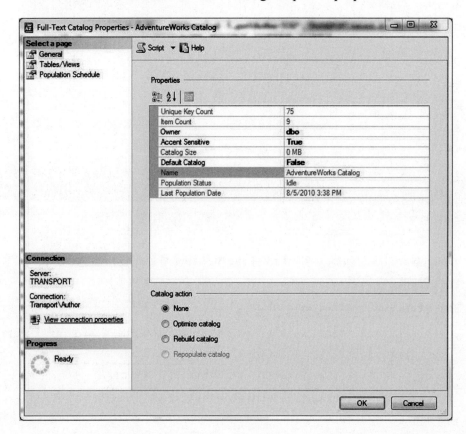

LAB 22
WORKING WITH TRANSACTIONS AND LOCKS

This lab contains the following exercise and activity:

Exercise 22.1   Identifying and Rectifying the Cause of a Block

Exercise 22.1	Identifying and Rectifying the Cause of a Block
Scenario	You have a SQL Server instance that has been running fine for several months. Recently, though, your developers created some new stored procedures and pushed them into production. When only a few users are connected to the system, everything runs fine, but when the traffic starts to pick up, users start complaining that they cannot access data. The most common complaint is that when the user tries to retrieve data, the system seems to hang and the query never completes. You recognize this as a block, and you decide to troubleshoot it using the sys.dm_exec_requests system view and the KILL command.
Duration	This task should take approximately 20 minutes.
Setup	For this task, you need access to the machine you installed SQL Server on in Exercise 2.1 and the AdventureWorks database installed with the sample data.
Procedure	In this task, you will simulate a blocking condition using the TABLOCKX and HOLDLOCK query hints. This tells SQL Server to place an exclusive lock on the table and hold the lock until the query completes, which will block other users from accessing the table in question. You will then query the sys.dm_exec_requests system view to find the blocking session ID and use the KILL command to end the session and release the lock.

Equipment	See Setup.
Objective	To simulate a block, troubleshoot it, and rectify it.
Criteria for Completion	This task is complete when you have simulated a block, queried the sys.dm_exec_requests system view to find the errant session, and used the KILL command to end it.

■ PART A: Setting Up the Laboratory Exercise

1. Open **SQL Server Management Studio** and start a new query.

2. Enter and execute the following Transact-SQL code:

```
USE AdventureWorks
GO
CREATE TABLE dbo.TestTable
(
RowNumber int null,
TextData char(10) null
)
GO
INSERT TestTable (RowNumber) VALUES (1)
GO
```

■ PART B: Identifying and Rectifying the Cause of a Block

1. To start a locking session, open a new query in SQL Server Management Studio, and execute this command:

```
USE AdventureWorks
GO
BEGIN TRAN
SELECT * FROM TestTable WITH (TABLOCKX, HOLDLOCK)
```

> **NOTE** *The WITH (TABLOCKX, HOLDLOCK) are called Table Hints. These are provided to the Query Optimizer, which takes them as orders.*

2. Now to create a blocked session, open a new query, and execute this code:

```
USE AdventureWorks
GO
UPDATE TestTable SET TextData = 'test' WHERE RowNumber = 1
```

3. Notice that the second query does not complete because the first query is holding an exclusive lock on the table. To find the session that is doing the blocking, open a third query window.

4. In the third query window, query the sys.dm_exec_requests system view for any session that is being blocked with this code:

```
SELECT session_id, status, blocking_session_id
FROM sys.dm_exec_requests WHERE blocking_session_id > 0
```

5. The blocking_session_id is the session causing the problem. To end it, execute the KILL command with the blocking_session_id value. For example, if the blocking_session_id is 53, you would execute this:

```
KILL 53
```

6. Switch to the second query (from Step 2); it should now be complete with one row affected.

■ PART C: Verifying Results

If you were successful, the query from Step 6 in Part B will complete with one row affected.

LAB 23
MOVING DATA

This lab contains the following exercise and activity:

Exercise 23.1   Using the Copy Database Wizard

Exercise 23.1	Using the Copy Database Wizard
Scenario	Your company has a SQL Server instance in production and another SQL Server instance that is reserved specifically for development and testing. Your developers have been hard at work on a new database for several weeks, and they are now ready to move the database from the development server to the production server. You have decided to use the Copy Database Wizard to accomplish the task.
Duration	This task should take approximately 15 minutes.
Setup	For this task, you need access to the machine you installed SQL Server on in Exercise 2.1 and the Second instance of SQL Server you installed in Exercise 2.2.
Caveat	The SQL Server Agent service must be running on both the default instance and the second instance for this to be successful.
Procedure	In this task, you'll copy the JobTest database from the default instance of SQL Server to the second instance using the Copy Database Wizard.
Equipment	See Setup.
Objective	To copy the JobTest database using the Copy Database Wizard.
Criteria for Completion	This task is complete when you have successfully copied the JobTest database from the default instance of SQL Server to the second instance using the Copy Database Wizard.

■ PART A: Creating the Jobtest Database

1.   Open **SQL Server Management Studio** by selecting it from the Microsoft SQL Server group. Connect and open a **New Query**.

2.   Enter the following Transact-SQL code into the Query Editor to create the JobTest database:

```
CREATE DATABASE JobTest ON PRIMARY (NAME = JobTest_dat,
FILENAME = 'C:\Practice\JobTest.mdf', SIZE = 10 MB, MAXSIZE = 15,
FILEGROWTH = 10%)
```

3.   Click the **Execute** button.

4.   If necessary, click on **Databases** in **Object Explorer** and press **F5** to refresh the display.

■ PART B: Using the Copy Database Wizard

> **NOTE**
>
> *The destination server must be running SQL Server 2005 Service Pack 2 or a later version to use all of the features of the wizard. This exercise uses basic features. Also, the wizard may be run on a computer separate from the source or destination servers.*

1.   Open **SQL Server Management Studio** by selecting it from the Microsoft SQL Server group under Programs on the Start menu, expand your server, and expand Databases.

2.   Right-click the **JobTest** database, go to **Tasks**, and select **Copy Database**. You will see the welcome screen.

3.   Click **Next**.

4. On the second screen, you are asked to select a source server. Select the default instance of your server and the proper authentication type (usually Windows Authentication), and click **Next**.

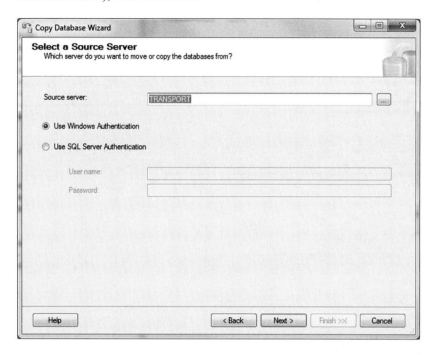

5. On the next screen, you need to select a destination, so click the ellipsis button, Click the Second instance, and click **OK**. Choose the appropriate security, and click **Next**.

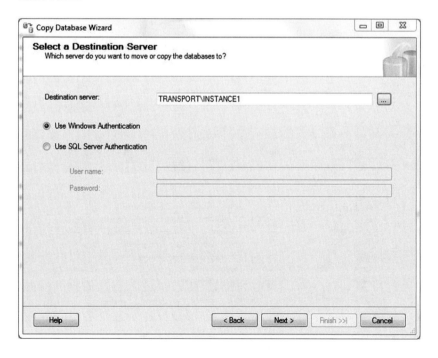

6. Next you are asked which method you would like to use. Attach/detach is useful for copying databases between servers that are in remote locations from each other; it requires the database to be taken offline. The SQL Management Object transfer method allows you to keep the database online and gives you the flexibility to make a copy on the same server, so select the **SQL Management Object Method** option, and click **Next**.

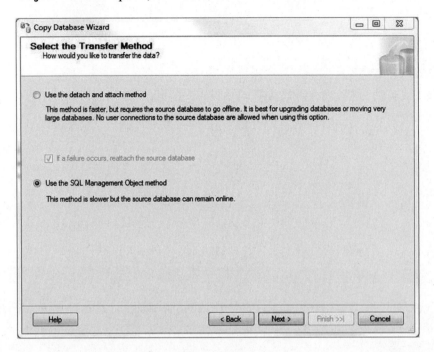

7. Next you are asked which database you would like to move or copy. Check the **Copy** box next to **JobTest**, and click **Next**.

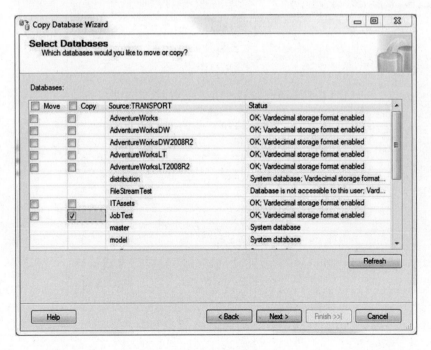

8. On the **Configure Destination Database** screen, accept the defaults, and click **Next**.

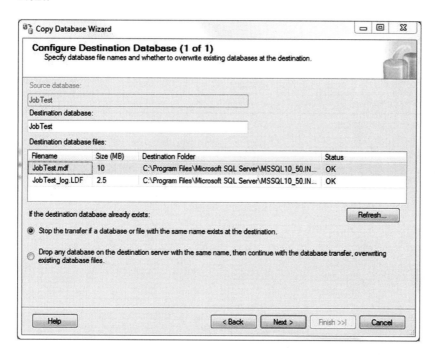

9. On the next screen, you are given the option to copy additional database objects. This is especially useful if the destination server does not have all the logins required to access the database or if additional stored procedures are used for business logic in your applications. Leave the defaults here, and click **Next**.

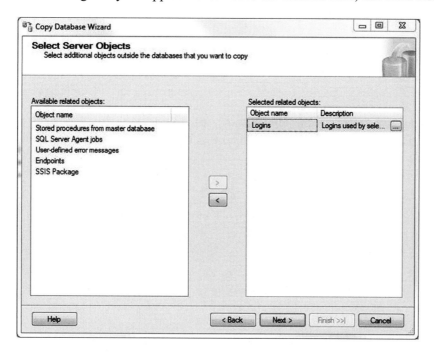

10. You now have the option to change the name of the package that will be created; this matters only if you plan to save the package and execute it later. Accept the defaults, and click **Next**.

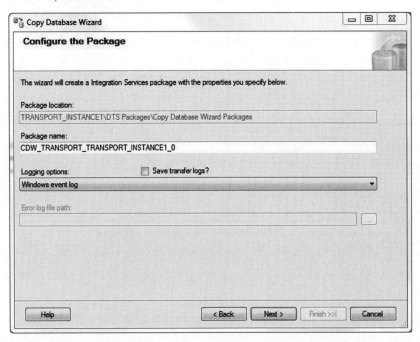

11. On the next screen, you are asked when you would like to run the SSIS job created by the wizard. Select **Run Immediately**, and click **Next**.

12. The final screen summarizes the choices you have made. Click **Finish** to copy the Test database.

13. You will see the **Log Detail** screen, which shows you each section of the job as it executes. Clicking the **Report** button will show each step of the job and its outcome.

14. Click **Close** on the **Performing Operation** screen to complete the wizard.

■ PART C: Verifying Results

You should see the **JobTest** database listed in **Object Explorer** under **Databases** on the second instance.

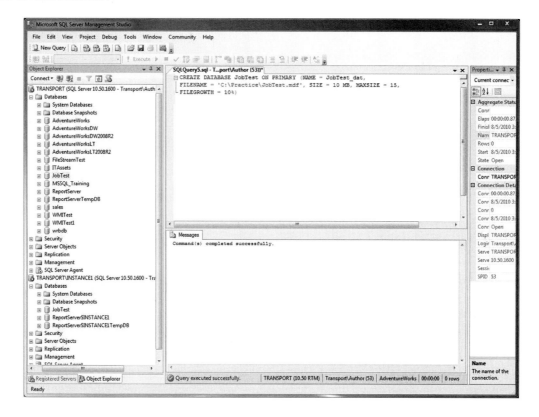

LAB 24
WORKING WITH XML DATA

This lab contains the following exercise and activity:

Exercise 24.1   Using the XML Data Type

Exercise 24.1	Using the XML Data Type
Scenario	Your company has asked you to work with a business-to-business customer who wants to share data using XML. You need to get up to speed using this technology.
Duration	This task should take approximately 30 minutes.
Setup	For this task, you need access to the machine you installed SQL Server on in Exercise 2.1.and to the database you created in Exercise 5.1.
Caveat	The SQL Server Agent service must be running on the default instance.
Procedure	In this task, you'll create a new table with a XML data type column, add some data, and then manipulate the data.
Equipment	See Setup.
Objective	To create a new table, add and then manipulate XML data.
Criteria for Completion	This task is complete when you have successfully performed a query method, value method, exist method, and modify method.

■ PART A: To Declare an XML Column

1. In the **Connect to Database Engine** dialog box, specify the following values, and then click **Connect**.

Property	Value
Server type	Database Engine
Server name	\<YourServerName\>
Authentication	Windows Authentication

2. Use the following code to create a table with an XML column:

```
-- Create a table with an xml column
USE Sales
GO
CREATE TABLE      Invoices
(InvoiceID        int,
SalesDate         datetime,
CustomerID        int,
ItemList          xml);
```

3. On the toolbar, click **Execute**. This creates a table with a column for untyped XML.

■ PART B: To Implicitly Cast a String to XML

1. Use the following code to assign an XML variable and column:

```
-- Use implicit casting to assign an xml variable and column
DECLARE @itemString nvarchar(2000)
SET @itemString = '<Items>
<Item ProductID="2" Quantity="3"/>
<Item ProductID="4" Quantity="1"/>
</Items>'
DECLARE @itemDoc xml
SET @itemDoc = @itemString
INSERT INTO Invoices
VALUES (1, GetDate(), 2, @itemDoc)
INSERT INTO Invoices
VALUES
(1, GetDate(), 2, '<Items>
<Item ProductID="2" Quantity="3"/>
<Item ProductID="4" Quantity="1"/>
</Items>')
SELECT * FROM Invoices
```

2. On the toolbar, click **Execute**. This code assigns an nvarchar variable to an XML variable and inserts it into the table. The code then inserts a string constant into the XML column directly.

3. Review the results, noting that the XML string has been stored in the table for both INSERT statements.

■ PART C: To Insert a Well-Formed Document

1. Perform the following steps to insert a well-formed document into the XML data type. This will succeed:

```
-- Well-formed document. This will succeed
INSERT INTO Invoices
VALUES
(1, GetDate(), 2, '<?xml version="1.0" ?>
<Items>
<Item ProductID="2" Quantity="3"/>
<Item ProductID="4" Quantity="1"/>
</Items>')
```

2. On the toolbar, click **Execute**. This code inserts a well-formed XML document into the table. Then:

```
SELECT * FROM Invoices
```

3. Click **Execute**. Review the results, noting that the XML string has been stored in the table. Note also that the XML version information is not stored.

■ PART D: To Attempt to Insert XML That Is Not Well Formed

1. Perform the following steps to attempt to insert XML that is not well formed into the XML data type. This will fail:

```
-- Not well formed. This will fail
INSERT INTO Invoices
VALUES
(1, GetDate(), 2, '<Items>
<Item ProductID="2" Quantity="3"/>
<Item ProductID="4" Quantity="1"/>')
```

2. On the toolbar, click **Execute**. This code attempts to insert a string that is not well-formed XML into the table.

3. Review the results, noting that the insert failed.

■ PART E: To Execute XML Methods

1. Perform the following steps to create a table with an XML column named Invoices and populate the table with data:

```
-- Create a table that includes xml data
USE Sales
CREATE TABLE Stores
(StoreID integer IDENTITY PRIMARY KEY,
StoreName nvarchar(40),
Manager nvarchar(40),
Invoices xml)
INSERT INTO Stores
VALUES
('Astro Mountain Bike Company', 'Jeff Adell', '<InvoiceList
xmlns="http://schemas.adventure-works.com/Invoices">
<Invoice InvoiceNo="1000">
<Customer>Kim Abercrombie</Customer>
<Items>
<Item Product="1" Price="1.99" Quantity="2"/>
<Item Product="3" Price="2.49" Quantity="1"/>
</Items>
</Invoice>
<Invoice InvoiceNo="1001">
<Customer>Sean Chai</Customer>
<Items>
<Item Product="1" Price="2.45" Quantity="2"/>
</Items>
</Invoice>
</InvoiceList>')
INSERT INTO Stores
VALUES
('Clocktower Sporting Goods', 'Karen Berge', '<InvoiceList
xmlns="http://schemas.adventure-works.com/Invoices">
<Invoice InvoiceNo="999">
<Customer>Sarah Akhtar</Customer>
<Items>
<Item Product="8" Price="2.99" Quantity="3"/>
</Items>
</Invoice>
<Invoice InvoiceNo="1000">
```

```
<Customer>Bei-Jing Guo</Customer>
<Items>
<Item Product="1" Price="1.95" Quantity="7"/>
<Item Product="100" Price="112.99" Quantity="1"/>
</Items>
</Invoice>
</InvoiceList>')
INSERT INTO Stores
VALUES
('HiaBuy Toys', 'Scott Cooper', NULL)
```

2. On the toolbar, click **Execute** to execute the entire script.

■ PART F: To Examine the Results of the Query Method

1. This code uses the query method in a SELECT statement to retrieve XML data from the Invoices column:

```
-- Use the query method
SELECT StoreName, Invoices.query('declare default element
namespace "http://schemas.adventure-works.com/Invoices";
<SoldItems>
{ for $i in /InvoiceList/Invoice/Items/Item
return $i }
</SoldItems>') SoldItems
FROM Stores
```

2. In the results pane, examine the results returned by the SELECT statement. The result set has two columns—StoreName and SoldItems.

■ PART G: To Examine the Results of the Value Method

1. This code uses the value method in a SELECT statement to retrieve a single value from the Invoices column:

```
-- Use the value method
SELECT StoreName, Invoices.value('declare default element
namespace
"http://schemas.adventure-works.com/Invoices";
(InvoiceList/Invoice/@InvoiceNo)[1]', 'int') FirstInvoice
FROM Stores
```

2. In the results pane, examine the results returned by the SELECT statement. The result set has two columns—StoreName and FirstInvoice.

■ PART H: To Examine the Results of the Exist Method

1. This code uses the exist method in a SELECT statement to find rows that contain an Invoice element in the Invoices column:

```
-- Use the exist method
SELECT StoreName StoresWithInvoices
FROM Stores
WHERE Invoices.exist('declare default element namespace
"http://schemas.adventure-works.com/Invoices";
InvoiceList/Invoice') = 1
```

2. In the results pane, examine the results returned by the SELECT statement. The result set has one column named StoresWithInvoices.

■ PART I: To Examine the Results of Binding Relational Columns

1. This code uses the query method in a SELECT statement to retrieve XML data that includes the StoreName relational column:

```
-- Bind a relational column
SELECT Invoices.query('declare default element namespace
"http://schemas.adventure-works.com/Invoices";
<Invoices>
<Store>{sql:column("StoreName")}</Store>
{ for $i in /InvoiceList/Invoice
return $i }
</Invoices>') InvoicesWithStoreName
FROM Stores
```

2. In the results pane, examine the results returned by the SELECT statement. (The result set has a single column, InvoicesWithStoreName.)

■ PART J: To Examine the Results of Using the Modify Method to Insert XML

1. Use the modify method to insert XML. This code uses the modify method in an UPDATE statement to insert a SalesPerson element into the Invoice column. The modified XML is then returned by a SELECT statement:

```
-- Use the modify method to insert xml
UPDATE Stores
SET Invoices.modify('declare default element namespace
"http://schemas.adventure-works.com/Invoices";
```

```
insert element SalesPerson {"Alice"}
as first into (/InvoiceList/Invoice)[1]')
WHERE StoreID = 1
SELECT Invoices.query('declare default element namespace
 "http://schemas.adventure-works.com/Invoices";
(InvoiceList/Invoice)[1]') InsertedSalesPerson
FROM Stores WHERE StoreID = 1
```

> **NOTE**
>
> *This exercise uses basic features. Also, the wizard may be run on a computer You have learned that Transact-SQL code is case insensitive but that is not necessarily true of CLR code. Try this: change the word insert in the fifth line of code to INSERT. Block this code segment and check the syntax (CNTL-F5 or click the blue check mark next to the execute button in the Query Editor). The code passes. Now Execute. The code fails. You now know that the syntax check itself is case insensitive even when the code itself is case sensitive.*

2. In the results pane, examine the results returned by the SELECT statement. The result set has a single column—InsertedSalesPerson.

■ PART K: To Examine the Results of Using the Modify Method to Update XML

1. This code uses the modify method in an UPDATE statement to update a SalesPerson element in the Invoice column. The modified XML is then returned by a SELECT statement:

```
-- Use the modify method to update xml
UPDATE Stores
SET Invoices.modify('declare default element namespace
"http://schemas.adenture-works.com/Invoices";
replace value of (/InvoiceList/Invoice/SalesPerson/text())[1]
with "Holly"') WHERE StoreID = 1
SELECT Invoices.query('declare default element namespace
"http://schemas.adventure-works.com/Invoices";
(InvoiceList/Invoice)[1]') UpdatedSalesPerson
FROM Stores
WHERE StoreID = 1
```

2. In the results pane, examine the results returned by the SELECT statement. The result set has a single column—UpdatedSalesPerson.

■ PART L: To Examine the Results of Using the Modify Method to Delete XML

1. This code uses the modify method in an UPDATE statement to delete a SalesPerson element in the Invoice column. The modified XML is then returned by a SELECT statement:

```
-- Use the modify method to delete xml
UPDATE Stores
SET Invoices.modify('declare default element namespace
"http://schemas.adventure-works.com/Invoices";
delete (/InvoiceList/Invoice/SalesPerson)[1]')
WHERE StoreID = 1
SELECT Invoices.query('declare default element namespace
"http://schemas.adventure-works.com/Invoices";
(InvoiceList/Invoice)[1]') DeletedSalesPerson
FROM Stores WHERE StoreID = 1
```

2. In the results pane, examine the results returned by the SELECT statement. The result set has a single column—DeletedSalesPerson.

■ PART M: To Examine the Results of Using the Nodes Method

1. This code uses the nodes method with the APPLY operator to extract relational data from an XML column:

```
-- Use the nodes method to extract relational data
SELECT nCol.value('../../@InvoiceNo[1]', 'int') InvoiceNo,
nCol.value('@Product[1]', 'int') ProductID,
nCol.value('@Price[1]', 'money') Price,
nCol.value('@Quantity[1]', 'int') Quantity
FROM Stores CROSS APPLY Invoices.nodes('declare default element
namespace
"http://schemas.adventure-works.com/Invoices";
/InvoiceList/Invoice/Items/Item') AS nTable(nCol)
ORDER BY InvoiceNo
```

2. In the results pane, examine the results returned by the SELECT statement. The resultset has four columns—InvoiceNo, ProductID, Price, and Quantity.

3. Close SQL Server Management Studio and Windows Explorer. Click No if prompted to save files when closing SQL Server Management Studio.

LAB 25
WORKING WITH HIGH-AVAILABILITY METHODS

This lab contains the following exercises and activities:

Exercise 25.1	Implementing Database Mirroring
Exercise 25.2	Implementing Log Shipping
Exercise 25.3	Creating a Database Snapshot
Exercise 25.4	Reverting from a Database Snapshot

Exercise 25.1	Implementing Database Mirroring
Scenario	You created a database for your sales department several months ago, and your sales staff has started to rely on it quite heavily. In fact, if the database were to go down, your sales managers have told you that their staff would not be able to get their work done. This means lost sales, lost productivity, and possibly even lost customers. This is not something you can let happen; you know that the database must be available to your sales staff at all times because the sales representatives make sales calls at all hours of the day and night. To ensure that the database is always available, you decide to implement a high-safety database mirror.
Duration	This task should take approximately 60 minutes.
Setup	For this task, you need access to the machine you installed SQL Server on in Exercise 2.1, the second instance of SQL Server you installed in Exercise 2.2, and the Sales database you created in Exercise 5.1

Caveat	Even though everyone started the class with the same setup, a variety of configurations have doubtless resulted by the time this exercise starts. You may have named your instances differently than other students. Therefore, start by creating a table for personal reference:
	<table><tr><td>*Instance Name*</td><td>*Role*</td></tr><tr><td></td><td>Principle</td></tr><tr><td></td><td>Mirror</td></tr></table>
Procedure	In this task, you will make a backup of the Sales database and then restore it to the second instance of SQL Server in the RECOVERY state. You will then create a high-safety database mirror of the Sales database on the second instance.
Equipment	See Setup.
Objective	To implement database mirroring.
Criteria for Completion	This task is complete when you have successfully mirrored the Sales database from the default instance on your machine to the second instance.

■ PART A: Backing Up the Sales Database from the Default Instance

1. Open **SQL Server Management Studio**, expand **Databases**, right-click **Sales**, point to **Tasks**, and click **Back Up**.

2. In the **Back Up** dialog box, make sure **Sales** is the selected database to back up and **Backup Type** is **Full**.

3. Leave the default name in the **Name** box. In the **Description** box, enter **Full Backup of Sales**.

4. Under **Destination**, a disk device may already be listed. If so, select the device, and click **Remove**.

5. Under **Destination**, click **Add**.

6. In the **Select Backup Destination** box, click **File Name**, and in the text box enter **C:\Practice\Sales.bak**. Click **OK**.

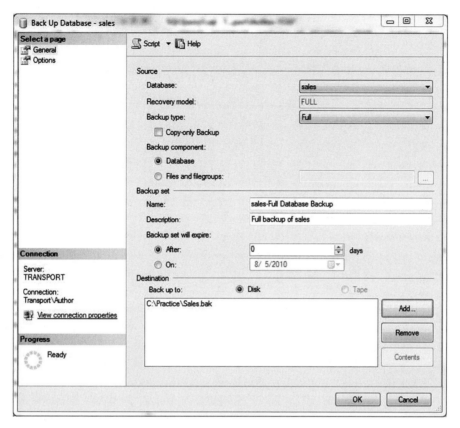

7. Click **OK** to start the backup.

8. When the backup is complete, you will get a notification; click **OK** to close it.

■ PART B: Backing Up the Transaction Log

1. Open **SQL Server Management Studio**, expand **Databases**, right-click **Sales**, point to **Tasks**, and click **Back Up**.

2. In the **Back Up** dialog box, make sure **Sales** is the selected database to back up and **Backup Type** is **Transaction Log**.

3. Leave the default name in the **Name** box. In the **Description** box, enter **Transaction Log Backup of Sales**.

4. Make sure **C:\Practice\Sales.bak** is the only device listed, and click **OK**.

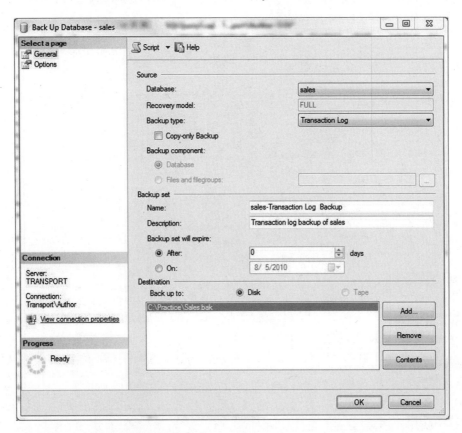

5. Click **OK** to start the backup.

6. When the backup is complete, you will get a notification; click **OK** to close it.

■ PART C: Restoring the Database to the Second Instance

> **NOTE**
>
> *In a production environment you need two servers each with a licensed copy of SQL Server and each must be the same edition: standard-to-standard or enterprise-to-enterprise. A witness server also requires a copy of SQL Server, which can be another production server or even Express Edition running on a workstation.*

1. Open **SQL Server Management Studio**, and connect to the second instance by selecting **Server\Instance1** from the Server Name drop-down list. One way to get there is by clicking **Connect** in your Object Explorer. The Connect to Server dialog box appears. Choose **Database Engine**, then Server name.

2. Right-click **Databases**, and select **Restore Database**.

3. Enter **Sales** in the **To Database** box.

4. Under **Source for restore**, select **From Device**. Click the **ellipsis (…)** button next to the text box to select a device.

5. In the Specify Backup dialog box, select **File** from the **Backup media** drop-down list box, and click **Add**.

6. In the **Locate Backup File** dialog box, find the Sales.bak file, and click **OK**.

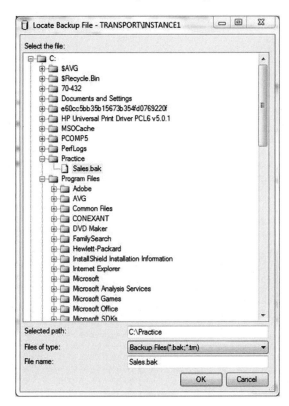

7. Click **OK** to close the Specify Backup dialog box.

8. Under **Select the Backup Sets to Restore**, check the boxes for both backups of Sales.

9. On the **Options** page, in the **Restore the Database Files As** grid, under the **Restore As** column, make these changes:

    *   Change Sales_data.mdf to Sales_data_mir.mdf
    *   Change Sales_data2.ndf to Sales_data_mir2.ndf
    *   Change Sales_data3.ndf to Sales_data_mir3.ndf
    *   Change Sales_log.ldf to Sales_log_mir.ldf.

10. Also on the **Options** page, make sure the **RESTORE WITH NORECOVERY** option is selected.

11. Click **OK** to begin the restore process.

12. Click **OK** in the dialog box that opens after the restore is complete.

■ PART D: Configuring Database Mirroring

1. Open **SQL Server Management Studio**, and connect to the default instance.

2. Expand **Databases**, right-click **Sales**, point to Tasks, and click **Mirror**.

3. Click the **Configure Security** button to start the Configure Database Mirroring Security Wizard, which will create the endpoints required for mirroring.

4. On the welcome screen, click **Next**.

5. Select **No** on the **Include Witness Server** screen, and then click **Next**.

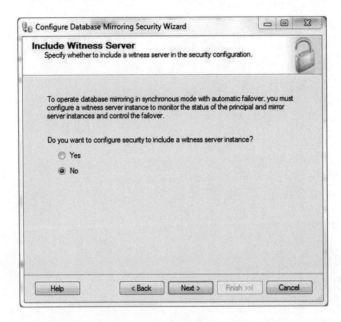

6. On the **Principal Server Instance** screen, note the settings and click **Next**.

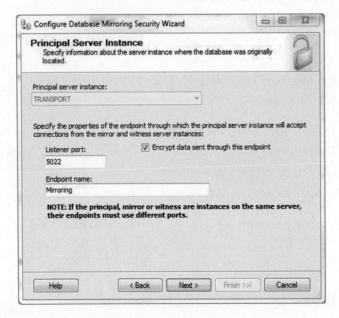

7. On the **Mirror Server Instance** screen, select the second instance of SQL
    Server, and click the **Connect** button. Then click **Connect**. Accept the defaults
    that are filled in for you, and click **Next**.

8. On the **Service Accounts** screen, leave both account names blank because you
    configured the services to use the same accounts. Click **Next**.

9. On the **Complete the Wizard** screen, click **Finish**.

10. Click **Close** when the wizard is complete.

11. In the **Database Properties** dialog box that opens, click **Start Mirroring**.

12. Click **OK** to close the **Database Properties** dialog box.

Question 1	*How quickly can the mirror respond to users after the production server fails? Compare with restoring from a full backup to a cold standby server. How quickly can you restore services to users without mirroring?*

■ PART E: Verifying Results

1. Connect to both instances and look at the **Sales** database in **Object Explorer**.

2. On the default instance, you should see (Principal, Synchronized) next to the Sales database.

3. On the Second instance you should see (Mirror, Synchronized/Restoring) next to Sales.

4. The label for the Sales database will show you what role it plays in the database-mirroring session.

Exercise 25.2	Implementing Log Shipping
Scenario	Your accounting department has come to rely on SQL Server to get their work done. They need it to be up and running at all times during the day, so you know you need to implement some form of high availability. In the past, some contract workers, who were not familiar with your systems, accidentally updated the data incorrectly, and you do not want future mistakes to be propagated to the standby server right away. Bearing this in mind, you decide to implement log shipping so you can control the delay of the restore on the secondary server.
Duration	This task should take approximately 60 minutes.
Setup	For this task, you need access to the machine you installed SQL Server on in Exercise 2.1, the second instance of SQL Server you installed in Exercise 2.2, and the AdventureWorks database installed with the sample data.
Procedure	In this task, you will make a backup of the AdventureWorks database and restore it to the second instance of SQL Server in the RECOVERY state. You will then ship the AdventureWorks database logs to the second instance.
Equipment	See Setup.
Objective	To back up the AdventureWorks database from the default instance.
Criteria for Completion	This task is complete when you have successfully configured log shipping for the AdventureWorks database from the default instance on your machine to the second instance.

■ PART A: Backing Up Adventureworks from the Default Instance

1. Open **SQL Server Management Studio**, expand **Databases**, right-click **AdventureWorks**, point to **Options**, and set the **Recovery Model** to **Full**.

2. Open **SQL Server Management Studio**, expand **Databases**, right-click **AdventureWorks**, point to **Tasks**, and click **Back Up**.

3. In the **Back Up Database** dialog box, make sure **AdventureWorks** is the selected database to back up and **Backup Type** is **Full**.

4. Leave the default name in the Name box. In the Description box, enter **Full Backup of AdventureWorks**.

5. Under **Destination**, a disk device may already be listed. If so, select the device, and click **Remove**.

6. Under **Destination**, click **Add**.

7. In the **Select Backup Destination** box, click **File Name**, and in the text box enter **C:\Practice\AdvWorks.bak**. Click **OK**.

8. Click **OK** to start the backup.

9. When the backup is complete, you will get a notification; click **OK** to close it.

■ PART B: Backing Up the Transaction Log for Adventureworks on the Default Instance

1. Right-click **AdventureWorks** again, point to **Tasks** and choose **Back Up.**

2. In the **Back Up Database** dialog box, make sure **AdventureWorks** is the selected database to back up and **Backup Type** is **Transaction Log**.

3. Leave the default name in the **Name** box. In the **Description** box, enter **Transaction Log Backup of AdventureWorks**.

4. Make sure C:\Practice\AdvWorks.bak is the only device listed.

5. Click **OK** to start the backup.

6. When the backup is complete, you will get a notification; click **OK** to close it.

■ PART C: Restoring the Database to the Second Instance

1. Open **SQL Server Management Studio**, and connect to the second instance by selecting <YourServerName>\Instance1 from the **Server Name** drop-down list.

2. Right-click **Databases**, and select **Restore Database**.

3. Enter **AdventureWorks** in the **To Database** box.

4. Under **Source for Restore**, select **From Device**. Click the **ellipsis (…)** button next to the text box to select a device.

5. In the **Specify Backup** dialog box, select **File** from the **Backup Media** drop-down list box, and click **Add**.

6. In the **Locate Backup File** dialog box, find the **AdvWorks.bak** file, and click **OK**.

7. Click **OK** to close the Specify Backup dialog box.

8. Under **Select the Backup Sets to Restore**, check the boxes for both backups of **AdventureWorks**.

9. On the **Options** page, in the **Restore the Database Files As** grid, under the **Restore As** column, make these changes so you do not accidentally overwrite the original AdventureWorks data and log files:

   - Change AdventureWorks_data.mdf to AdventureWorks_data_ls.mdf
   - Change AdventureWorks_log.ldf to AdventureWorks_log_ls.ldf
   - Change AdventureWorks Catalog to AdventureWorks Catalog LS (if it exists)

10. Also on the **Options** page, make sure the **RESTORE WITH STANDBY** option is selected.

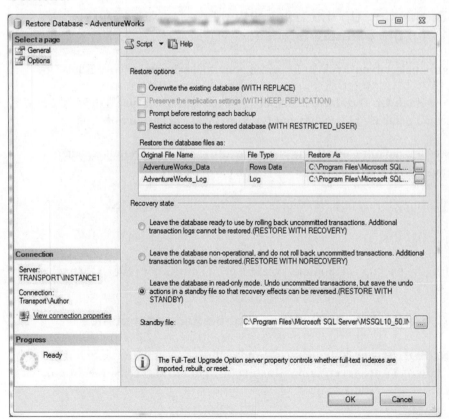

11.   Click **OK** to begin the restore process.

12.   Click **OK** in the dialog box that opens after the restore is complete.

■ PART D: Configuring Log Shipping

1.   Open **SQL Server Management Studio**, and connect to the default instance.

2.   Expand **Databases**, right-click **AdventureWorks**, point to **Tasks**, and click **Ship Transaction Logs**.

3.   Check the box next to **Enable This As a Primary Database in a Log Shipping Configuration**.

4.   Click the **Backup Settings** button.

5.   Enter a network path for the backup folder by typing **\\<YourServerName>\c$\Practice** in the first text box.

6.   Enter a local path for the backup folder by typing **C:\Practice** in the second text box.

7.   Select the defaults for the job schedules and file deletion, and click **OK** to return to the **Database Properties** dialog box.

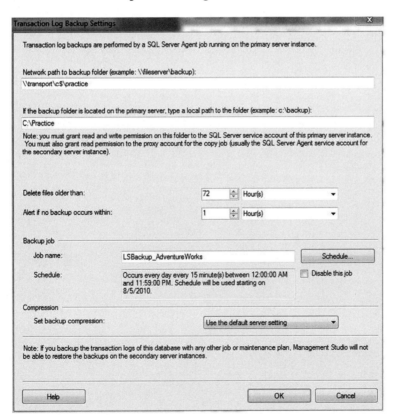

8. Click the **Add** button under the **Secondary Server Instances and Databases** grid.

9. Click the **Connect** button next to the Secondary Server Instance text box, and connect to the second instance.

10. On the **Initialize Secondary Database** tab, make sure the **No, the Secondary Database Is Initialized** option is selected.

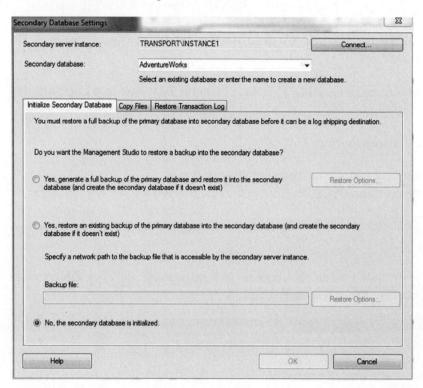

11.   On the **Copy Files** tab, enter **C:\Practice\copy**.

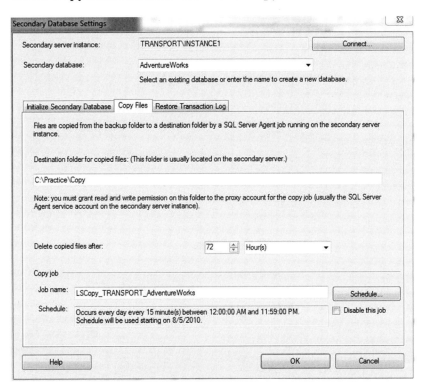

12.   On the **Restore Transaction Log** tab, select the standby mode option to allow users read-only access to the standby database.

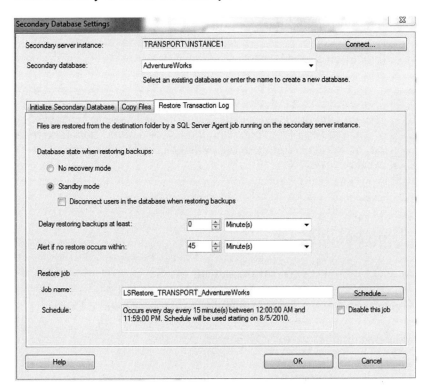

13. Click **OK** to return to the **Database Properties** dialog box.

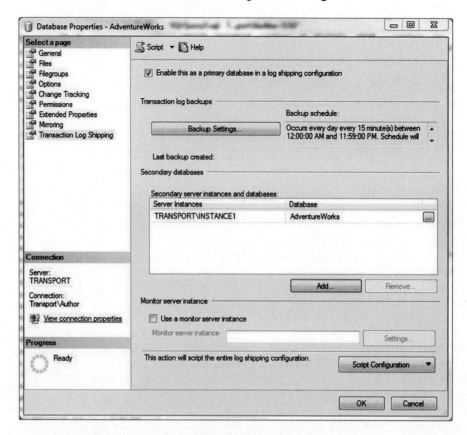

14. Click **OK** again to finish configuring log shipping.

15. Close the **Configuration** dialog box when it is complete.

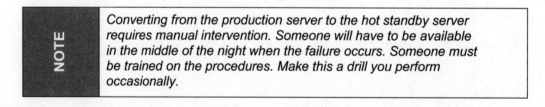

> NOTE
>
> *Converting from the production server to the hot standby server requires manual intervention. Someone will have to be available in the middle of the night when the failure occurs. Someone must be trained on the procedures. Make this a drill you perform occasionally.*

■ PART E: Verifying Results

1. Open a new query in **SQL Server Management Studio**.

2. From the **Query** menu, hover over **Connection**, and click **Change Connection**.

3. Connect to the default instance of SQL Server.

4. To create a new record to ship to the second instance, enter and execute the following code:

```
USE AdventureWorks
GO
INSERT HumanResources.Shift(Name, StartTime, EndTime,
ModifiedDate)
VALUES('Test Shift 3', getdate( ) + 1, getdate( )+ 2,
getdate( ))
```

5. Wait approximately 15 minutes for the log-shipping jobs to run.

6. Clear the query window. From the Query menu, hover over **Connection**, and click **Change Connection**.

7. Connect to the second instance of SQL Server.

8. Run this query to see whether the log was successfully shipped:

```
USE AdventureWorks
SELECT * FROM HumanResources.Shift
```

9. You should see the new 'Test Shift 3' record after the logs are shipped. If the logs do not ship, make sure the SQL Server Agent is running on both instances.

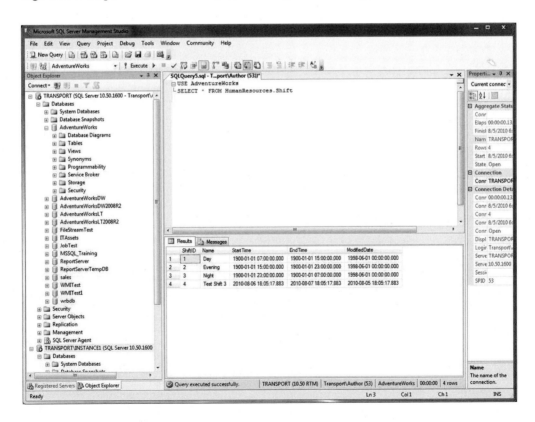

Exercise 25.3	Creating a Database Snapshot
Scenario	You have created a new database for your engineering department to store their data, some of which is important test results for new products. Your chief engineer is naturally concerned about keeping the database available, but he does not want the database copied to another server for security reasons. You decide that the best way to protect against disaster, and get the data back as fast as possible, is to create a database snapshot.
Duration	This task should take approximately 30 minutes.
Setup	For this task, you need access to the machine you installed SQL Server on in Exercise 2.1.
Caveat	In production, you should give the snapshot a more descriptive name, using the date and time of the snapshot, because you can create more than one per day. A good example is Test_Snapshot_20100629_1130AM.mdf.
Procedure	In this task, you will create a new database named Test, create a new table in the database, and then create a snapshot of the new database.
Equipment	See Setup.
Objective	To create a database snapshot.
Criteria for Completion	This task is complete when you have created a new database named Test, created a new table named TestResults in that database, and created a snapshot of the new Test database.

■ PART A: Creating the Test Database and Inserting a New Table

1. Start **SQL Server Management Studio** by selecting **Start**, **Programs**, **Microsoft SQL Server** and **Management Studio**.

2. Connect to your default instance of SQL Server.

3. Right-click **Databases**, and choose **New Database** from the context menu.

4. On the **General** page of the Database properties sheet, enter the database name **Test,** and leave the owner as <default>.

5. Accept the all the defaults, and click **OK** to create the Test database.

6. In **Object Explorer**, expand the **Test** database.

7. Right-click the **Tables** icon, and select **New Table** to open the table designer.

8. In the first row, under Column Name, enter **ProdID** with a data type of **int**, and uncheck **Allow Nulls**.

9. In the second row under Column Name, enter Results with a data type of
    nvarchar(100), and uncheck **Allow Nulls**.

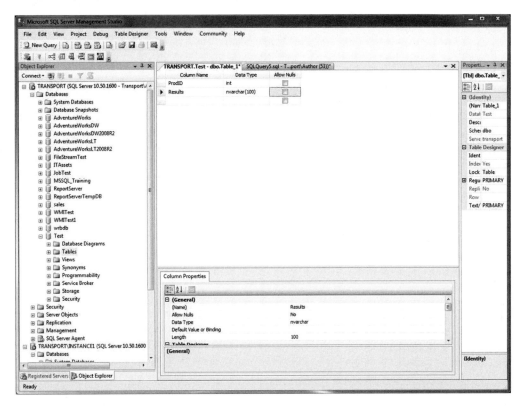

10. Click the **Save** button (it looks like a floppy disk) on the left side of the toolbar.

11. In the **Choose Name** box that opens, enter **TestResults**.

12. Close the table designer screen by clicking the black X in the upper-right corner
    of the window.

13. To create a new record in the **TestResults** table, enter and execute the following
    code:

```
USE Test
GO
INSERT dbo.TestResults(ProdID,Results) VALUES(1, 'Success')
```

■ PART B: Creating a Snapshot of the Test Database

1. Open a new query in **SQL Server Management Studio**.

2. To create a snapshot of Test on the C drive, execute the following code (note that
    you should replace the C:\ with the drive on which you installed SQL Server):

```
CREATE DATABASE Test_Snapshot ON ( NAME = Test, FILENAME =
'C:\Practice\Test_snapshot.mdf' ) AS SNAPSHOT of Test
```

3.   In the results pane (on the bottom) in the query window, you should see a message stating that the command completed successfully.

4.   To verify that the snapshot has been created, expand your server in **Object Explorer**, and then expand **Database Snapshots**. You should see **Test_Snapshot** in the list of available snapshots.

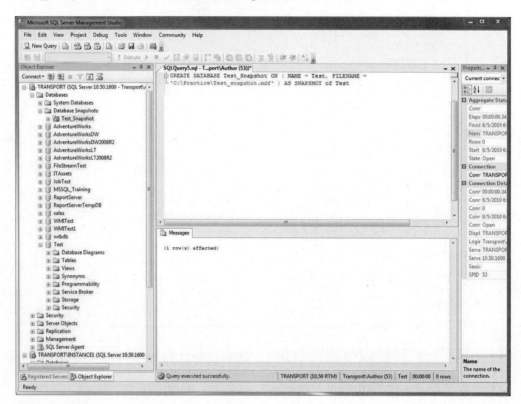

Question 2	*Your management decrees that no more than 10 minutes of data shall be lost under any circumstances. Can you create a snapshot every 10 minutes? If yes, what are the costs? What are the procedures? What are the alternative methods? Log shipping every 10 minutes? Log backup every 10 minutes?*

■ PART C: Verifying Results

1.   Open a new query in **SQL Server Management Studio**.

2.   To create a new record in the TestResults table, enter and execute the following code:

```
USE Test
GO
INSERT dbo.TestResults(ProdID,Results) VALUES(2,'Fail')
```

3. Clear the query window (control-shift-delete), and run this query to see whether the update was applied to the snapshot:

```
USE Test_snapshot
GO
SELECT * FROM dbo.TestResults
```

4. You should see only the record that existed before that snapshot was taken, which is the ProdID: 1, Results: Success record.

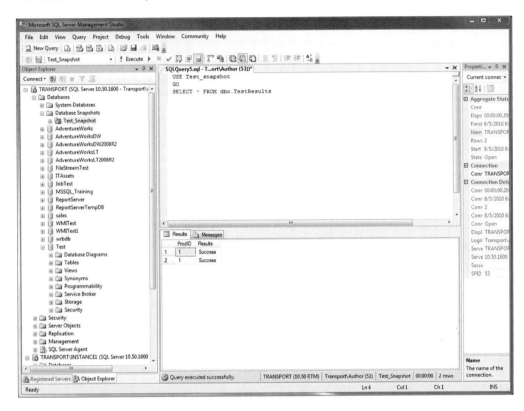

Exercise 25.4	Reverting from a Database Snapshot
Scenario	Your chief engineer recently asked you to help protect his database and keep it available, so you decided to create regular snapshots of the database. Today, one of the engineers accidentally updated several records in the database, indicating that several products had passed safety tests when in fact they had failed, and the engineer doesn't remember which records were updated in error. You need to get the database back to the point before the errors were introduced, so you decide that the fastest method is to revert from the most recent snapshot.
Duration	This task should take approximately 15 minutes.
Setup	For this task, you need access to the machine you installed SQL Server on in Exercise 2.1 and the Test database and Test_Snapshot database snapshot you created in Exercise 25.3.

Caveat	In a production environment, you should perform a full backup of your database after reverting from a snapshot.
Procedure	In this task, you will revert the Test database from the Test_Snapshot database snapshot.
Equipment	See Setup.
Objective	To revert from a database snapshot.
Criteria for Completion	This task is complete when you have reverted from the Test_Snapshot database snapshot.

■ PART A: Creating the Test Database and Inserting a New Table

1. Start **SQL Server Management Studio** by selecting Start Programs, Microsoft SQL Server and Management Studio.

2. To view all the records in the **TestResults** table of the original database, run the following query (you should see two records):

    ```
    USE Test
    GO
    SELECT * FROM TestResults
    ```

3. To view all the records in the **TestResults** table of the snapshot, run the following query (you should see one record):

    ```
    USE Test_Snapshot
    GO
    SELECT * FROM TestResults
    ```

4. To revert from the snapshot, clear the query window, and enter and execute the following code:

    ```
    USE Master
    GO
    RESTORE DATABASE Test FROM DATABASE_SNAPSHOT = 'Test_Snapshot'
    ```

5. Your original database should now match your snapshot. To view all the records in the TestResults table of the original database, run the following query (you should now see one record):

    ```
    USE Test
    GO
    SELECT * FROM TestResults
    ```

6. To remove the now defunct snapshot, expand **Database Snapshots** in **Object Explorer**, right-click **Test_Snapshot**, and click **Delete**.

7. Click **OK** in the **Delete an Object** dialog box.

Question 3	*How do you recover the data lost since the last snapshot? Do you have plan. Has the plan been rehearsed? Can you guarantee management data integrity?*

■ PART B: Verifying Results

1. Examine the data in the original TestResults table of the Test database.

2. You will have only one surviving record.

LAB 26
AUTOMATING MAINTENANCE

This lab contains the following exercises and activities:

Exercise 26.1	Configuring Database Mail
Exercise 26.2	Creating an Operator
Exercise 26.3	Creating a Job
Exercise 26.4	Creating an Alert
Exercise 26.5	Creating a Database Maintenance Plan
Exercise 26.6	Creating a SQL Server Performance Alert
Exercise 26.7	Creating a WMI Alert

Exercise 26.1	Configuring Database Mail
Scenario	You work for a medium-sized company that has SQL Server installations at major offices throughout the country. You need to make sure the systems are up and running at all times, but it is not always easy for you to check the servers' status because they are geographically scattered. You have decided the best way to keep track of your servers is to have them email you when there is a notable status change, such as an error or a completed job. To make that happen, you need to configure the MSDB database as a mailhost database.
Duration	This task should take approximately 30 minutes.
Setup	For this task, you need access to the machine you installed SQL Server on in Exercise 2.1.

Procedure	In this task, you will configure a mailhost, and then you will configure the SQL Server Agent service to use the mailhost.
Equipment	See Setup.
Objective	To configure a mailhost.
Criteria for Completion	This task is complete when you have configured a mailhost and configured the SQL Server Agent service to use the mailhost to send mail.

■ PART A: Creating a Mail Profile

> **NOTE**
>
> *You may create a mail profile for both SQL Mail and Database Mail. Be sure you know the differences and why you might want to use the newer mail system over the legacy mail system.*

1. Open **SQL Server Management Studio**, and connect to your server.

2. Expand **Management** in Object Explorer, right-click **Database Mail**, and select **Configure Database Mail**. On the welcome screen, click **Next**.

3. On the Select Configuration Task screen, select **Set Up Database Mail by Performing the Following Tasks**, and click **Next**.

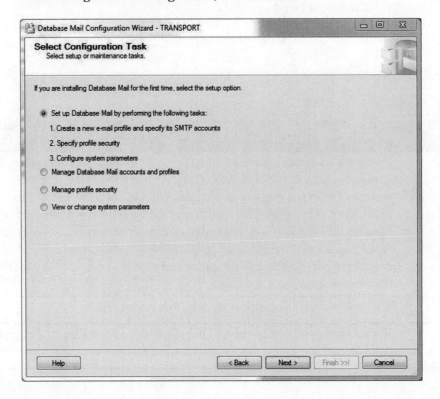

4. If a dialog box opens and asks you whether you would like to enable Database Mail, click **Yes**.

5. On the New Profile screen, create a mail profile, and associate it with a mail server account:

    a. Enter **SQLAgentProfile** in the **Profile Name** box.

    b. Under **SMTP Accounts**, click **Add**.

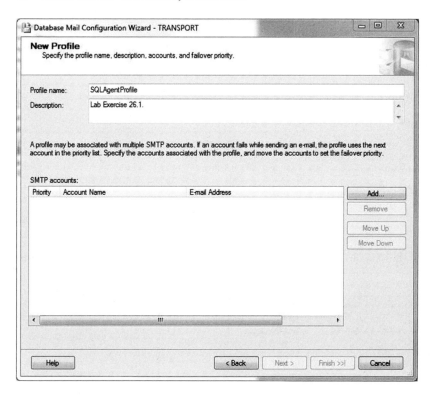

    c. In the **Account Name** box, enter **Mail Provider Account 1**.

    d. In the **Description** box, enter **Email account information.**

    e. Enter your outgoing mail server information using the information provided by your ISP or network administrator.

f. If your email server requires you to log in, select the **Basic Authentication** radio button, and enter your login information.

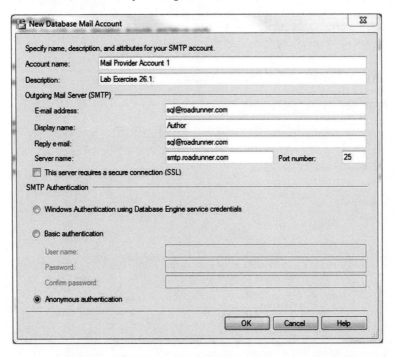

g. Click **OK** to return to the wizard. Your account should now be listed under SMTP Accounts.

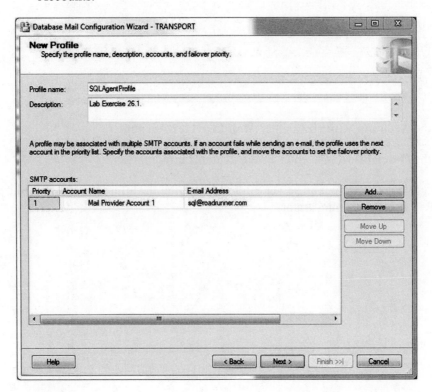

6. Click **Next**.

7. On the **Manage Profile Security** screen, check the **Public** box next to the mail profile you just created to make it accessible to all users. Set the **Default Profile** option to **Yes,** and click **Next.**

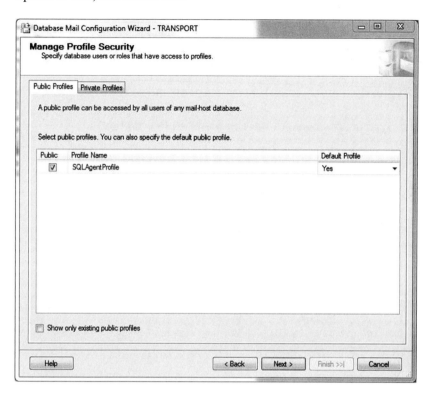

8. On the **Configure System Parameters** screen, accept the defaults, and click **Next.**

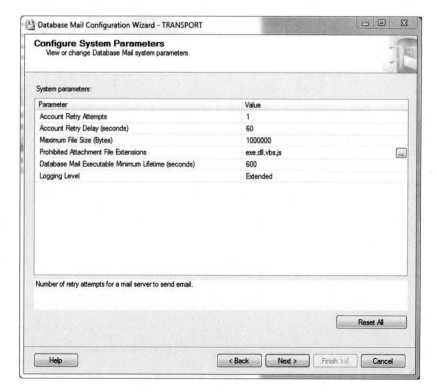

9.   On the **Complete the Wizard** screen, review all your settings, and click **Finish**.

10.   When the system is finished setting up Database Mail, click **Close**.

■ PART B: Configuring SQL Server Agent

1.   In **Object Explorer**, right-click **SQL Server Agent**, and select **Properties**.

2.   On the **Alert System** screen, check the **Enable Mail Profile** box.

3.   Select **Database Mail** from the **Mail System** drop-down list.

4.   Select **SQLAgentProfile** from the **Mail Profile** drop-down list.

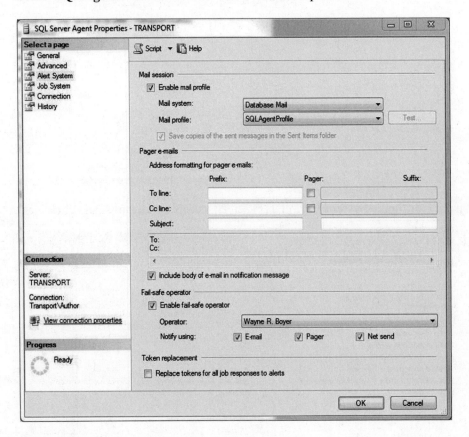

5.   Click **OK**.

6.   In Object Explorer, right-click **SQL Server Agent**, and click **Restart**.

7.   Click **Yes** in the subsequent dialog box that opens.

■ PART C: Verifying Results

1. Expand **Management** in Object Explorer, right-click **Database Mail**, and select **Send Test E-mail**.

2. Enter your email address in the **To** text box, and click **Send Test E-mail**.

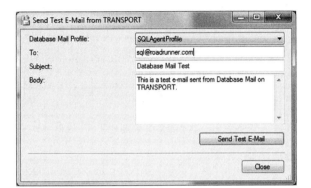

> **NOTE**
>
> *Firewall and antivirus controls may require answering several pop-up Windows requests.*

3. Wait for the email to arrive in your inbox. When it arrives, click **OK** in the dialog box that opens.

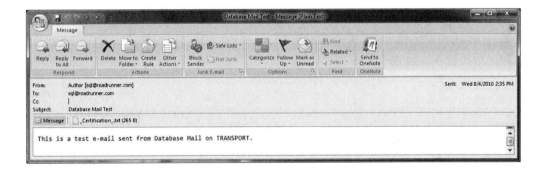

> **NOTE**
>
> *Unless Windows Server is configured with the Post Office Protocol (POP-3), this step will fail. POP-3 is not loaded by default. You must insert the Server distribution disk to add and configure the required utilities.*

Exercise 26.2	Creating an Operator
Scenario	You work for a medium-sized company that has SQL Server installations at major offices throughout the country. You are the lead DBA, and you have several assistant DBAs working for you at the remote offices. You need to make sure you are alerted to problems on the servers when they arise and you want to make sure the appropriate assistant DBA is alerted as well, so you have decided to create operators for yourself and your assistants. You also want to make sure coverage exists 24/7, so you have decided to configure yourself as the fail-safe operator.
Duration	This task should take approximately 15 minutes.
Setup	For this task, you need access to the machine you installed SQL Server on in Exercise 2.1.
Caveat	Make sure you have Database Mail configured and a valid email service to receive the message.
Procedure	In this task, you will create an operator and configure that operator as the fail-safe operator.
Equipment	See Setup.
Objective	To create an operator.
Criteria for Completion	This task is complete when you have successfully created an operator and configured the SQL Server Agent to use that operator as the fail-safe operator.

■ **PART A: Creating an Operator**

1.   Open **SQL Server Management Studio**.

2.   In **Object Explorer**, expand your server, and then expand **SQL Server Agent**.

3.   Right-click **Operators**, and select **New Operator**.

4.   In the Name box, enter **Administrator**.

5.   If you configured your system to use Database Mail, enter your email address as the email name. If you didn't configure your system to use email, skip this step.

6.   Enter your email address in the **E-mail Address** box.

7. If you carry a device capable of receiving email, and you've configured Database Mail, you can enter your PDA or cell phone email address in the E-mail Name box.

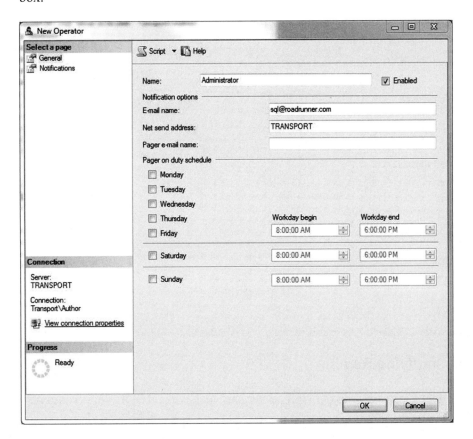

8. Click **OK** to create the operator.

Question 1	What is a Fail-Safe Operator? How does this operator differ from what you just created?

■ PART B: Configuring SQL Server Agent

1. In **SQL Server Management Studio**, right-click the **SQL Server Agent** icon in **Object Explorer**, and select **Properties**.

2. On the **Alert System** screen, check the **Enable Fail-Safe Operator** box.

3. Select **Administrator** in the **Operator** drop-down list.

4. Check the box next to **E-mail** so you'll receive messages as a fail-safe operator.

5. Click **OK** to apply the changes.

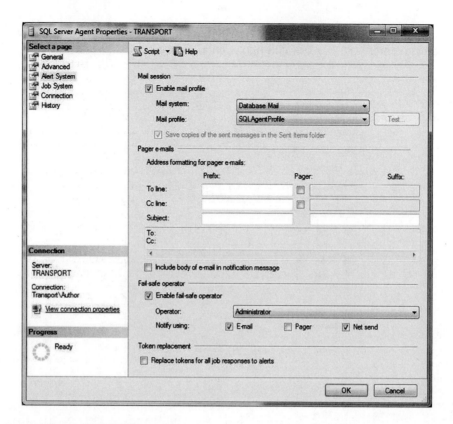

■ PART C: Verifying Results

1. In **Object Explorer**, expand your server, and then expand **SQL Server Agent**.

2. Expand **Operators**; you should see the Administrator operator listed.

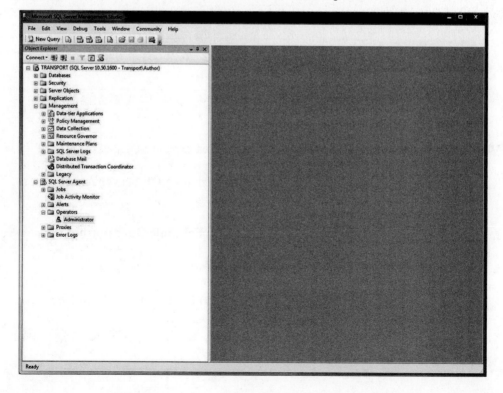

Exercise 26.3	Creating a Job
Scenario	You work for a medium-sized company that has SQL Server installations at major offices throughout the country. As the lead DBA, it is up to you to make sure maintenance takes place regularly on the databases. You know that the best way to guarantee this is to create jobs to automate the maintenance tasks.
Duration	This task should take approximately 30 minutes.
Setup	For this task, you need access to the machine you installed SQL Server on in Exercise 2.1 and the operator you created in Exercise 26.2.
Caveat	This database was created in Exercise 14.1. You will need to delete the database in order to complete this exercise.
Procedure	In this task, you'll create a job that builds a database named JobTest and then backs it up.
Equipment	See Setup.
Objective	To create a job that builds and backs up a new database.
Criteria for Completion	This task is complete when you have successfully created a job that builds and backs up a database named JobTest.

■ **PART A: Creating a Job**

Question 2	You can create a job in SQL Server or you can schedule a batch file in the operating system. Both can perform exactly the same functions. Which is preferred? Why?

1. Open **SQL Server Management Studio** by selecting it from the SQL Server group under Programs on the Start menu.

2. Expand your server in Object Explorer, and then expand **SQL Server Agent**.

3. Right-click **Jobs**, and select **New Job**.

4. In the Name box, enter **Create JobTest Database** (leave the rest of the boxes on this screen with the default settings).

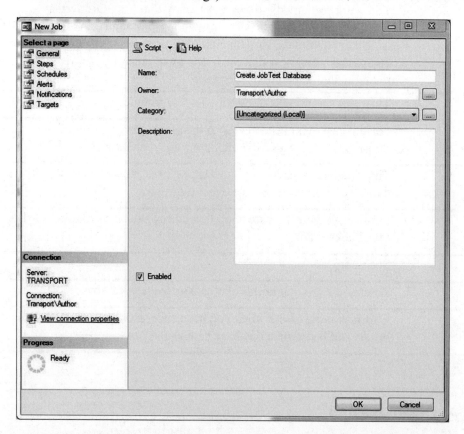

5. Go to the Steps page, and click the **New** button to create a new step.

6. In the Step Name box, enter **Create Database**.

7. Leave **Type** as **Transact-SQL**, and enter the following code in the **Command** text box to create a database named JobTest on the C:\ drive:

```
CREATE DATABASE JOBTEST ON PRIMARY (NAME = jobtest_dat,
FILENAME = 'C:\Practice\jobtest.mdf', SIZE = 10 MB, MAXSIZE = 15,
FILEGROWTH = 10%)
```

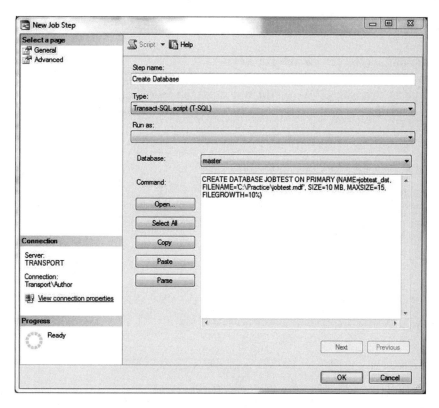

8. Click the **Parse** button to verify you entered the code correctly, and then move to the **Advanced** page.

9. On the **New Job Step** page, verify that **On Success Action** is set to **Go to the Next Step** and that **On Failure Action** is set to **Quit the Job Reporting Failure**. Click **OK**.

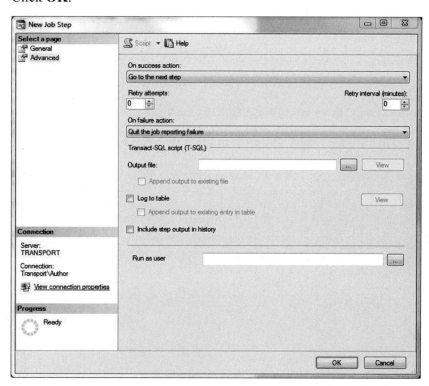

10. To create the second step of the job, click the **New** button.

11. In the **Step name** box, enter **Back Up Test**.

12. Leave **Type** as **Transact-SQL Script**, and enter the following code in the **Command** text box to back up the database once it has been created:

```
EXEC sp_addumpdevice 'disk', 'JobTest_Backup',
'C:\Practice\JobTest_Backup.dat'
BACKUP DATABASE JOBTEST TO JobTest_Backup
```

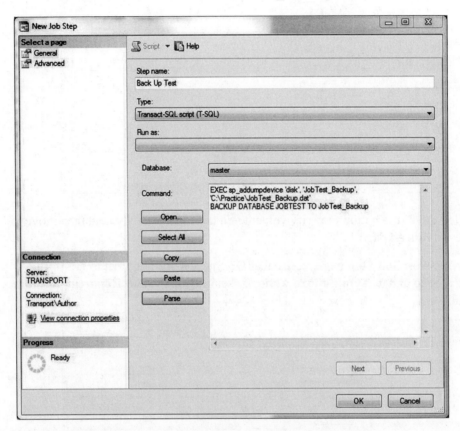

13. Click the **Parse** button to verify you entered the code correctly.

14. Click **OK** to create the step; you should now have two steps listed on the Steps page.

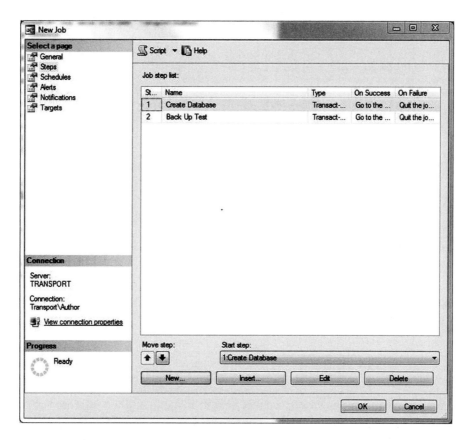

15. Move to the **Schedules** page, and click the **New** button to create a schedule that will instruct SQL Server when to fire the job.

16. In the Name box, enter **Create and Back Up Database**.

17. Select **One Time** from the **Schedule Type** drop-down list. Set the time to be five minutes from the time displayed in the system tray (usually at the bottom-right corner of your screen).

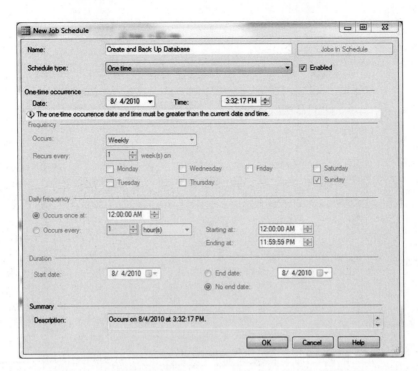

18. Click **OK** to create the schedule, and move to the **Notifications** tab.

19. On the **Notifications** page, check the box next to E-mail (if you configured Database Mail earlier), choosing Administrator as the operator to notify. Next to each, select **When the Job Completes** from the list box (this will notify you no matter what the outcome of the job is).

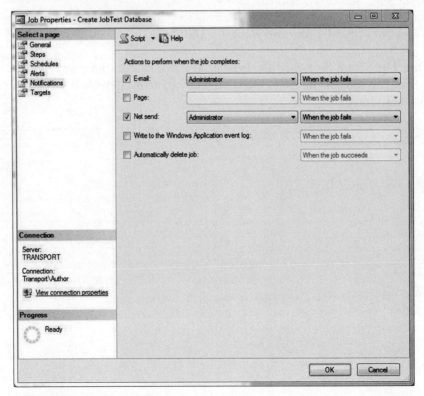

20. Click **OK** to create the job.

■ PART B: Verifying Results

1.   Wait until the time set in Step 17.

2.   At that time, you should see a message pop up on your screen, notifying you of completion. You can then check for the existence of the JobTest database in SQL Server Management Studio and the C:\Practice\JobTest_Backup.dat file. You should see the JobTest database in Object Explorer after the job runs.

Exercise 26.4	Creating an Alert
Scenario	You have a sales database on your SQL Server that contains customer information. Part of the information stored there is the customer credit limit. Your sales manager wants to be notified when someone on his team tries to increase a customer's credit limit to greater than $10,000. You know no built-in error message will handle this task, so you decide to create a custom error message and fire it using the RAISERROR( ) command.
Duration	This task should take approximately 15 minutes.
Setup	For this task, you need access to the machine you installed SQL Server on in Exercise 2.1 and the operator you created in Exercise 26.2.
Caveat	Database Mail must be configured to send an email message. A valid email address must be used to receive the message.
Procedure	In this task, you'll create a custom error message that accepts a string parameter and then create an alert based on the custom error message.
Equipment	See Setup.
Objective	To create an alert that is based on a custom error message.
Criteria for Completion	This task is complete when you have successfully created an alert based on a custom error message that accepts a string parameter.

■ PART A: Creating an Alert

> **NOTE**
>
> *Don't focus on this specific example that only generates an alert message for an undeclared situation; instead, work through this exercise thinking about what are good candidate alerts. How about running out of log disk space? How about exceeding 80 percent CPU usage most of the time?*

1.   Open a new SQL Server query by clicking the **New Query** button in SQL Server Management Studio.

2. Enter and execute the following code to create a new error that is logged to the Windows event log every time it fires:

```
USE master
GO
EXEC sp_addmessage @msgnum = 50001, @severity = 10,
@msgtext = N' This is a custom error by %ls. ', @with_log = 'TRUE'
GO
```

3. In **Object Explorer**, expand your server, and then expand **SQL Server Agent**.

4. Right-click **Alerts**, and select **New Alert**.

5. In the **Name** box, enter **Custom Alert**.

6. Select the **Error Number** radio button, and enter **50001** in the Error Number text box.

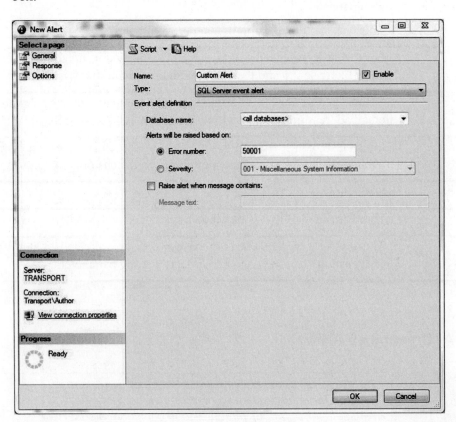

7. On the **Response** page, check the **Notify Operators** box, and check the E-mail box next to Administrator.

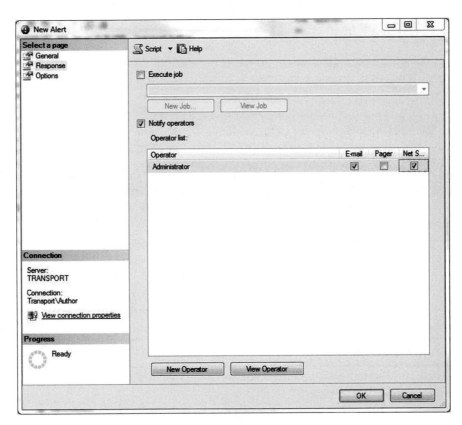

8.   On the **Options** page, check the E-mail box to include the entire text of the error message in the alert, and click **OK** to create the alert.

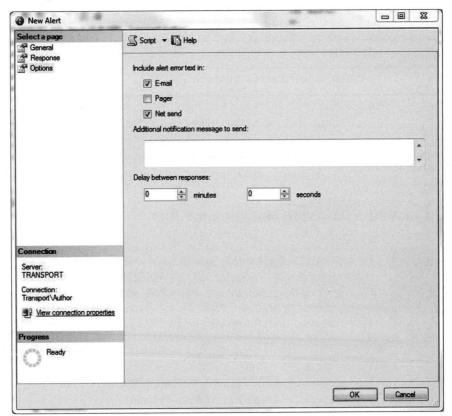

■ PART B: Verifying Results

1. To test the new alert, open a new query, and execute the following code:

    ```
    RAISERROR(50001, 10, 1, 'SQL Guru')
    ```

2. When the email message opens, note the detail it gives you.

Exercise 26.5	Creating a Database Maintenance Plan
Scenario	As the database administrator for your company, you know how important it is to keep the database system running smoothly at all times. You know quite a few maintenance tasks need to be run regularly to keep the system tuned, such as index reorganizing, database and log backups, file maintenance, and so on. These tasks should be performed during off-peak hours, so you know you need to schedule all these tasks; however, you do not want to create separate jobs for each of these tasks. To make the task easier, you decide to use the Maintenance Plan Wizard.
Duration	This task should take approximately 30 minutes.
Setup	For this task, you need access to the machine you installed SQL Server on in Exercise 2.1.
Caveat	Make sure you have SQL Server Integration Services (SSIS) running before starting this task.
Procedure	In this task, you'll create a database maintenance plan for all the databases on your server using the Maintenance Plan Wizard.
Equipment	See Setup.
Objective	To create a database maintenance plan.
Criteria for Completion	This task is complete when you have successfully created a database maintenance plan for all the databases on the default instance of SQL Server using the Maintenance Plan Wizard.

■ PART A: Creating a Database Maintenance Plan

> **NOTE**
>
> Check Books Online for sqlmaint located at Program Files\Microsoft SQL Server\MSSQL.1\MSSQL\Binn. This runs SQL Server 2000 maintenance plans and works from a command prompt and can, thus, be a scheduled batch file. This will be removed from future versions of SQL Server, however.

1. In **SQL Server Management Studio**, expand **Management**, right-click **Maintenance Plans**, and select **Maintenance Plan Wizard**.

2. On the welcome screen, click the **Next** button. The Select Plan Properties screen is displayed.

3. On the **Select Plan Properties** screen, enter **Maintenance Plan 1** in the **Name** box and enter a description if you'd like. Select **Separate schedules for each task**. Click **Next**.

4. On the **Select Maintenance Tasks** screen, check the boxes for all the available tasks except **Execute SQL Server Agent Job**, and click **Next**.

5. On the next screen, you can set the order in which these tasks are performed. Leave the default, and click **Next**.

6. The next screen allows you to select the databases on which you want to perform integrity checks. When you click the drop-down list, you'll see several choices:

    - **All Databases:** This encompasses all databases on the server in the same plan.
    - **System Databases:** This choice affects only the master, model, and MSDB databases.

- **All User Databases:** This affects all databases (including AdventureWorks) except the system databases.
- **These Databases:** This choice allows you to be selective about which databases to include in your plan.

For this task, select **All Databases**, click **OK**, and then click **Next**.

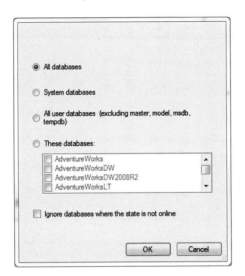

7. On the **Define Shrink Database Task** screen, select **All Databases**, and then click **Next**.

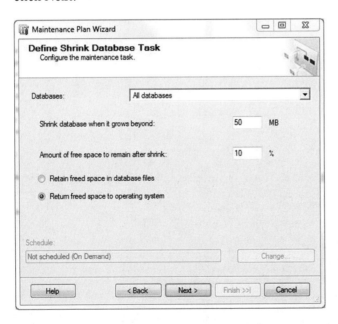

8. On the **Define Reorganize Index Task** screen, select **All Databases** from the Databases drop-down list, and then click **Next**.

9. The **Define Rebuild Index Task** screen gives you a number of options for rebuilding your indexes:

- **Reorganize Pages with the Default Amount of Free Space:** This regenerates pages with their original fill factor.
- **Change Free Space per Page Percentage To:** This creates a new fill factor. If you set this to 10, for example, your pages will contain 10 percent free space.

Again, select **All Databases**, accept the defaults, and then click **Next**.

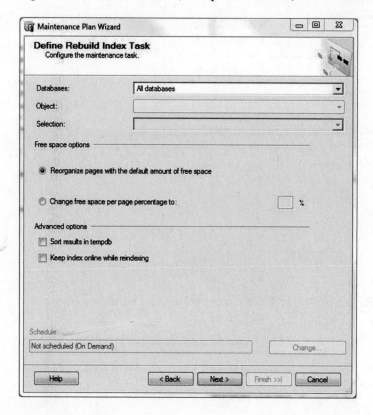

10.   Next comes the **Define Update Statistics Task** screen. Again, select **All Databases**, and then click **Next**.

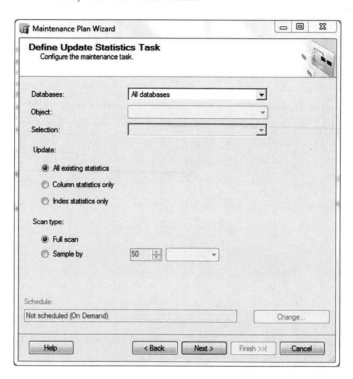

11.   Next is the **Define History Cleanup Task** screen. All the tasks performed by the maintenance plan are logged in the MSDB database. This list is referred to as the history, and it can become quite large if you don't prune it occasionally. On this screen, you can set when and how the history is cleared from the database so you can keep it in check. Again, accept the defaults, and click **Next**.

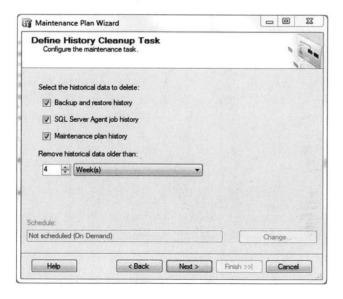

12. The next screen allows you to control how full backups are performed. Select **All Databases** from the drop-down list, accept the defaults, and then click **Next**.

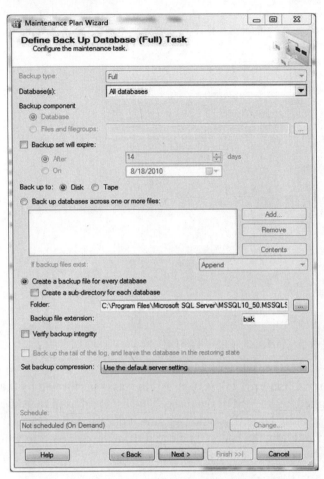

13.   The next screen allows you to control how differential backups are performed. Select **All Databases** from the drop-down list, accept the defaults, and then click **Next**.

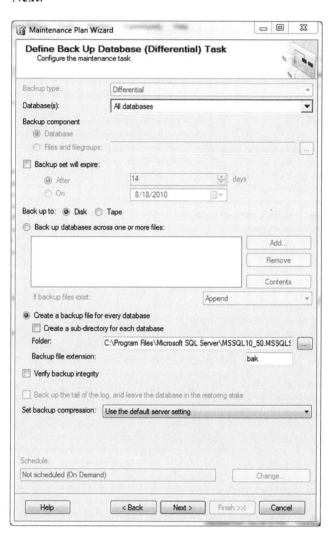

14. The next screen allows you to control how transaction log backups are performed. Select **All Databases** from the drop-down list, accept the defaults, and click **Next**.

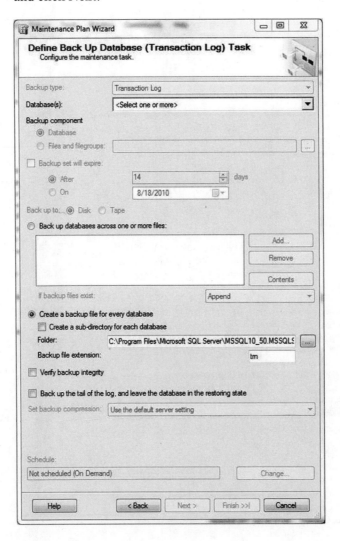

15.   On the **Define Maintenance Cleanup Task** page, understand the options available and then accept the defaults by clicking **Next**.

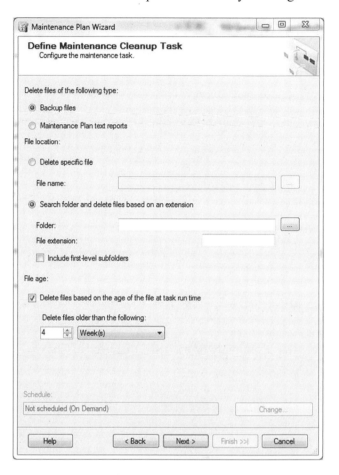

16. On the **Select Report Options** screen, you can write a report to a text file every time the job runs, and you can email the report to an operator. In this case, write a report to C:\ and click **Next**.

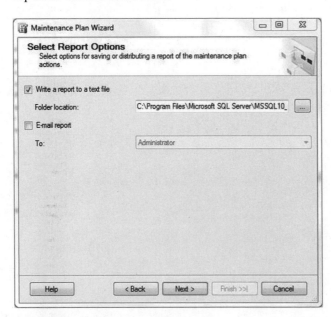

17. On the next screen, you can view a summary of the tasks to perform. Click **Finish** to create the maintenance plan.

18. Once SQL Server is finished creating the maintenance plan, you can click **Close**.

Question 3	*You need to run such utilities as backup, DBCC SHRINKFILE, DBCC SHRINKDATABASE, ALTER DATABASE to compact indexes and others. If you don't use the Maintenance Wizard what are your options?*

■ PART B: Verifying Results

1. In **SQL Server Management Studio**, expand **Management**, and then expand **Maintenance Plans**. You should see **Maintenance Plan 1** listed.

2. Double-click **Maintenance Plan 1** to open **Design** view. You can view and modify all the options you set for the maintenance plan on this screen.

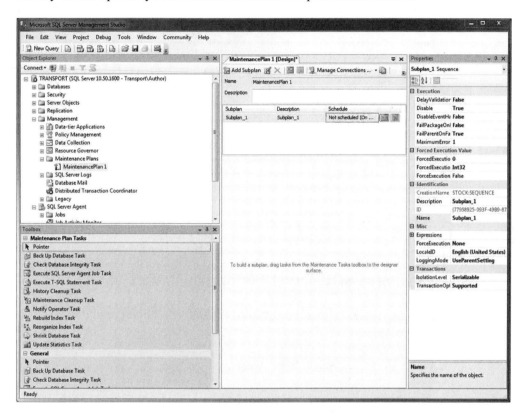

3. Close **Design** view.

Exercise 26.6	Creating a SQL Server Performance Alert
Scenario	As the lead database administrator (DBA) for your company, you understand how important it is to keep SQL Server up and running at top speed, and you want to make certain that all the databases are available at all times. You have had some trouble with the Sales database, which is heavily used. Occasionally under heavy usage, the transaction log fills to 100 percent, and the users are locked out. You can't find a reliable pattern for when this happens, but you still need to prevent it. You have decided that the best way to keep the log from filling to capacity is to create a performance alert that runs a backup job to clear the log before it gets to 100 percent full.
Duration	This task should take approximately 15 minutes.

Setup	For this task, you need access to the machine you installed SQL Server on in Exercise 2.1, the AdventureWorks database installed with the sample data, and the operator you created in Exercise 26.2.
Caveat	In this task, you will create an alert that fires when the log is less than 100 percent full. On your production systems, you should set such an alert to fire when the log is about 70 percent full and then fire a job that will back up (and thus clear) the transaction log. You will need Database Mail to be configured as well as having a usable email address.
Procedure	In this task, you'll create an alert that fires when the transaction log for the AdventureWorks database is less than 100 percent full, and you will then disable the alert.
Equipment	See Setup.
Objective	To create a performance alert in SQL Server Management Studio.
Criteria for Completion	This task is complete when you have created a performance alert that notifies you when the transaction log of the AdventureWorks database is less than 100 percent full.

■ PART A: Creating a SQL Server Performance Alert

1. Open **SQL Server Management Studio**, expand your server, and then expand **SQL Server Agent**.

2. Right-click **Alerts**, and select **New Alert**.

3. In the **Name** box, enter **Performance Alert**.

4. In the **Type** list, select **SQL Server Performance Condition Alert**.

5. In the **Object** box, select **SQLServer:Databases**.

6. In the **Counter** box, select **Percent Log Used**.

7. In the **Instance** box, select **AdventureWorks**.

8. Make sure **Alert If Counter** is set to **Falls Below**.

9. In the Value box, enter **100**.

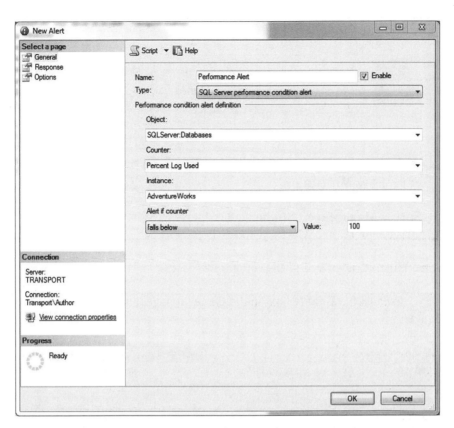

10.   Select the **Response** page, check the **Notify Operators** box, and check the
       E-mail box next to your operator name.

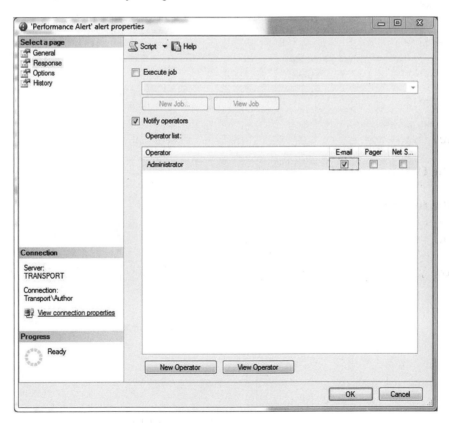

11. Click **OK** to create the alert.

Question 4	Which is better—performance alerts or SQL Server Agent alerts? Which would you prefer to use and why?

■ PART B: Disabling the Error Message to Prevent It from Popping Up Every Few Minutes

1. In **SQL Server Management Studio**, under **Alerts** in **SQL Server Agent**, double-click **Performance Alert** to expose its properties.

2. Check the **History** page. Verify the counter increases.

3. To stop it, uncheck the **Enable** box on the **General** page, and click **OK** to apply the changes.

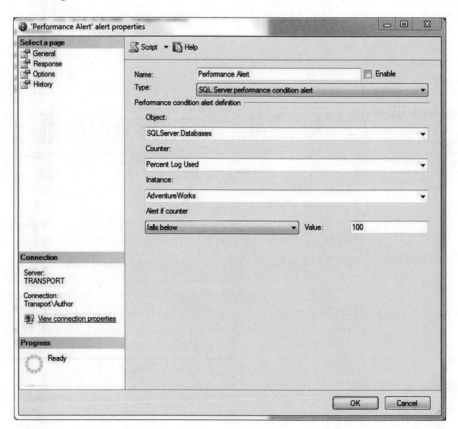

■ PART C: Verifying Results

While enabled, the history counter starts increasing and your mail box fills up.

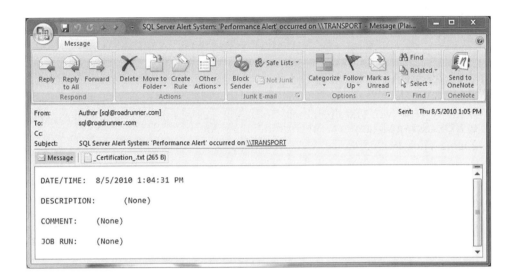

Exercise 26.7	Creating a WMI Alert
Scenario	You are the database administrator (DBA) for a medium-sized company that employs several developers, many of whom create SQL Server objects on a regular basis. Management has implemented a change control program to keep track of what objects are changed and when, and management wants all the developers to follow this new protocol. You have been asked to help make sure no database objects are changed in the production environment without a change control document in place and approved. You could prevent the developers from modifying production objects, but you would have to remove the permissions they need to do their jobs, so you decide to create a WMI alert to notify yourself and management when a production object is modified so you can check for a corresponding change request.
Duration	This task should take approximately 15 minutes.
Setup	For this task, you need access to the machine you installed SQL Server on in Exercise 2.1 and the operator you created in Exercise 26.2.
Caveat	You must have Database Mail configured. You must have a valid email address.
Procedure	In this task, you will create a WMI alert that fires when a new database is created. You will then disable the alert.
Equipment	See Setup.

Objective	To create a Windows Management Instrumentation (WMI) alert in SQL Server Management Studio.
Criteria for Completion	This task is complete when you have created a performance alert that notifies you when someone has created a new database.

■ PART A: Creating A WMI Alert

1. Open **SQL Server Management Studio**, expand your server, and then expand **SQL Server Agent**.

2. Right-click **Alerts**, and select **New Alert**.

3. In the **Name** box, enter **WMI Alert**.

4. In the **Type** list, select **WMI Event Alert**.

5. Make sure Namespace is set to **\\.\root\Microsoft\SqlServer\ServerEvents\ MSSQLSERVER**.

6. Enter this query in the Query box:

```
SELECT * FROM CREATE_DATABASE
```

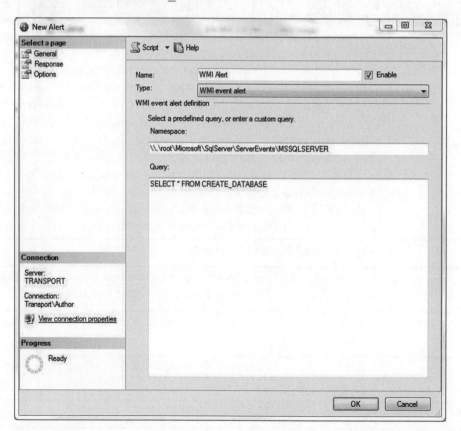

7. Select the **Response** page, check the **Notify Operators** box, and check the **E-mail** box next to your operator name.

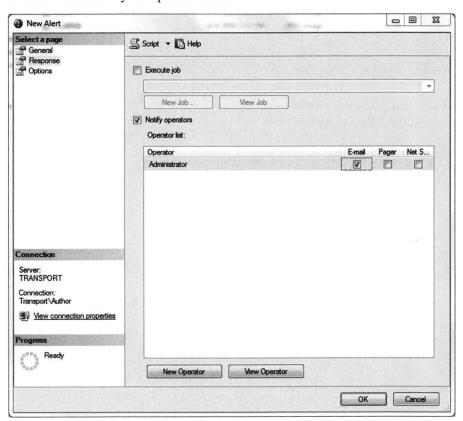

8. On the Options page, check the **E-Mail** box under **Include Alert Error Text In**, and click **OK** to create the alert.

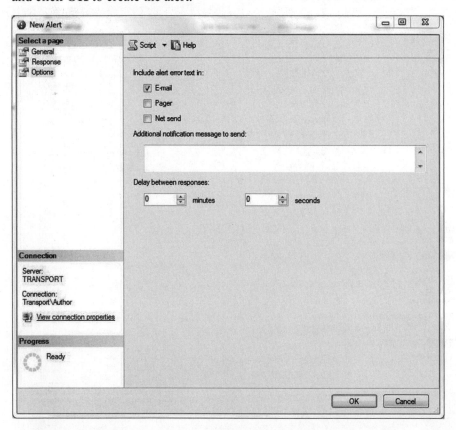

9. Open a new SQL Server query in **SQL Server Management Studio** by clicking the **New Query** button.

10. Enter and execute the following code to fire the new alert:

```
USE Master
GO
CREATE DATABASE WMITest ON PRIMARY ( NAME = N'WMITest',
FILENAME = N'C:\Practice\WMITest.mdf' , SIZE = 3072KB ,
MAXSIZE = UNLIMITED, FILEGROWTH = 1024KB ) LOG ON
( NAME = N'WMITest_log', FILENAME = N'C:\Practice\
WMITest_log.ldf' ,
SIZE = 504KB , MAXSIZE = UNLIMITED, FILEGROWTH = 10% )
```

11.   The alert is received as email.

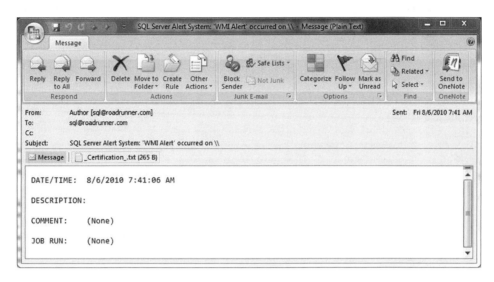

12.   To disable the alert, open it, uncheck the Enable box, and click **OK**.

■ PART B: Verifying Results

Confirm the **Number of occurrences:** increased from zero to one.

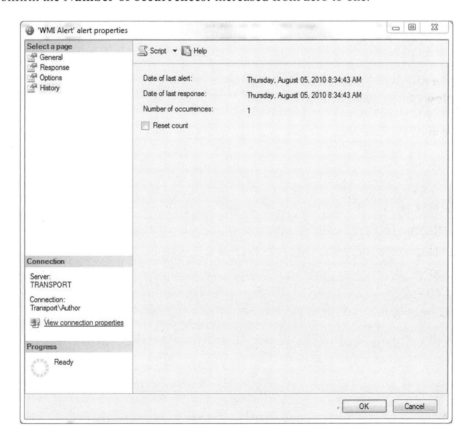

LAB 27
MONITORING AND OPTIMIZING

This lab contains the following exercises and activities:

Exercise 27.1	Using Windows System Monitor
Exercise 27.2	Creating an Alert in Windows System Monitor
Exercise 27.3	Running a Trace in Profiler
Exercise 27.4	Creating a Workload File in Profiler
Exercise 27.5	Using the Database Engine Tuning Advisor

Exercise 27.1   Using Windows System Monitor

Scenario	As the lead database administrator (DBA) for your company, you understand how important it is to keep SQL Server up and running at top speed. You want to make sure all the subsystems on the server are working in harmony and none is being overloaded. The best way to accomplish that goal is to view the data in Windows System Monitor on a regular basis.
Duration	This task should take approximately 15 minutes.
Setup	For this task, you need access to the machine you installed SQL Server on in Exercise 2.1.
Procedure	In this task, you will work with the graph and report views in Windows System Monitor.
Equipment	See Setup.
Objective	To work with Windows System Monitor.
Criteria for Completion	This task is complete when you have familiarized yourself with Windows System Monitor.

■ PART A: Using Windows System Monitor

1. Log on to Windows as Administrator.

2. From the **Start** menu, select **Programs**, **Administrative Tools**, and then **Performance**. In the **Performance Monitor** dialog box, click on **Performance Monitor**. Notice that the graph is already populated with with the **% Processor Time** counter.

3. On the toolbar, click the **Add** button (it looks like a + sign) to open the **Add Counters** dialog box.

4. In the **Select counters from computer:** expand **Memory**.

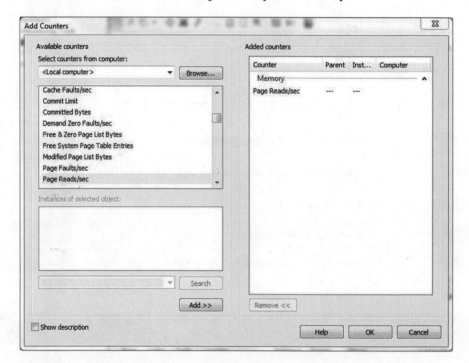

5. From the expanded list, **select Available Bytes**, and **click Add**.

6.   Click **OK**, and notice the graph being created on the screen.

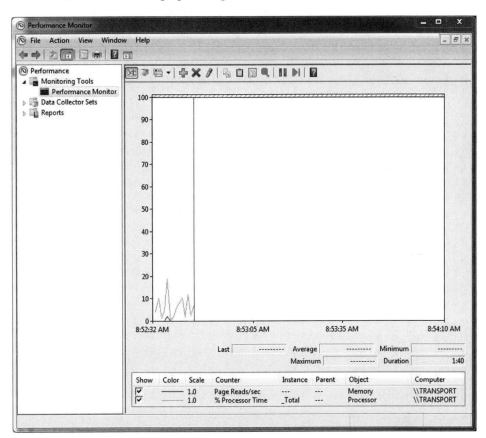

7.   Press **Ctrl+H**, and notice the current counter changes color. This can make the chart easier to read.

8. On the toolbar, click the **Change the Graph Type** down button (it looks like a sheet of paper), and select **Reports**. Notice how the same data appears in report view.

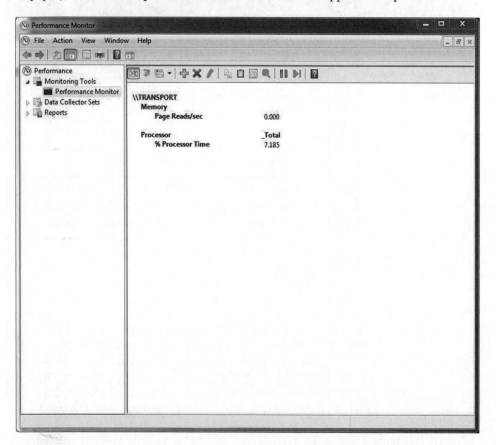

■ PART B: Verifying Results

Look at each of the other performance objects and counters.

Question 1	Do you understand how each can be used and the importance of each? If not, check Books Online for "Monitoring Resource Usage (System Monitor)."

Exercise 27.2	Creating an Alert in Windows System Monitor
Scenario	As the lead database administrator (DBA) for your company, you understand how important it is to keep SQL Server up and running at top speed. You want to make sure all the subsystems on the server are working in harmony and none is being overloaded. The best way to accomplish that goal is to view the data in Windows System Monitor on a regular basis. You need to be notified if a subsystem suddenly becomes overloaded as well, so you decide to create some alerts in Windows System Monitor to keep you updated.
Duration	This task should take approximately 15 minutes.

Setup	For this task, you need access to the machine you installed SQL Server on in Exercise 2.1.
Caveat	In this task, you will create an alert that notifies you when the Processor:% Processor Time counter is less than 70 percent (which is just an arbitrary value that we use in this task). In production, this would be more than 75 percent.
Procedure	In this task, you will create an alert in Windows System Monitor.
Equipment	See Setup.
Objective	To work with Windows System Monitor.
Criteria for Completion	This task is complete when you have created an alert that notifies you when the Processor:% Processor Time counter is less than 70 percent, which you should see in Event Viewer as outlined in the earlier task details.

■ PART A: Creating an Alert in Windows System Monitor

1. Log on to Windows as Administrator.

2. From the **Start** menu, select **Programs**, **Administrative Tools** and then **Performance**.

3. In the left pane, expand **Data Collector Sets**, right-click **User Defined** and select **Create new Data Collector Set** and choose **Performance Counter Alert**.

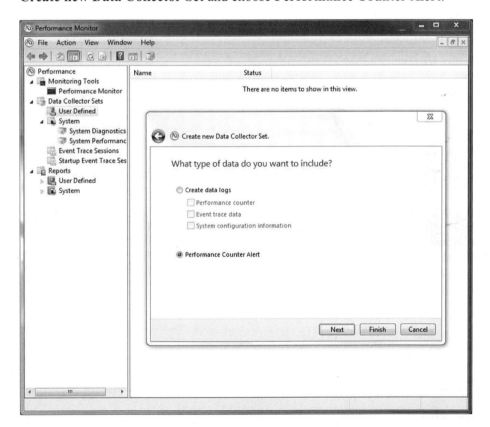

4. In the **Alert Settings** dialog box, enter **Test Alert** in the **Comment** field.

5. Click **Add**. Select the **Processor** object and the **% Processor Time** counter, and click **Add**; then click **OK**.

Question 2	How many objects and counters can you use to create alerts?

6. Select **Below** from the **Alert When** drop-down list, enter **70** for **Limit**, and click **Next**. This will generate an alert if the processor is not busy 70 percent of the time. In the real world, you would set this to more than 70 percent, thus warning you just before it becomes a serious problem.

7. To modify your settings, right-click and select **Properties**. Note the location of the file. You should perform regular maintenance at this location to avoid a "Disk Full" error.

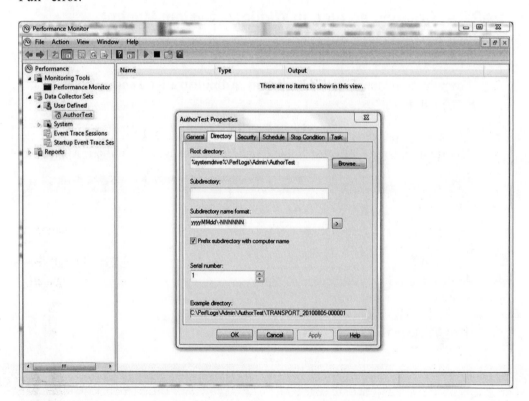

8. To configure your data collection, right-click and select **Properties**. Check each of the tabs in turn.

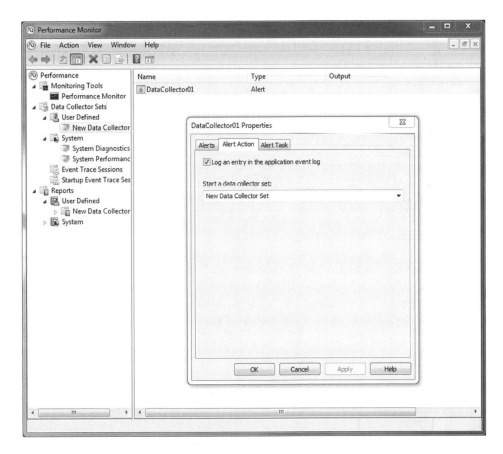

9. Click **OK** to create the alert. Right-click your alert and select **Start** to enable it.

■ PART B: Verifying Results

1. To view the alerts, open **Event Viewer**, and look for them in the Application log.

2. Watch the alerts generated for a short time, then select the alert, and finally press the **Delete** key. If asked whether you want to continue deleting a running alert, click **OK**.

3. Exit **System Monitor** and **Event Viewer**.

Exercise 27.3	Running a Trace in Profiler
Scenario	You are the database administrator (DBA) for a medium-sized company with several SQL Server users. Recently your users have started complaining that they are having trouble retrieving data from SQL Server. Some users cannot access the data they need at all, and others can access it, but it is slow. You realize that this could be any number of problems ranging from network connectivity to security issues. It could even be a combination of these problems. You realize that the best way to troubleshoot this problem is to run a trace in Profiler.
Duration	This task should take approximately 15 minutes.

Setup	For this task, you need access to the machine you installed SQL Server on in Exercise 2.1 and the AdventureWorks database installed with the sample data.
Procedure	In this task, you will configure and run a trace in Profiler.
Equipment	See Setup.
Objective	To create and run a trace in Profiler.
Criteria for Completion	This task is complete when you have created and run a trace in Profiler.

■ PART A: Running a Trace in Profiler

1. From the **Start** menu, select **All Programs**, **Microsoft SQL Server**, **Performance Tools** and then **SQL Server Profiler**.

2. From the **File** menu, select **New Trace**.

3. Connect to your default server instance using the proper authentication; this opens the **Trace Properties** dialog box.

4. In the **Trace Name** box, enter **Monitor**.

5. Use the Standard (default) template.

6. Check the **Save to File** box, and click **Save** to accept the default name and location. Leave the **Enable File Rollover** box checked and the **Server Processes Trace Data** box unchecked.

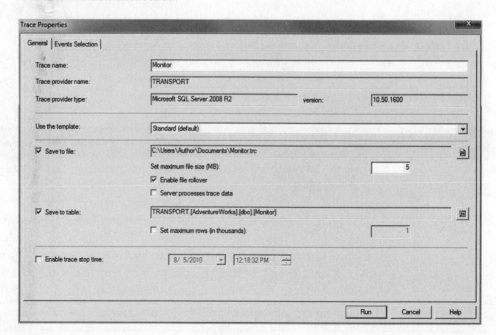

7.   Check the **Save to Table** box, log on to your default server instance, and fill in the following:

- Database: **AdventureWorks**
- Owner: **dbo**
- Table: **Monitor**

8.   Click **OK** once you have made these changes.

9.   Click the **Events Selection** tab, and check the **Show All Events** box toward the bottom of the tab.

10. In the **Events** grid, expand **Security Audit** (if it is not already expanded), and check the box to the left of **Audit Schema Object Access Event**. This will monitor the opening and closing of objects, such as tables.

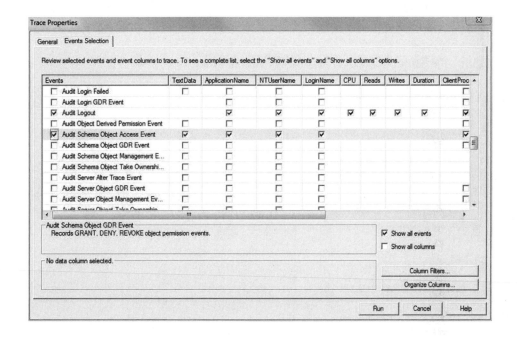

11. Click **Run** to start the trace.

12. Leave **Profiler** running, and open a new SQL Server query in **SQL Server Management Studio**.

13. Execute the following query:

```
USE AdventureWorks
GO
SELECT * FROM Person.Contact
```

14.   Switch to **Profiler**, and click the **Pause** button (double blue lines). In Profiler, notice the amount of data that was collected.

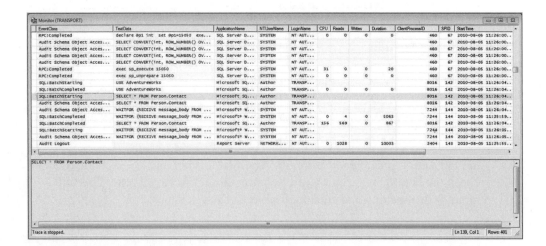

15.   Click the **Stop** button (the red box) to stop the trace.

16.   Close **Profiler** and **SQL Server Management Studio**.

> NOTE
>
> *When the Server Processes Trace Data box is checked, SQL Server processes the trace. This can slow server performance, but no events are missed. If the box is unchecked, the client processes the trace data. This results in faster performance, but some events may be missed under a heavy server load.*

■ PART B: Verifying Results

You should see a list of database activity in the task details.

Exercise 27.4	Creating a Workload File in Profiler
Scenario	You have a SQL Server instance that has been running well for several months. Over the past couple of weeks, though, users have started complaining about performance. They tell you that queries are taking an excessive amount of time to return data. After doing some research into the problem, you realize the users have begun to query on columns that are not indexed, and some of the indexes currently in place may not be used any longer. You know that the most efficient way to fix this problem is by using the Database Engine Tuning Advisor; however, before you can do that, you need to create a workload file.
Duration	This task should take approximately 15 minutes.

Setup	For this task, you need access to the machine you installed SQL Server on in Exercise 2.1, the AdventureWorks database installed with the sample data, and the Monitor table you created in Exercise 27.3.
Procedure	In this task, you will create a workload file by configuring a trace in Profiler based on the Tuning trace template.
Equipment	See Setup.
Objective	To create a workload file in Profiler.
Criteria for Completion	This task is complete when you have created a workload file in Profiler.

■ PART A: Creating a Workload File in Profiler

> **NOTE**
>
> *In a production environment, you would run suspect conditions in Profiler during a typical interval (perhaps two weeks) to capture actual user workloads. This exercise manufactures a problem that can be expeditiously repaired.*

1.   First you need to remove the indexes from the test table, so open **SQL Server Management Studio**, and expand **Databases**, **AdventureWorks** and then **Tables**.

2.   Right-click **Monitor**, and select **Design**.

3.   Right-click the key icon by the **RowNumber** column, and select **Remove Primary Key**.

4.   Click the **Save** button on the toolbar to remove the indexes from the table.

5.   To stop any excess traffic on the server, right-click **SQL Server Agent** in **Object Explorer**, select **Stop**, then click **Yes** or **No**.

6.   From the **Start** menu, select **Programs**, **Microsoft SQL Server**, **Performance Tools** and then **Profiler**.

7.   From the **File** menu, select **New Trace** to open the **Trace Properties** dialog box.

8.   Connect to your default server instance using the proper authentication.

9.   In the **Trace Name** box, enter **Tuning**.

10.   Use the **Tuning** template.

11. Check the **Save to File** box, and click **Save** to accept the default name and location. Leave the **Enable File Rollover** box checked and the **Server Processes Trace Data** box unchecked.

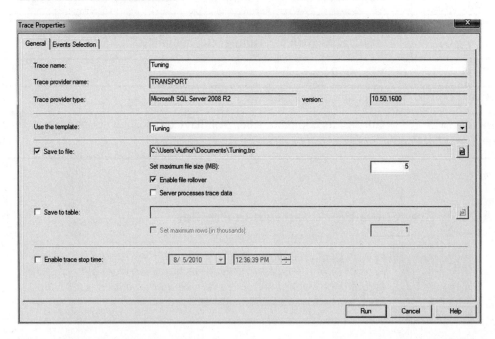

12. Click **Run** to start the trace.

13. Leave **Profiler** running, and open a new SQL Server query in **SQL Server Management Studio**.

14. Execute the following query (make sure to insert your username in the WHERE clause):

```
USE AdventureWorks
GO
SELECT textdata FROM monitor WHERE NTUserName =
'<YourUserName>'
```

15. Switch to Profiler, click the **Stop** button (red box), and then close **Profiler**.

■ PART B: Verifying Results

You should see a list of database activity.

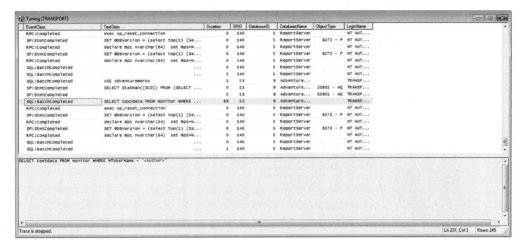

Question 3	What tools can you use to identify suspect conditions to avoid the overhead of monitoring everything?

Exercise 27.5	Using the Database Engine Tuning Advisor
Scenario	You have a SQL Server instance that has been running well for several months. Over the past couple of weeks, though, users have started complaining about performance. They tell you queries are taking an excessive amount of time to return data. After doing some research into the problem, you realize that the users have begun to query on columns that are not indexed, and some of the indexes currently in place may not be used any longer. Because you have already created a workload file, you are ready to tune the database using the Database Engine Tuning Advisor.
Duration	This task should take approximately 15 minutes.
Setup	For this task, you need access to the machine you installed SQL Server on in Exercise 2.1, the AdventureWorks database installed with the sample data, the Monitor table you created in Exercise 27.3, and the workload file you created in Exercise 27.4.
Procedure	In this task, you will tune the AdventureWorks database using the Database Engine Tuning Advisor and the workload file you created in Exercise 5.9.
Equipment	See Setup.
Objective	To run the Database Engine Tuning Advisor.
Criteria for Completion	This task is complete when you have used the Database Engine Tuning Advisor to create an index on the Monitor table in the AdventureWorks database using the Tuning.trc workload file created in Exercise 27.4. You should see a new index on the Monitor table.

■ PART A: Using the Database Engine Tuning Advisor

1. From the **Start** menu, select **All Programs**, **Microsoft SQL Server**, **Performance Tools** and then the **Database Engine Tuning Advisor**.

2. Connect to your server using the appropriate authentication method. This will create a new session in the advisor.

3. In the **Session Name** box, enter **Tuning Session**.

4. In the Workload section, click the **Browse** button (it looks like a pair of binoculars), and locate the **Tuning.trc** trace file created earlier.

> **NOTE**
>
> *If you selected the wrong parameters for creating the workload file the Database Tuning Advisor will provide unoptimized suggestions.*

5. In the database for workload analysis: select **AdventureWorks** from the drop-down list and in the **Select databases and tables to tune:** put a checkmark beside AdventureWorks.

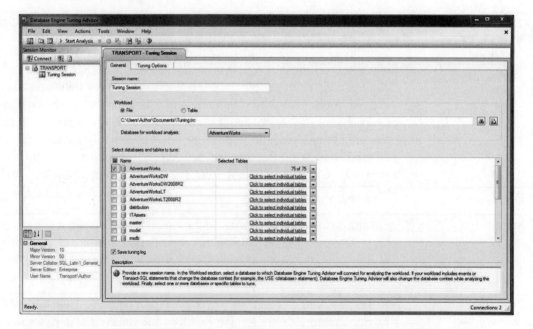

6. Switch to the **Tuning Options** tab. From here you can instruct the advisor what physical changes to make to the database; specifically, you can have the advisor create new indexes (clustered and nonclustered) and partition the database.

7. Leave the **Limit Tuning Time** option checked and set for the default time; this prevents the advisor from taking too many system resources.

8. Leave the default options for Physical Design Structures (PDS) to Use in Database, Partitioning Strategy to Employ, and Physical Design Structures (PDS) to Keep in Database.

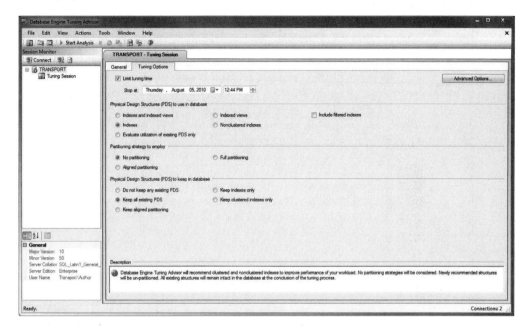

9. Click the **Advanced Options** button. From here you can set these options:

   - **Define Max. Space for Recommendations (MB):** Sets the maximum amount of space used by the recommended physical performance structures.
   - **All Recommendations Are Offline:** Generates recommendations that may require you to take the database offline to implement the change.
   - **Generate Online Recommendations Where Possible:** Return online recommendations even if a faster offline method is possible. If there is no online method, then an offline method is recommended.
   - **Generate Only Online Recommendations:** Returns only online recommendations.

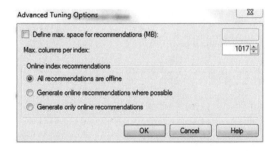

10. Click **Cancel** to return to the advisor.

11. Click the **Start Analysis** button on the toolbar.

12. You should see a progress status screen during the analysis phase.

13. After analysis is complete, you will be taken to the **Recommendations** tab; you should see a recommendation for creating an index on the Monitor table.

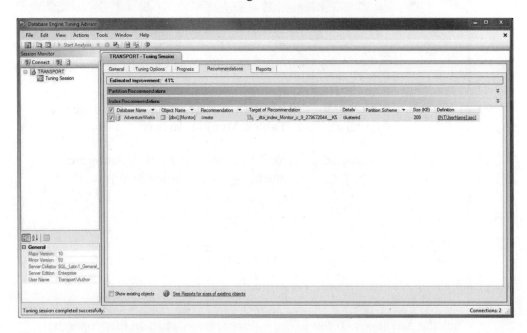

14. You can also check the **Reports** tab for more detailed information about the analysis process. Select **Statement Detail Report** from the Select Report drop-down list as an example.

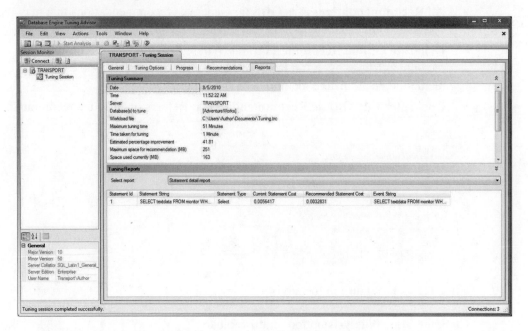

15. To apply these recommendations, select **Apply Recommendations** from the **Actions** menu.

16.   In the dialog box that opens, click **Apply Now**, and click **OK**.

17.   When the index has been created, click **Close**.

18.   Close the **Database Engine Tuning Advisor**.

■ **PART B: Verifying Results**

1.   Open **SQL Server Management Studio**, expand your server, and then select
      Databases, **AdventureWorks**, **Tables**, **Monitor**, **Indexes**.

2.   You should see a new index listed. This is an example of system-generated
      name. Consider renaming it to something more meaningful to you.

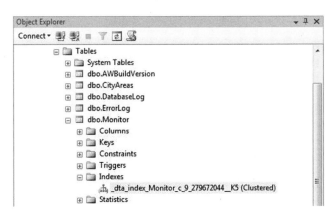

LAB 28
SQL SERVER MANAGEMENT TOOLS

This lab contains the following exercise and activity:

Exercise 28.1   Using the Resource Governor

Exercise 28.1	Using the Resource Governor
Scenario	You have many users running many different queries on a database. You want to prioritize these queries so that certain users and group have higher priority than others.
Duration	This task should take approximately 45 minutes.
Setup	For this task, you need access to the machine you installed SQL Server on in Exercise 2.1.
Procedure	In this task, you will configure the Resource Governor.
Equipment	See Setup.
Objective	To set up the necessary components for Resource Governor.
Criteria for Completion	This task is complete when the Resource Governor is running with the Resource pools and Workload groups.

■ PART A: Creating Resource Pools

1. Open **SQL Server Management Studio**.

2. Open a **New Query**.

3. Enter and execute the following code:

```
-- Setup content for Resource Governor
USE master
GO
CREATE RESOURCE POOL adminpool
WITH (max_cpu_percent = 100)
CREATE RESOURCE POOL busypool
WITH (max_cpu_percent = 75)
CREATE RESOURCE POOL lowpripool
WITH (max_cpu_percent = 25, max_memory_percent = 50)
```

■ PART B: Creating Workload Groups

1. Open a **New Query**.

2. Enter and execute the following code:

```
CREATE WORKLOAD GROUP admingroup
USING adminpool
CREATE WORKLOAD GROUP busygroup
USING busypool
CREATE WORKLOAD GROUP lazygroup
USING lowpripool
```

■ PART C: Creating the Classifier Function

1. Open a **New Query**.

2. Enter and execute the following code:

```
-- Classifier Function Code
USE master
GO
CREATE FUNCTION funct_classify( )
RETURNS SYSNAME WITH SCHEMABINDING
BEGIN
DECLARE @val sysname
IF SUSER_NAME( ) = 'Marketer'
BEGIN
SET @val = 'lazygroup'
END
```

```
IF APP_NAME( ) = 'Microsoft SQL Server Management Studio'
OR
SUSER_NAME( ) = 'Administrator'
BEGIN
SET @val = 'admingroup'
END
IF IS_MEMBER('regular_users') = 1
BEGIN
SET @val = 'busygroup'
END
RETURN @val
END
```

■ PART D: Turning On the Resource Governor

1. Open a **New Query**.

2. Enter and execute the following code:

```
ALTER RESOURCE GOVERNOR
    WITH (CLASSIFIER_FUNCTION = dbo.funct_classify)
ALTER RESOURCE GOVERNOR RECONFIGURE
GO
```

■ PART E: Verifying Results

1. In **Object Explorer**, underneath the server instance, expand **Management**.

2. Expand the **Resource Govenor** and all subsidiary levels to see the newly created Resource Pools and Workload Groups.

3. Click on **Resource Governor** and select **Properties**.

4. In the **Properties** window, note the **Classifier** function, the **Resource** pools, and the **Workload** groups that you created in the previous steps.

5.   Click **Cancel** to close the properties window.

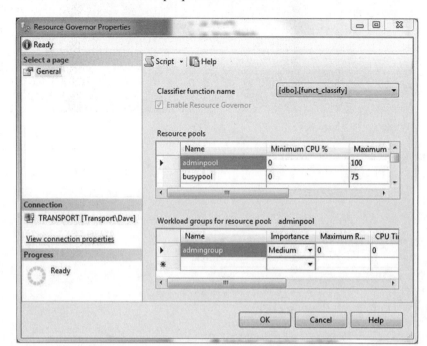

■ PART F: Stopping Resource Governor

1.   If you want to remove or otherwise stop the classification of processes being done by Resource Governor, you may need to go through a series of steps. Try right-clicking on some of the objects created in the earlier steps. You will not be able to delete them at first. This depends on whether processes are active. Also, pools cannot be deleted if there is a workload group assigned to the pool.

2.   Try entering and executing the following code:

```
ALTER RESOURCE GOVERNOR DISABLEALTER RESOURCE GOVERNOR
WITH (CLASSIFIER_FUNCTION = NULL)
ALTER RESOURCE GOVERNOR RECONFIGURE
GO
```

3.   These commands should disable the Resource Governor process, remove the classifier function, and then restart the Resource Governor without a classifier function.

LAB 29
TROUBLESHOOTING

This lab contains the following exercise and activity:

Exercise 29.1 Using the Dedicated Administrator Connection

Exercise 29.1	Using the Dedicated Administrator Connection
Scenario	You have a SQL Server instance that has been running well for several months. Just this morning, though, your developers pushed some new stored procedures into production. A few hours later, users started complaining that they could not connect to SQL Server to retrieve data. While trying to investigate the problem, you find that you cannot connect to SQL Server using SQL Server Management Studio either. You know that the only method left for troubleshooting is the DAC.
Duration	This task should take approximately 30 minutes.
Setup	For this task, you need access to the machine you installed SQL Server on in Exercise 2.1.
Procedure	In this task, you will connect to the DAC and run a query.
Equipment	See Setup.
Objective	To connect to the DAC and run a query.
Criteria for Completion	This task is complete when you have connected to the DAC and verified your results.

■ PART A: Using the Dedicated Administrator Connection

NOTE	*This is the only way you can access the RESOURCE hidden database.*

1. Open a **command prompt** on your server.

2. The following command connects to the server specified with the –S parameter using a trusted connection as specified by the –E parameter. The –A parameter specifies the DAC, or an administrative connection. Run the following command now:

```
sqlcmd -S (local) -A -E
```

NOTE	*This works for database repair only if the SQL Server service is running; if it is not, restart the service with sqlservr –m. Check BOL for further details.*

3. You should see a 1> prompt. From here you can enter a query. Type the following, and hit Enter:

```
SELECT session_id, status, blocking_session_id FROM
sys.dm_exec_requests
```

4. You should now see a 2> prompt. Type **GO**, and hit Enter to execute the query.

5. You should see a list of sessions in the results grid.

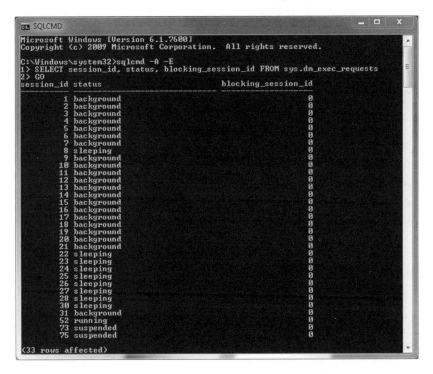

6. Close **SQL Server Management Studio**.

■ PART B: Verifying Results

You should see results from each query as outlined in the Part A of this task.

APPENDIX A
LAB SETUP GUIDE FOR MICROSOFT® SQL SERVER® 2008 IMPLEMENTATION AND MAINTENANCE (70-432)

■ PART A: First Considerations

1. The *Microsoft SQL Server 2008 Implementation and Maintenance* title of the Microsoft Official Academic Course (MOAC) series includes two books: a textbook and a lab manual. The exercises in the lab manual are designed for classroom use under the supervision of an instructor or a lab aide. In an academic setting, a computer classroom is commonly used by a variety of classes each day, so must plan your setup procedure accordingly. For example, you might consider automating the classroom setup procedure and using removable fixed disks in the classroom. You can use the automated setup procedure to rapidly configure the classroom environment, and then remove the fixed disks after class each day. Another alternative is to use Windows 7 and the included Microsoft Virtual PC to create an isolated SQL Server instance so as not to interfere with other uses of the computer.

2. The classroom labs and the textbook exercises use the Microsoft Windows default double-click setting: double-click to open an item (single-click to select) Do not configure the computers to use the optional setting (single-click to open an item; point to select).

3. The instructor's machine and each student workstation need an operating system. You lose some features (e.g., streaming) if you use Windows Server 2003; you

have all features by using Windows Server 2008 (the specialized features of Windows Server 2008 R2 are not used for the Technical Specialist course); all lab exercises have been tested and work with Windows 7 Professional both 64- and 32-bit versions.

4. As a user of this textbook, you have access to the Microsoft Academic Alliance software resources (contact your Wiley representative for details). Windows 7 is offered in the "N" version making it suitable for distribution to Europe; SQL Server is offered in the standard version, which won't support the lab exercises requiring the Enterprise Edition features.

■ PART B: Classroom Setup

1. This course can be taught in a classroom containing networked computers that students can use for hands-on experience:

   - **Isolate the classroom:** When taught in a classroom environment, this course requires a classroom with one computer for the instructor and one computer for each student. If possible, you should isolate the classroom from the rest of the network. Probably the best way to do this is to use a Network Address Translation (NAT) or firewall device. This will prevent IP addressing and name resolution issues with the rest of the campus. You can ask the administrator of your campus or classroom network if the configuration or services used in this setup guide will cause problems with other systems. If so, you will have to isolate the classroom by configuring a NAT/Firewall device or by simply disconnecting the classroom from the rest of the network. Alternatively, if you are running multiple MOAC courses simultaneously, consider using different names and IP addresses. For example, you might use 10.2.2.x as the IP range for the second classroom, 10.3.3.x for the third classroom, and so forth. You might use Instructor01a, Instructor01b, and Instructor01c for the first instructor computer in each room, respectively. Student computers can also be suffixed with a, b, and c. In this way, you won't have to isolate the classrooms using a NAT/Firewall device. Of course, you must still consider whether DHCP or other services might cause issues.

   - **Suggest a password:** Students commonly forget the passwords they assign to their Administrator account. For this reason, it is best for students to use a password that is known to you. A suggested password that meets the default password complexity requirements is *Pa$$w0rd*. To limit student access to the instructor's computer, you should use a different password for that machine.

   - **Adjust settings:** After the installation is complete, consider adjusting the Date/Time and Display settings to provide a better desktop appearance. You can adjust the Date/Time settings through the Date and Time icon in the Control Panel. To adjust the Display settings, right-click the desktop, click Personalize, and then click Settings. For example, you might set the computers to use a consistent resolution and color support with gadgets removed.

2. At some point, the operating system will ask you to activate the server. When that happens, follow the steps to activate the product. The Microsoft Academic Alliance support supplies unique activation numbers for each machine. This isn't an issue if you choose to use evaluation copies but you then have the separate issue of expiration dates that differ from product to product.

■ PART C: Instructor Computer Hardware and Software Requirements

1. All hardware must be published in the Windows Compatibility List Center. Consider also having:

   - One mouse
   - One network adapter card
   - One (or ideally two) display adapter(s) and monitor(s)
   - Audio capability and loud speakers for supplemental videos
   - Projector

2. The required software in this list is available for download from Microsoft:

   - Windows operating system
   - Microsoft PowerPoint Viewer
   - Microsoft Word Viewer

■ PART D: Student Computer Hardware and Software Requirements

All hardware must be published in the Windows Compatibility List Center. Consider also having:

   - One mouse
   - One network adapter card
   - One (or ideally two) display adapter(s) and monitor(s)

■ PART E: Classroom Configuration

1. Much of the actual classroom setup must be performed prior to student arrival. They must find a stand-alone operating system installation (Active Directory is not needed).

   - Provide a computer name (e.g., Computer21).

2. The instructor computer is configured similarly.

   - Provide a computer name (e.g., Instructor01).

   > **NOTE**
   >
   > *To avoid naming conflicts and TCP/IP addressing conflicts, isolate the classroom from the campus network by using a NAT/Firewall device or disconnecting the classroom from other networks.*

   > **NOTE**
   >
   > *The classroom setup described here assumes that you have a Dynamic Host Configuration Protocol (DHCP) server to provide IP addresses dynamically; otherwise you need to use static IP addresses.*

■ PART F: Computer Setup

1. The student needs to create a C:\Practice folder and populate it from the Wiley book companion site. This can be first populated on a shared resource on the instructor's machine and then the students can copy it.

2. Use one of the following options to install the operating system:

   - A DVD-ROM
   - A network share
   - An automated installation of Windows

   > **NOTE**
   >
   > *If you follow these setup instructions, your computer's hard disks will be repartitioned and reformatted. You'll lose all existing data on these systems.*

■ PART G: Using a DVDROM

1. Use your distribution DVD or download the .iso operating system edition of choice from Microsoft.com/downloads and transfer the file to DVD.

2. Set the BIOS to boot from DVD.

3. Reboot with the DVD inserted in the optical media tray.

4. Follow the setup instructions.

■ PART H: Using a Network Share

1. Copy the operating system of choice to a network share.

2. Start setup.exe and follow all subsequent prompts.

■ PART I: Using an Automated Installation of Windows

1. You can then use Windows Deployment Services (WDS) to accomplish student workstation installations. WDS is the updated and redesigned version of Remote Installation Services enabling you to remotely deploy Windows operating systems.

2. Check http://technet.microsoft.com/en-us/library/cc772106(WS.10).aspx for details on Window Server 2008 although this same scheme applies to Windows 7.

■ PART J: Supporting the SQL Server Installation

1. Follow the steps in the Textbook Exercises for installing SQL Server 2005 or the Hands-On Exercises for installing SQL Server 2008—both in Lab 2 of this lab manual.

2. Consider also:

    - By default, Windows supports paging, hibernation, and dump files. Disable hibernation and memory dumps if hard drive space is limited.

    - Using minimum requirements leads to students spending more time waiting than working constructively. Have a much better experience by using a CPU four times the minimum, RAM at two to four times the minimum, a hard drive disk at twice the minimum, and a flat screen monitor capable of a 1280 x 1024 pixel display minimum (two monitors per student can be helpful especially if the ebook edition of this course material is purchased).

    - Provide every student with a DVD copy of SQL Server to experience installation as they might in their enterprise environment. As an alternative provide access to a network share.

■ PART K: Setup Notes

And finally, some last considerations:

- VisualStudio, if supplied, sometimes fails to load a service pack on machines with less than 1 GB of system memory (memory left over after the integrated video card takes its share).
- Do NOT use Virtual PC without at least 3 GB of system memory (1 GB for the operating system and 2 GB for SQL Server).
- Microsoft Virtual PC supplied with Windows 7 Pro works well. Consider this if you have to share your computers with other classes or users and do not have removable drives. More memory is better (the 64-bit OS allows this although Microsoft Virtual PC supports only 32-bit emulation).
- Do NOT provide SQL Server 2005 without SP2 on Vista; go here to find out why: http://msdn.microsoft.com/en-us/library/aa905868(SQL.90).aspx.
- Dual booting is fine.
- At some point (except for evaluation copies) the operating system will ask each user to activate the software. Be prepared with the necessary activation code and follow the on-screen prompts.